SEAL TEAM 7

SOCOM: SEAL TEAM SEVEN

M. ZACHARY SHERMAN
WRITER

ROBERTO DE LA TORRE
ARTIST

ALEX JAEGER
PRODUCTION DESIGNER

RANDY GENTILE
LETTERER

FOR IMAGE COMICS

ERIK LARSEN · PUBLISHER
TODD MCFARLANE · PRESIDENT
MARC SILVESTRI · CEO
JIM VALENTINO · VICE-PRESIDENT
ERIC STEPHENSON · EXECUTIVE DIRECTOR
JIM DEMONAKOS · PR & MARKETING COORDINATOR
MIA MACHATTON · ACCOUNTS MANAGER
LAURENN MCCUBBIN · ART DIRECTOR
ALLEN HUI · PRODUCTION ARTIST
JOE KEATINGE · TRAFFIC MANAGER
JONATHAN CHAN · PRODUCTION ASSISTANT
DREW GILL · PRODUCTION ASSISTANT
TRACI HUI · ADMINISTRATIVE ASSISTANT

WWW.IMAGECOMICS.COM

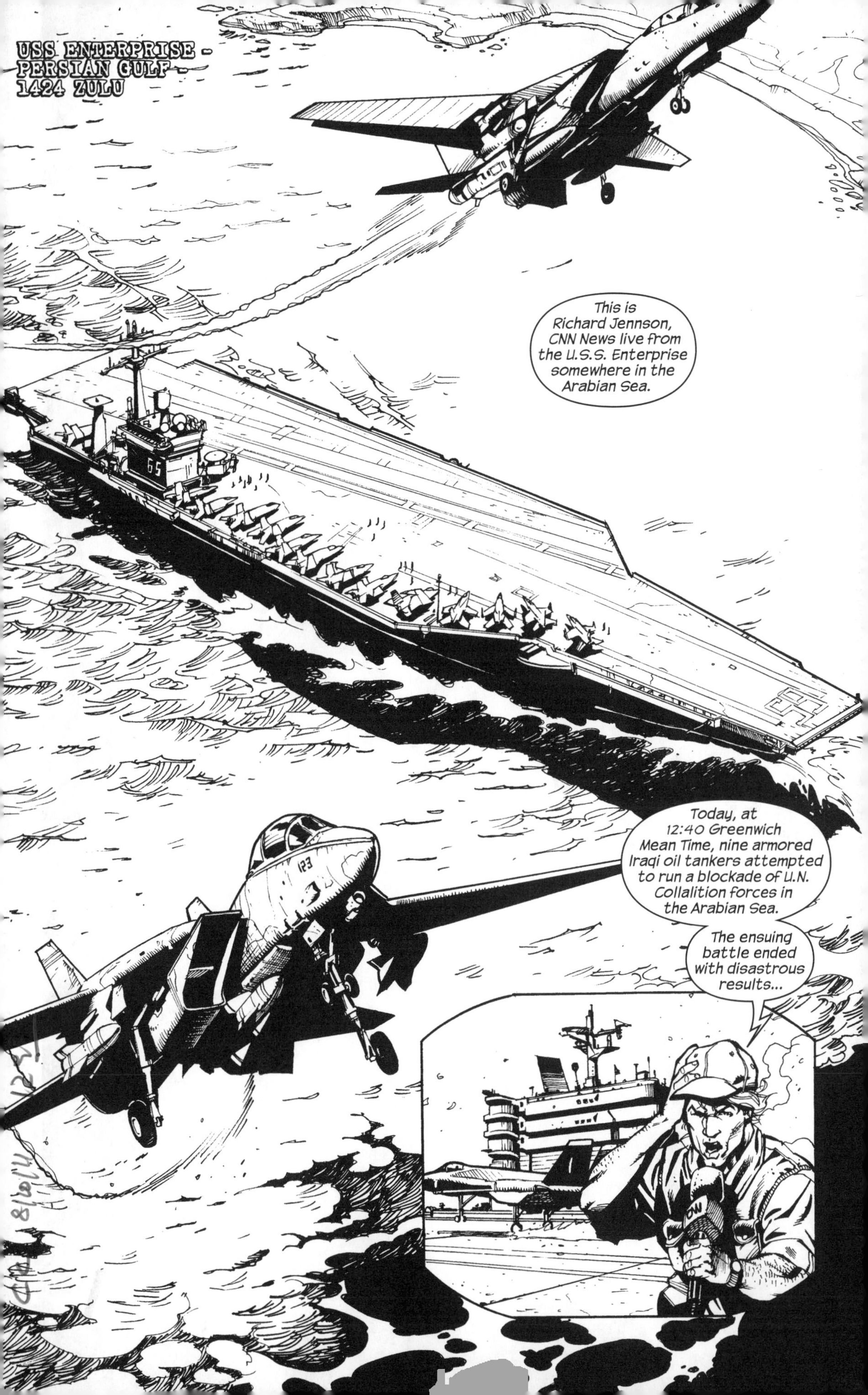
USS ENTERPRISE - PERSIAN GULF - 1424 ZULU
This is Richard Jennson, CNN News live from the U.S.S. Enterprise somewhere in the Arabian Sea.
Today, at 12:40 Greenwich Mean Time, nine armored Iraqi oil tankers attempted to run a blockade of U.N. Collalition forces in the Arabian Sea.
The ensuing battle ended with disastrous results...

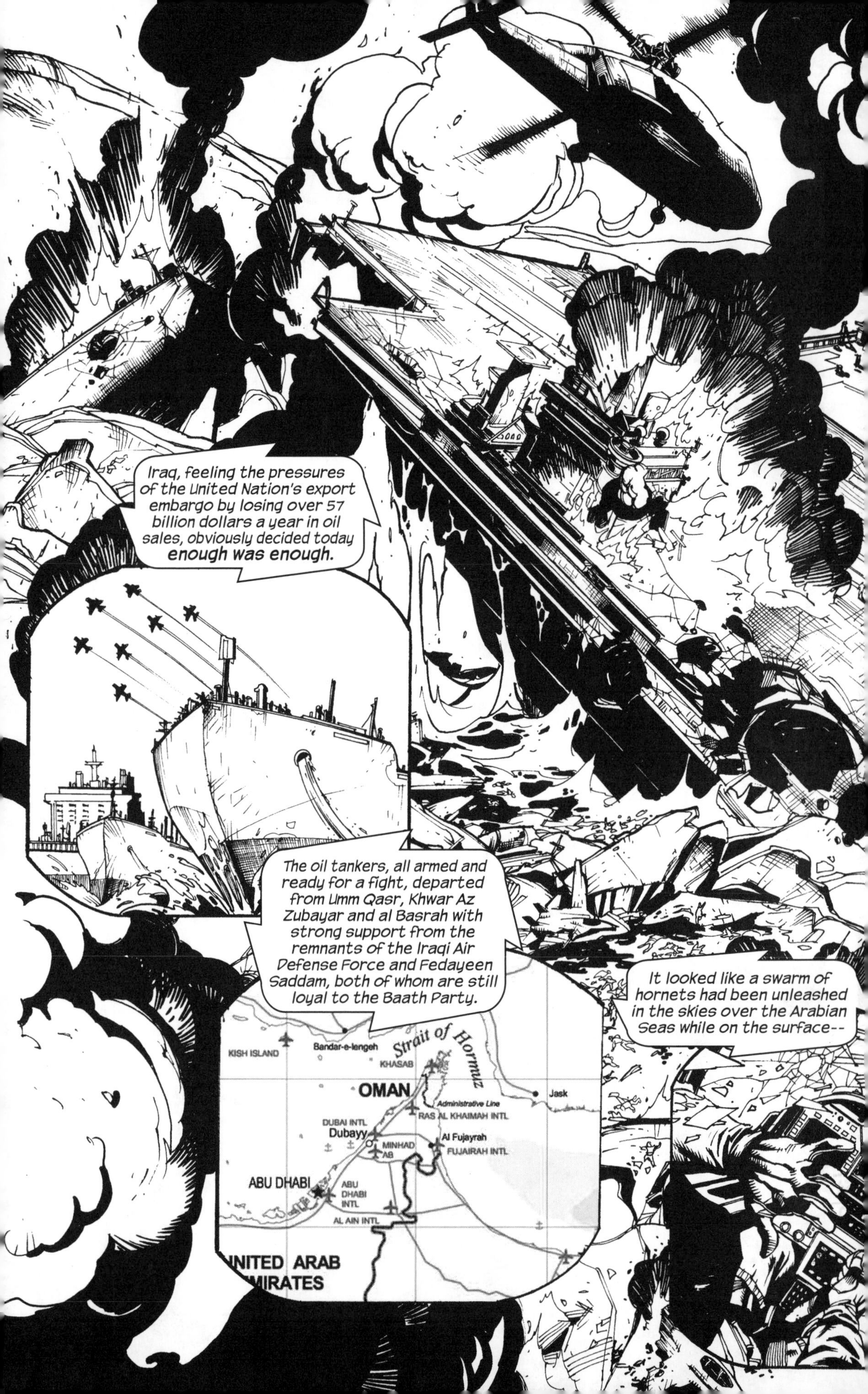
Iraq, feeling the pressures of the United Nation's export embargo by losing over 57 billion dollars a year in oil sales, obviously decided today **enough was enough.**
The oil tankers, all armed and ready for a fight, departed from Umm Qasr, Khwar Az Zubayar and al Basrah with strong support from the remnants of the Iraqi Air Defense Force and Fedayeen Saddam, both of whom are still loyal to the Baath Party.
KISH ISLAND
Bandar-e-lengeh
Strait of Hormuz
KHASAB
OMAN
Jask
Administrative Line
RAS AL KHAIMAH INTL
DUBAI INTL
Dubayy
MINHAD AB
Al Fujayrah
FUJAIRAH INTL
ABU DHABI
ABU DHABI INTL
AL AIN INTL
UNITED ARAB EMIRATES
It looked like a swarm of hornets had been unleashed in the skies over the Arabian Seas while on the surface--

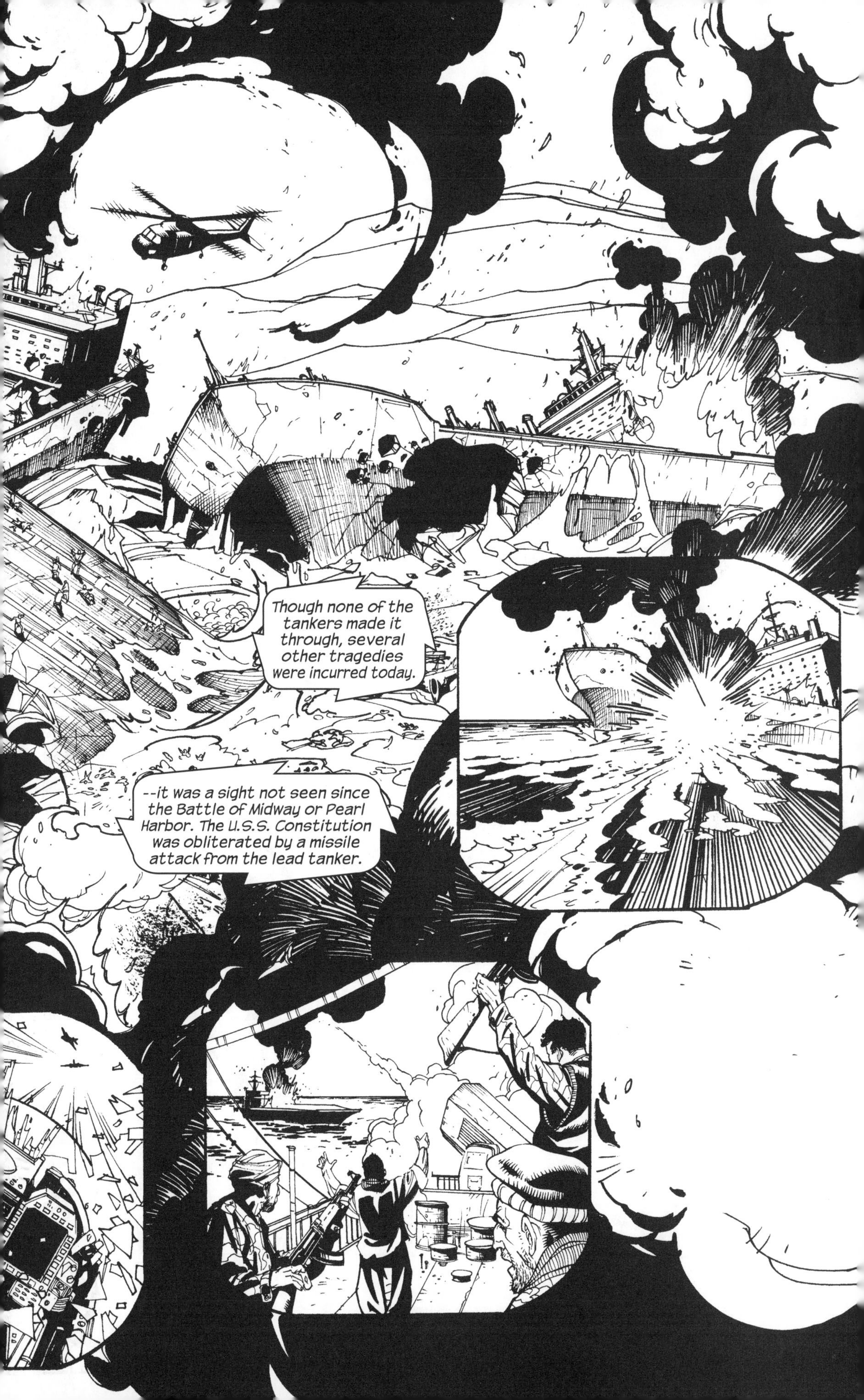
Though none of the tankers made it through, several other tragedies were incurred today.
--it was a sight not seen since the Battle of Midway or Pearl Harbor. The U.S.S. Constitution was obliterated by a missile attack from the lead tanker.

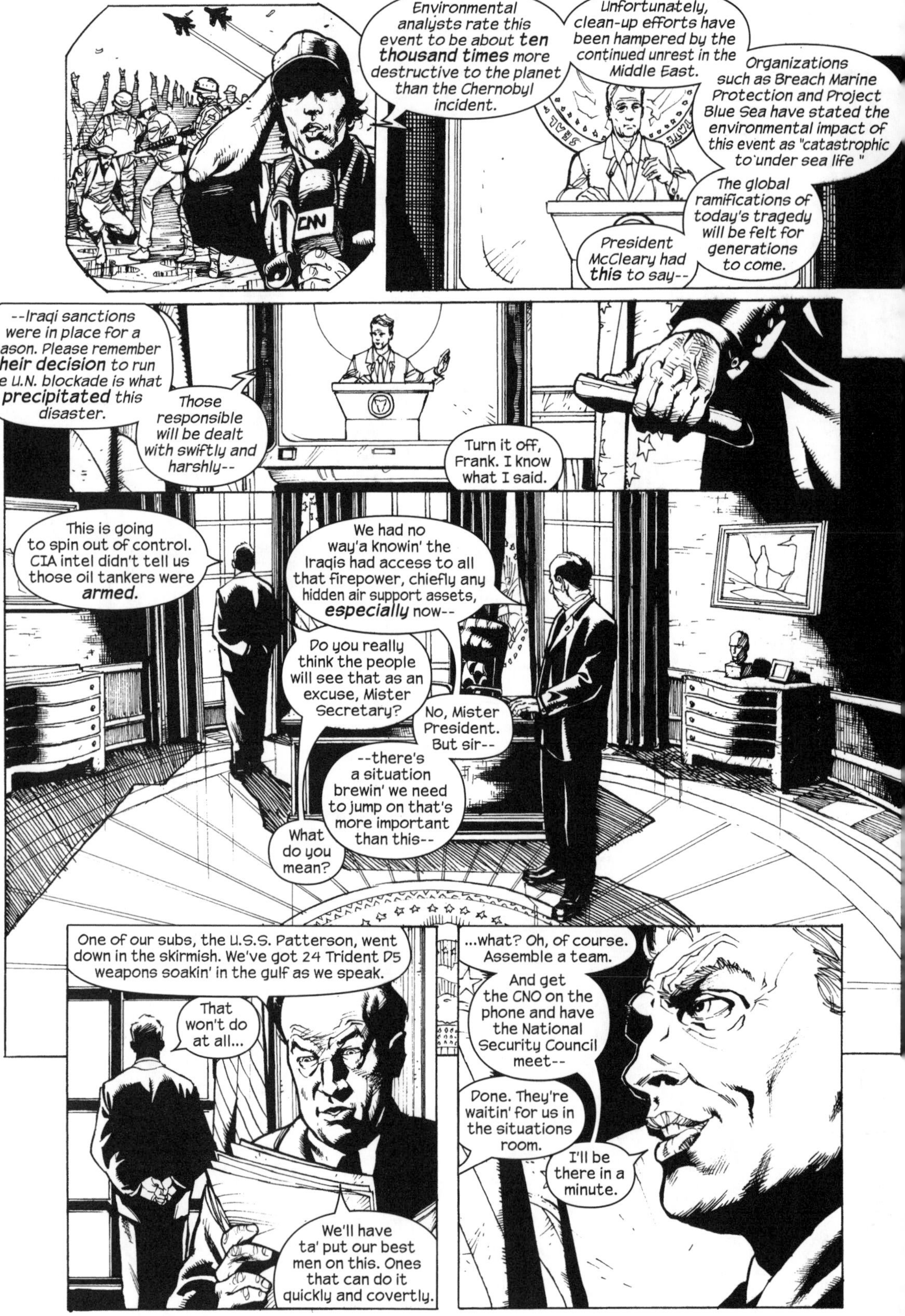

Environmental analysts rate this event to be about ten thousand times more destructive to the planet than the Chernobyl incident.
Unfortunately, clean-up efforts have been hampered by the continued unrest in the Middle East.
Organizations such as Breach Marine Protection and Project Blue Sea have stated the environmental impact of this event as "catastrophic to under sea life"
The global ramifications of today's tragedy will be felt for generations to come.
President McCleary had this to say--
--Iraqi sanctions were in place for a reason. Please remember their decision to run the U.N. blockade is what precipitated this disaster.
Those responsible will be dealt with swiftly and harshly--
Turn it off, Frank. I know what I said.
This is going to spin out of control. CIA intel didn't tell us those oil tankers were armed.
We had no way'a knowin' the Iraqis had access to all that firepower, chiefly any hidden air support assets, especially now--
Do you really think the people will see that as an excuse, Mister Secretary?
No, Mister President. But sir--
--there's a situation brewin' we need to jump on that's more important than this--
What do you mean?
One of our subs, the U.S.S. Patterson, went down in the skirmish. We've got 24 Trident D5 weapons soakin' in the gulf as we speak.
That won't do at all...
We'll have ta' put our best men on this. Ones that can do it quickly and covertly.
...what? Oh, of course. Assemble a team.
And get the CNO on the phone and have the National Security Council meet--
Done. They're waitin' for us in the situations room.
I'll be there in a minute.

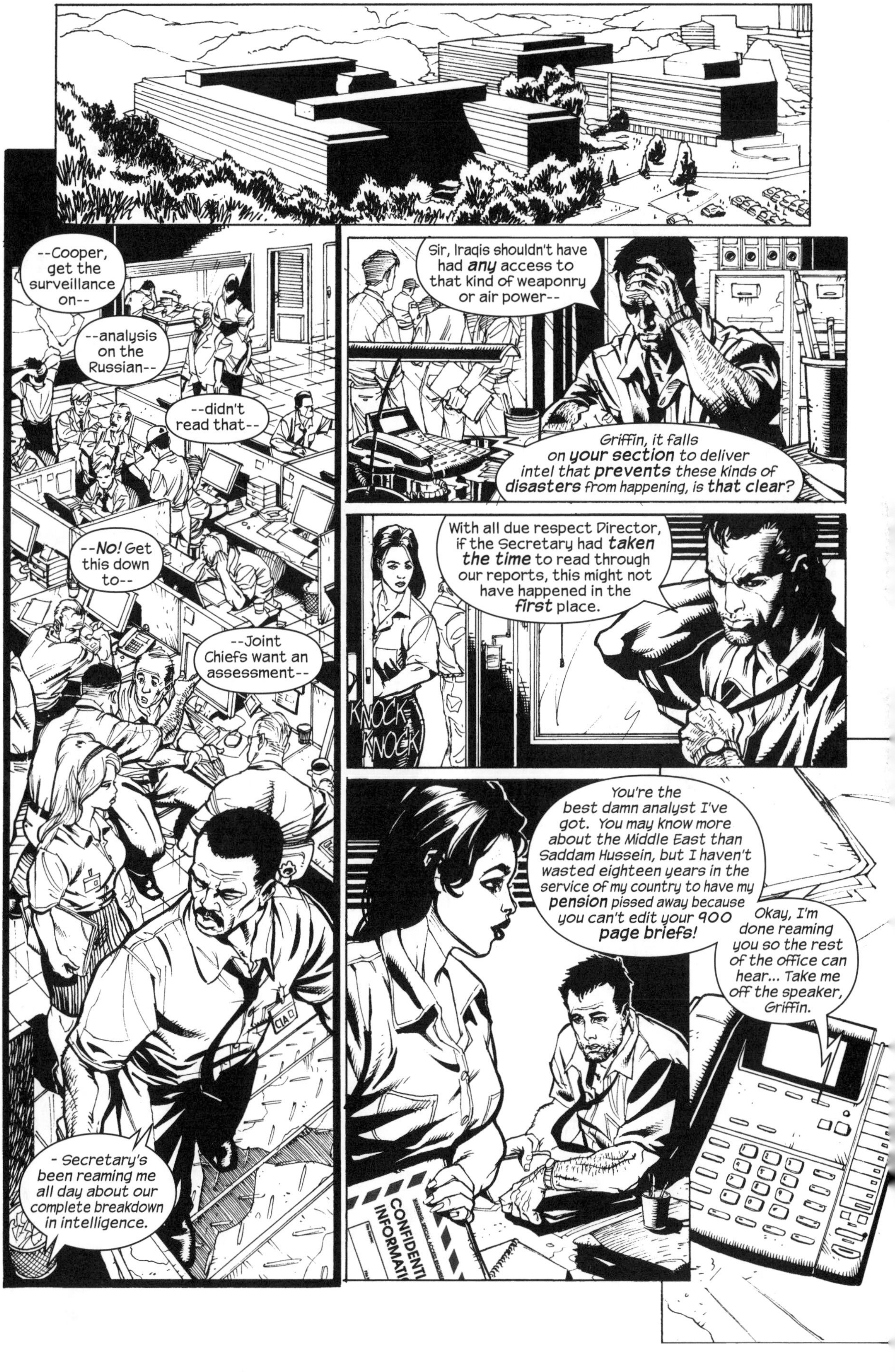
--Cooper, get the surveillance on--
--analysis on the Russian--
--didn't read that--
--No! Get this down to--
--Joint Chiefs want an assessment--
- Secretary's been reaming me all day about our complete breakdown in intelligence.
Sir, Iraqis shouldn't have had any access to that kind of weaponry or air power--
Griffin, it falls on your section to deliver intel that prevents these kinds of disasters from happening, is that clear?
With all due respect Director, if the Secretary had taken the time to read through our reports, this might not have happened in the first place.
KNOCK KNOCK
You're the best damn analyst I've got. You may know more about the Middle East than Saddam Hussein, but I haven't wasted eighteen years in the service of my country to have my pension pissed away because you can't edit your 900 page briefs!
Okay, I'm done reaming you so the rest of the office can hear... Take me off the speaker, Griffin.
CONFIDENTI
INFORMATI

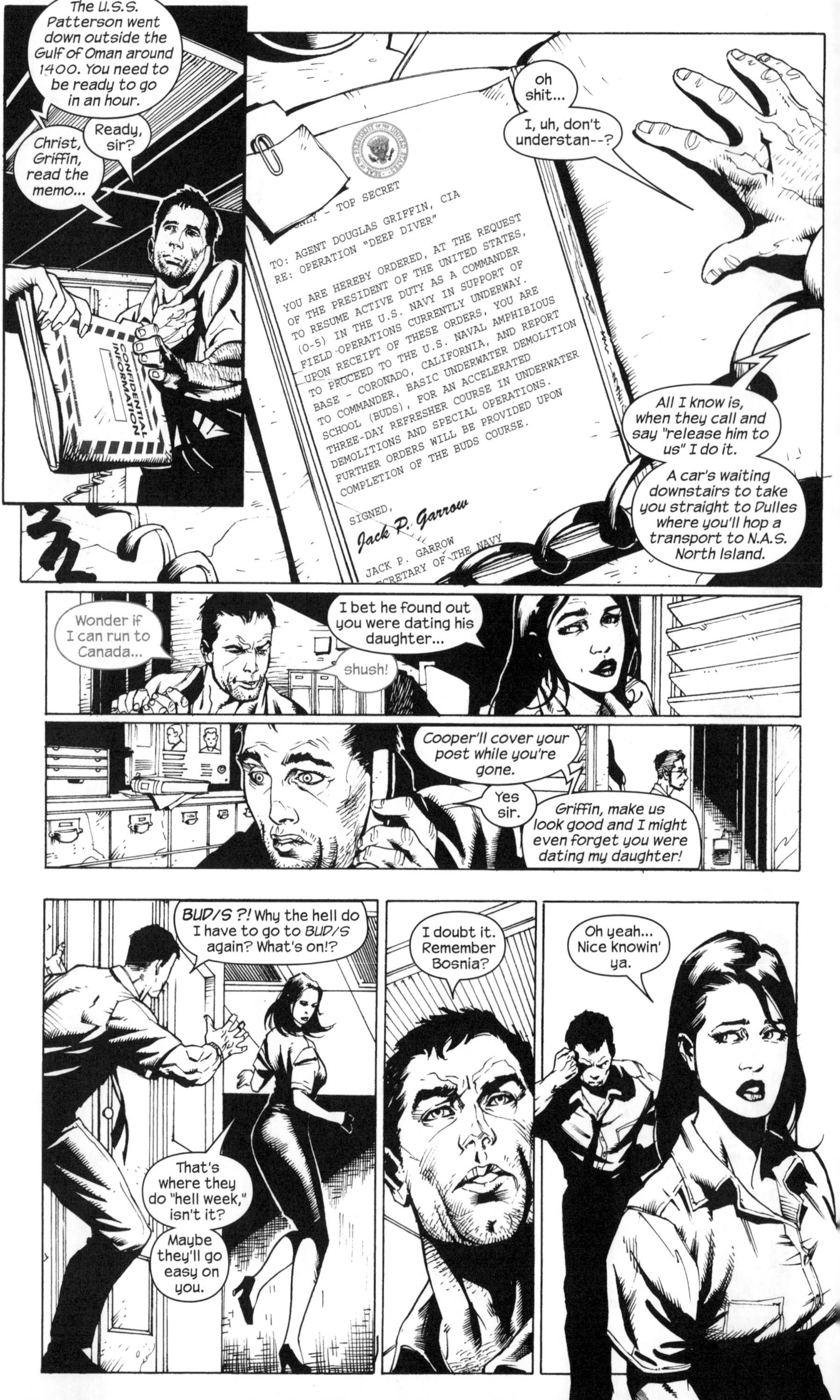

The U.S.S. Patterson went down outside the Gulf of Oman around 1400. You need to be ready to go in an hour.
Ready, sir?
Christ, Griffin, read the memo...
CONFIDENTIAL INFORMATION
ONLY - TOP SECRET
TO: AGENT DOUGLAS GRIFFIN, CIA
RE: OPERATION "DEEP DIVER"
YOU ARE HEREBY ORDERED, AT THE REQUEST OF THE PRESIDENT OF THE UNITED STATES, TO RESUME ACTIVE DUTY AS A COMMANDER (O-5) IN THE U.S. NAVY IN SUPPORT OF FIELD OPERATIONS CURRENTLY UNDERWAY. UPON RECEIPT OF THESE ORDERS, YOU ARE TO PROCEED TO THE U.S. NAVAL AMPHIBIOUS BASE - CORONADO, CALIFORNIA, AND REPORT TO COMMANDER, BASIC UNDERWATER DEMOLITION SCHOOL (BUDS), FOR AN ACCELERATED THREE-DAY REFRESHER COURSE IN UNDERWATER DEMOLITIONS AND SPECIAL OPERATIONS. FURTHER ORDERS WILL BE PROVIDED UPON COMPLETION OF THE BUDS COURSE.
SIGNED,
Jack P. Garrow
JACK P. GARROW
SECRETARY OF THE NAVY
oh shit...
I, uh, don't understan--?
All I know is, when they call and say "release him to us" I do it.
A car's waiting downstairs to take you straight to Dulles where you'll hop a transport to N.A.S. North Island.
Wonder if I can run to Canada...
I bet he found out you were dating his daughter...
shush!
Cooper'll cover your post while you're gone.
Yes sir.
Griffin, make us look good and I might even forget you were dating my daughter!
BUD/S ?! Why the hell do I have to go to BUD/S again? What's on!?
That's where they do "hell week," isn't it?
Maybe they'll go easy on you.
I doubt it. Remember Bosnia?
Oh yeah... Nice knowin' ya.

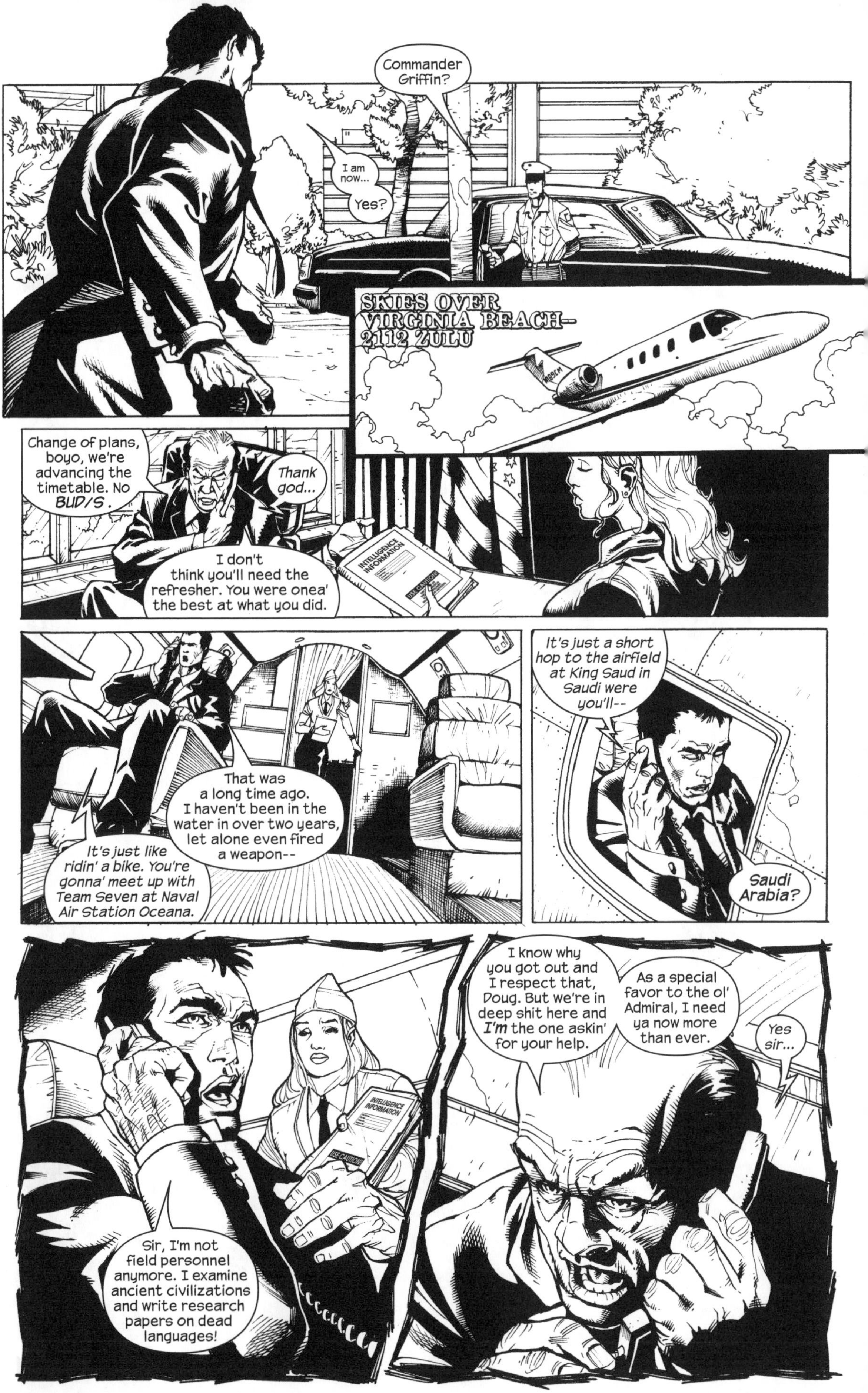
Commander Griffin?
I am now...
Yes?
SKIES OVER VIRGINIA BEACH- 2112 ZULU
Change of plans, boyo, we're advancing the timetable. No BUD/S.
Thank god...
I don't think you'll need the refresher. You were onea' the best at what you did.
INTELLIGENCE INFORMATION
USE CAUTION
That was a long time ago. I haven't been in the water in over two years, let alone even fired a weapon--
It's just like ridin' a bike. You're gonna' meet up with Team Seven at Naval Air Station Oceana.
It's just a short hop to the airfield at King Saud in Saudi were you'll--
Saudi Arabia?
Sir, I'm not field personnel anymore. I examine ancient civilizations and write research papers on dead languages!
I know why you got out and I respect that, Doug. But we're in deep shit here and I'm the one askin' for your help.
As a special favor to the ol' Admiral, I need ya now more than ever.
Yes sir...

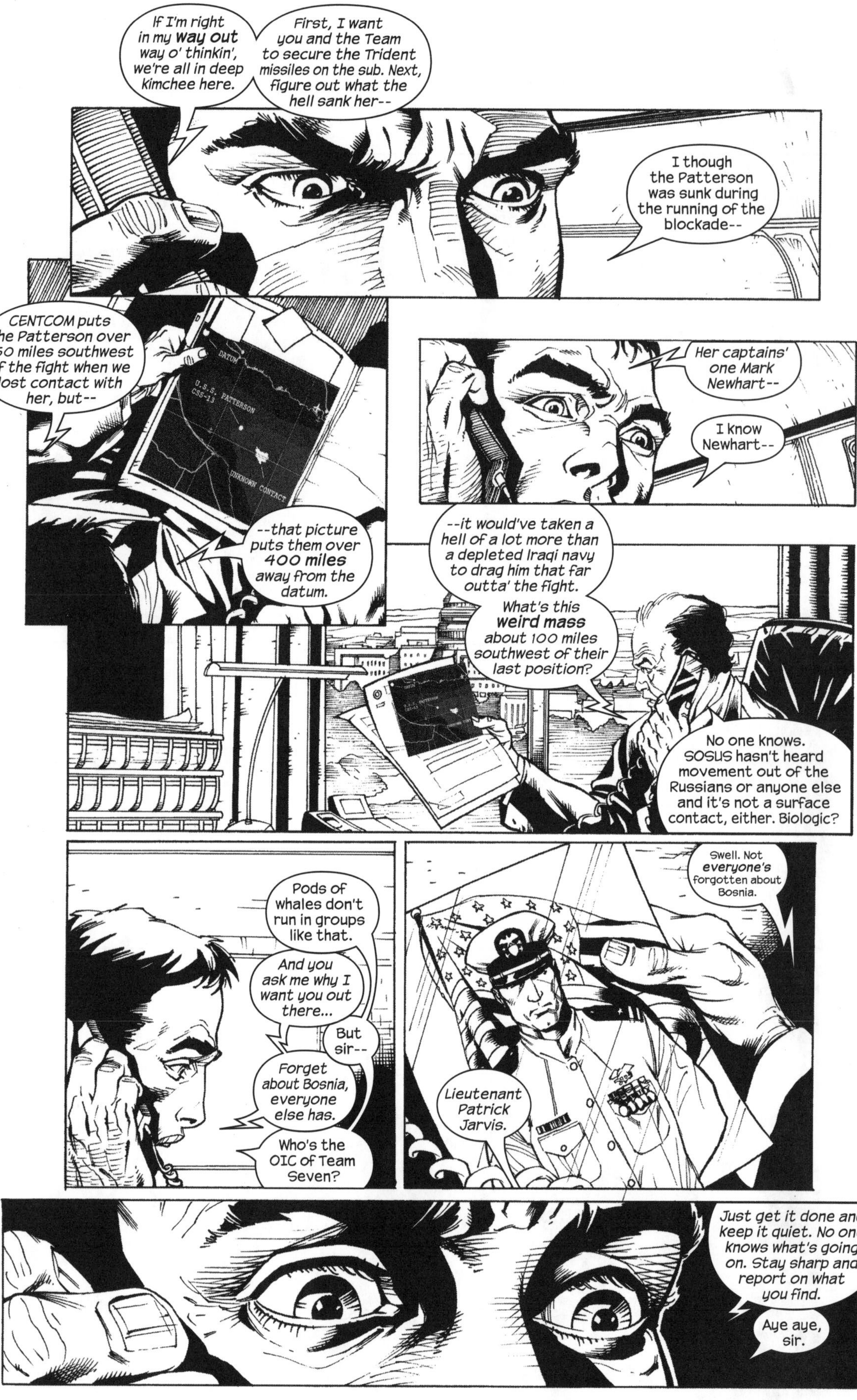
If I'm right in my **way out** way o' thinkin', we're all in deep kimchee here.
First, I want you and the Team to secure the Trident missiles on the sub. Next, figure out what the hell sank her--
I though the Patterson was sunk during the running of the blockade--
CENTCOM puts the Patterson over 150 miles southwest of the fight when we lost contact with her, but--
DATUM
U.S.S. PATTERSON
UNKNOWN CONTACT
Her captains' one Mark Newhart--
I know Newhart--
--that picture puts them over **400 miles** away from the datum.
--it would've taken a hell of a lot more than a depleted Iraqi navy to drag him that far outta' the fight.
What's this **weird mass** about 100 miles southwest of their last position?
No one knows. SOSUS hasn't heard movement out of the Russians or anyone else and it's not a surface contact, either. Biologic?
Pods of whales don't run in groups like that.
And you ask me why I want you out there...
But sir--
Forget about Bosnia, everyone else has.
Who's the OIC of Team Seven?
Swell. Not *everyone's* forgotten about Bosnia.
Lieutenant Patrick Jarvis.
Just get it done and keep it quiet. No one knows what's going on. Stay sharp and report on what you find.
Aye aye, sir.

SKIES OVER SAUDI ARABIA--0518 ZULU

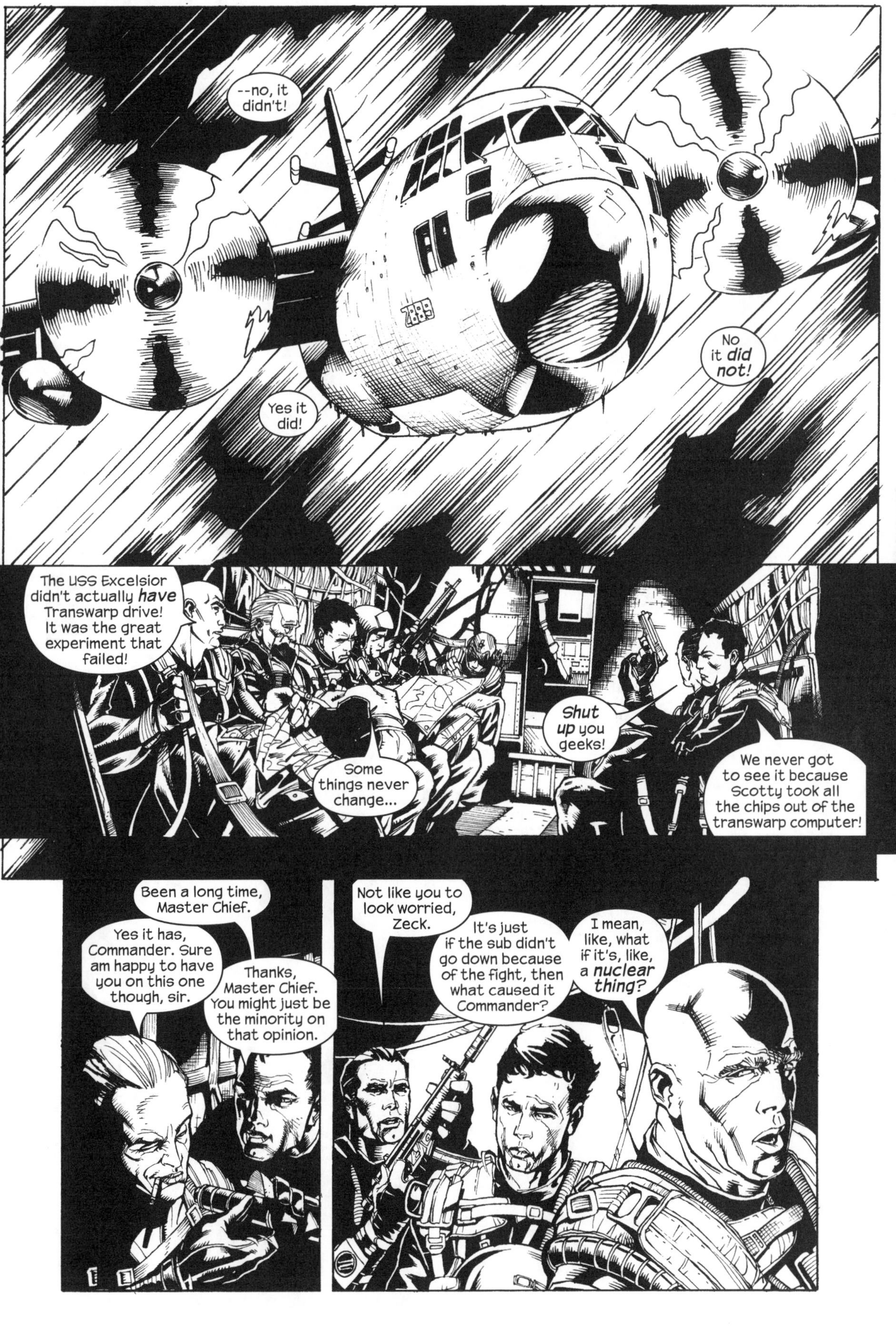
--no, it didn't!
Yes it did!
No it *did not!*
7889
The USS Excelsior didn't actually *have* Transwarp drive! It was the great experiment that failed!
Some things never change...
Shut up you geeks!
We never got to see it because Scotty took all the chips out of the transwarp computer!
Been a long time, Master Chief.
Yes it has, Commander. Sure am happy to have you on this one though, sir.
Thanks, Master Chief. You might just be the minority on that opinion.
Not like you to look worried, Zeck.
It's just if the sub didn't go down because of the fight, then what caused it Commander?
I mean, like, what if it's, like, a *nuclear thing?*

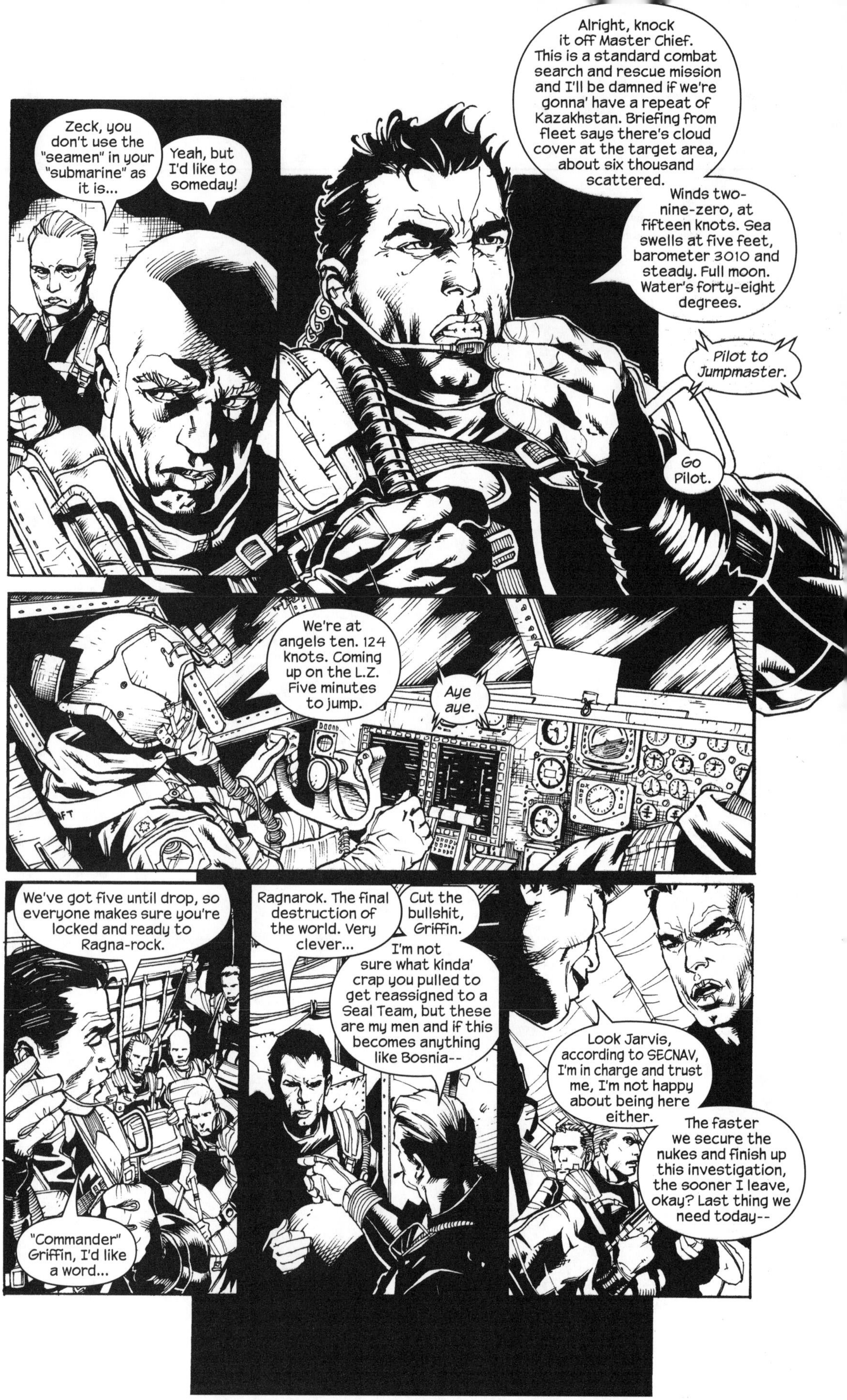
Zeck, you don't use the "seamen" in your "submarine" as it is...
Yeah, but I'd like to someday!
Alright, knock it off Master Chief. This is a standard combat search and rescue mission and I'll be damned if we're gonna' have a repeat of Kazakhstan. Briefing from fleet says there's cloud cover at the target area, about six thousand scattered.
Winds two-nine-zero, at fifteen knots. Sea swells at five feet, barometer 3010 and steady. Full moon. Water's forty-eight degrees.
Pilot to Jumpmaster.
Go Pilot.
We're at angels ten. 124 knots. Coming up on the L.Z. Five minutes to jump.
Aye aye.
We've got five until drop, so everyone makes sure you're locked and ready to Ragna-rock.
"Commander" Griffin, I'd like a word...
Ragnarok. The final destruction of the world. Very clever...
Cut the bullshit, Griffin.
I'm not sure what kinda' crap you pulled to get reassigned to a Seal Team, but these are my men and if this becomes anything like Bosnia--
Look Jarvis, according to SECNAV, I'm in charge and trust me, I'm not happy about being here either.
The faster we secure the nukes and finish up this investigation, the sooner I leave, okay? Last thing we need today--

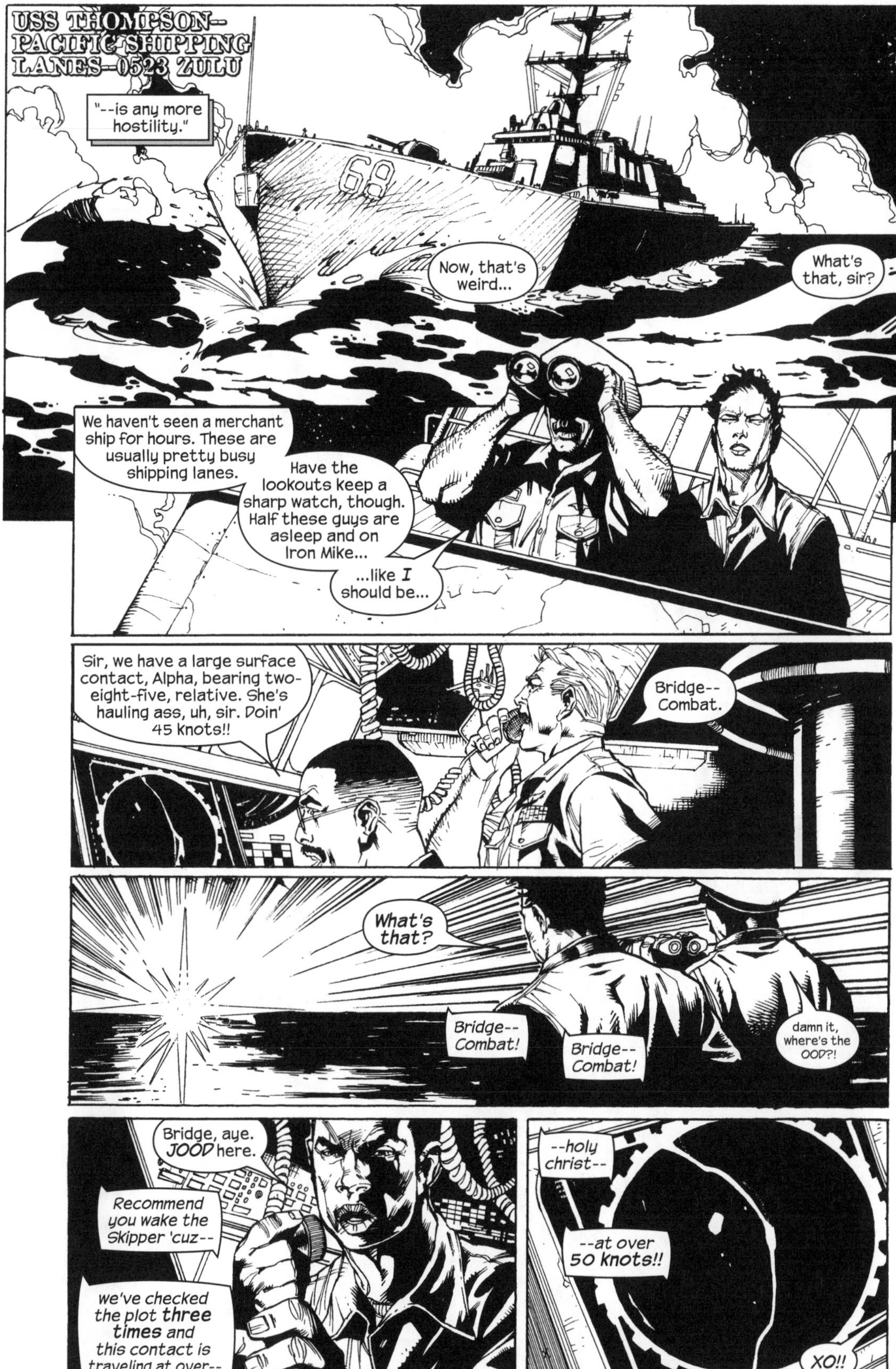
USS THOMPSON--
PACIFIC SHIPPING
LANES--0523 ZULU
"--is any more hostility."
Now, that's weird...
What's that, sir?
We haven't seen a merchant ship for hours. These are usually pretty busy shipping lanes.
Have the lookouts keep a sharp watch, though. Half these guys are asleep and on Iron Mike...
...like I should be...
Sir, we have a large surface contact, Alpha, bearing two-eight-five, relative. She's hauling ass, uh, sir. Doin' 45 knots!!
Bridge--Combat.
What's that?
Bridge--Combat!
Bridge--Combat!
damn it, where's the OOD?!
Bridge, aye. JOOD here.
Recommend you wake the Skipper 'cuz--
we've checked the plot three times and this contact is traveling at over--
--holy christ--
--at over 50 knots!!
XO!!

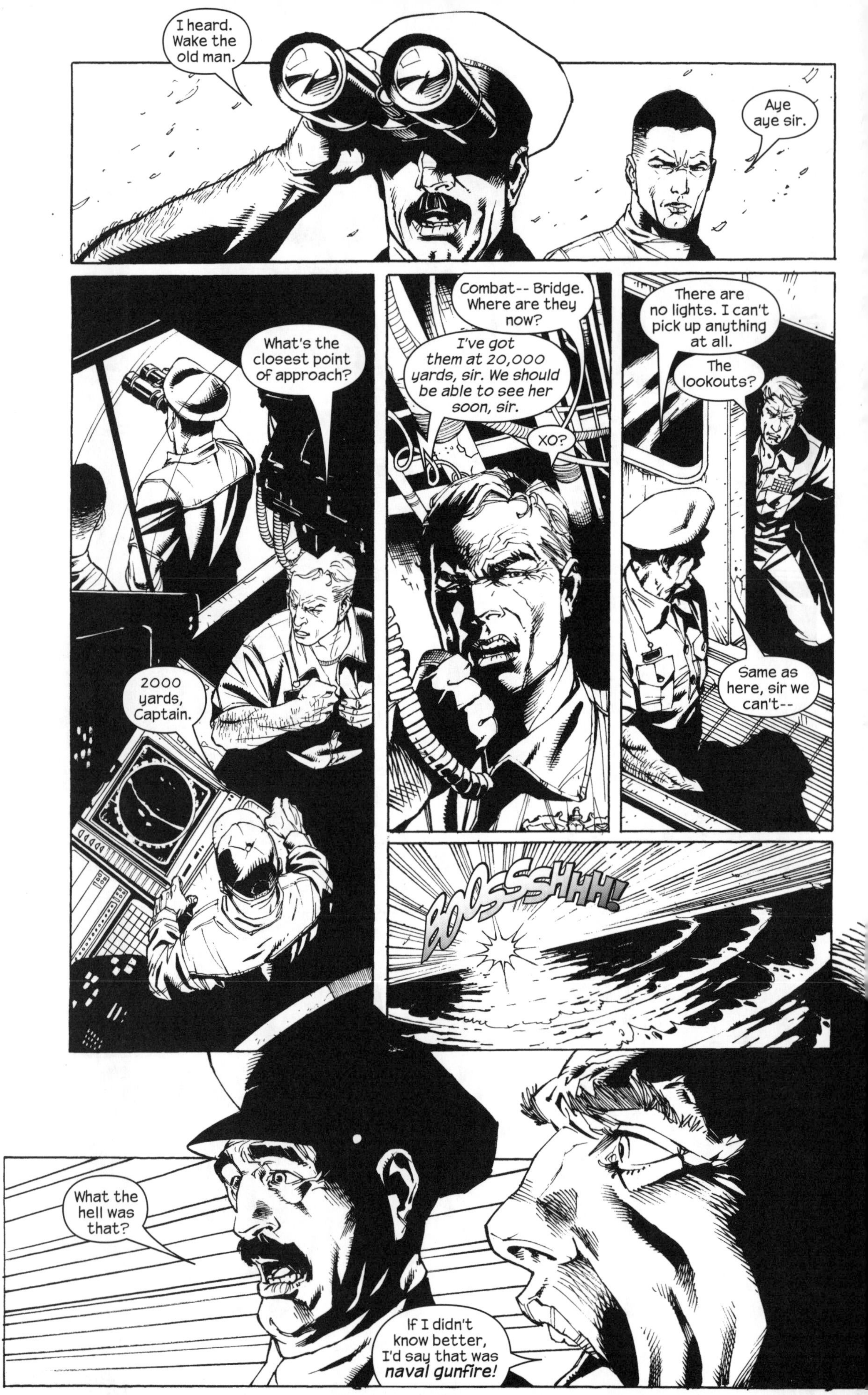
I heard. Wake the old man.
Aye aye sir.
What's the closest point of approach?
2000 yards, Captain.
Combat-- Bridge. Where are they now?
I've got them at 20,000 yards, sir. We should be able to see her soon, sir.
XO?
There are no lights. I can't pick up anything at all.
The lookouts?
Same as here, sir we can't--
BOOSSSHHH!
What the hell was that?
If I didn't know better, I'd say that was naval gunfire!

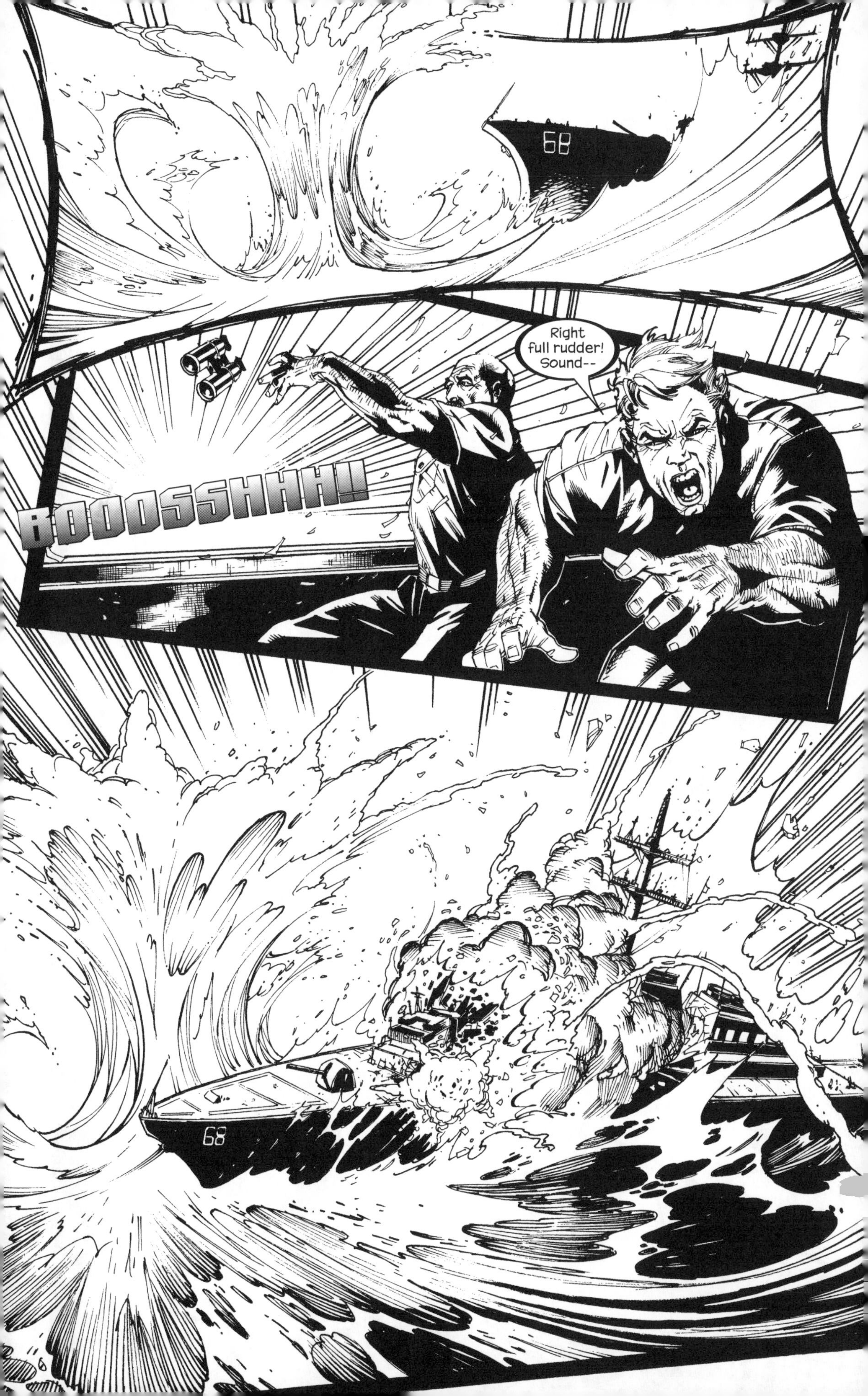
Right full rudder! Sound--
BOOOSSHHH!!

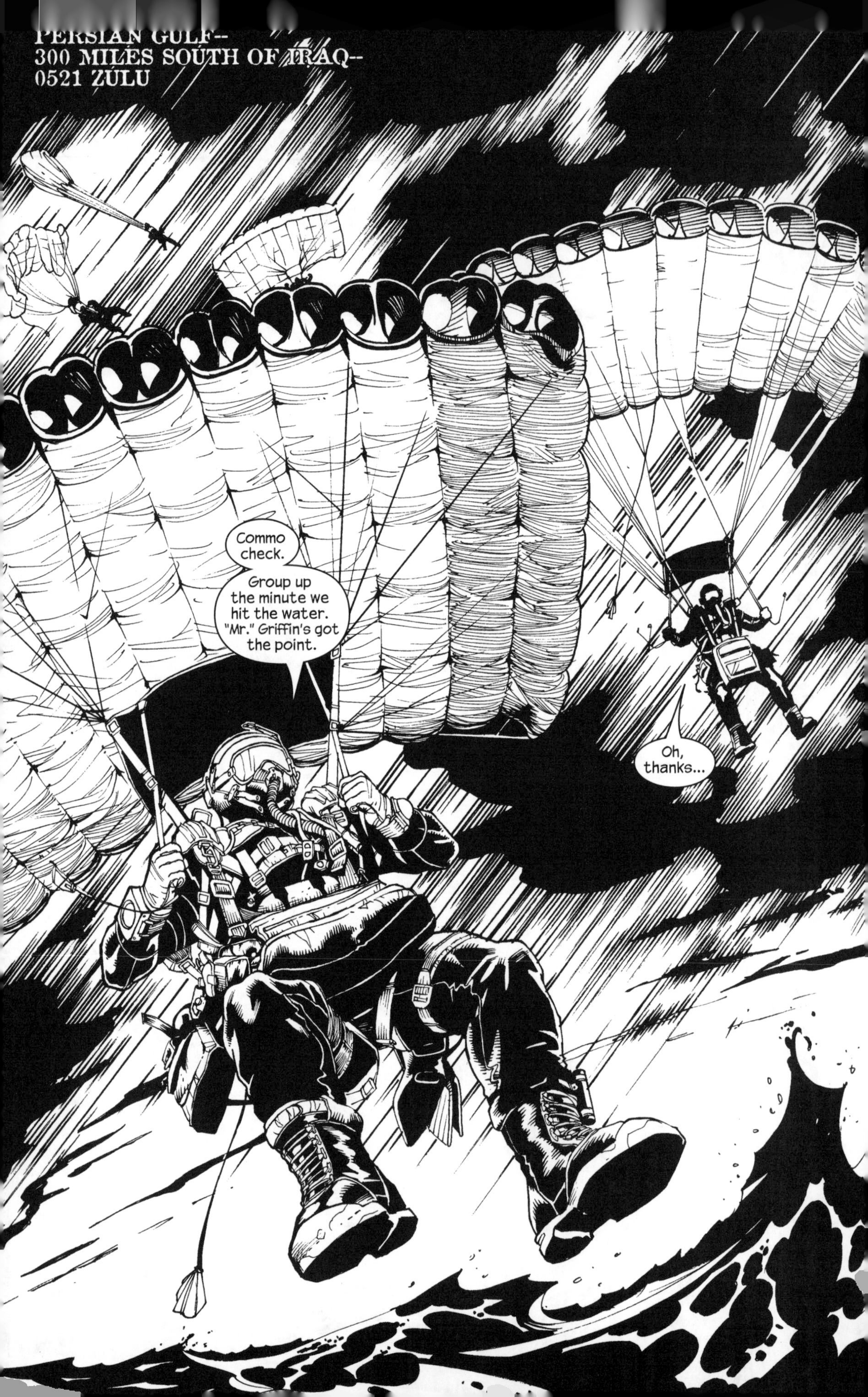
PERSIAN GULF--
300 MILES SOUTH OF IRAQ--
0521 ZULU
Commo check.
Group up the minute we hit the water. "Mr." Griffin's got the point.
Oh, thanks...

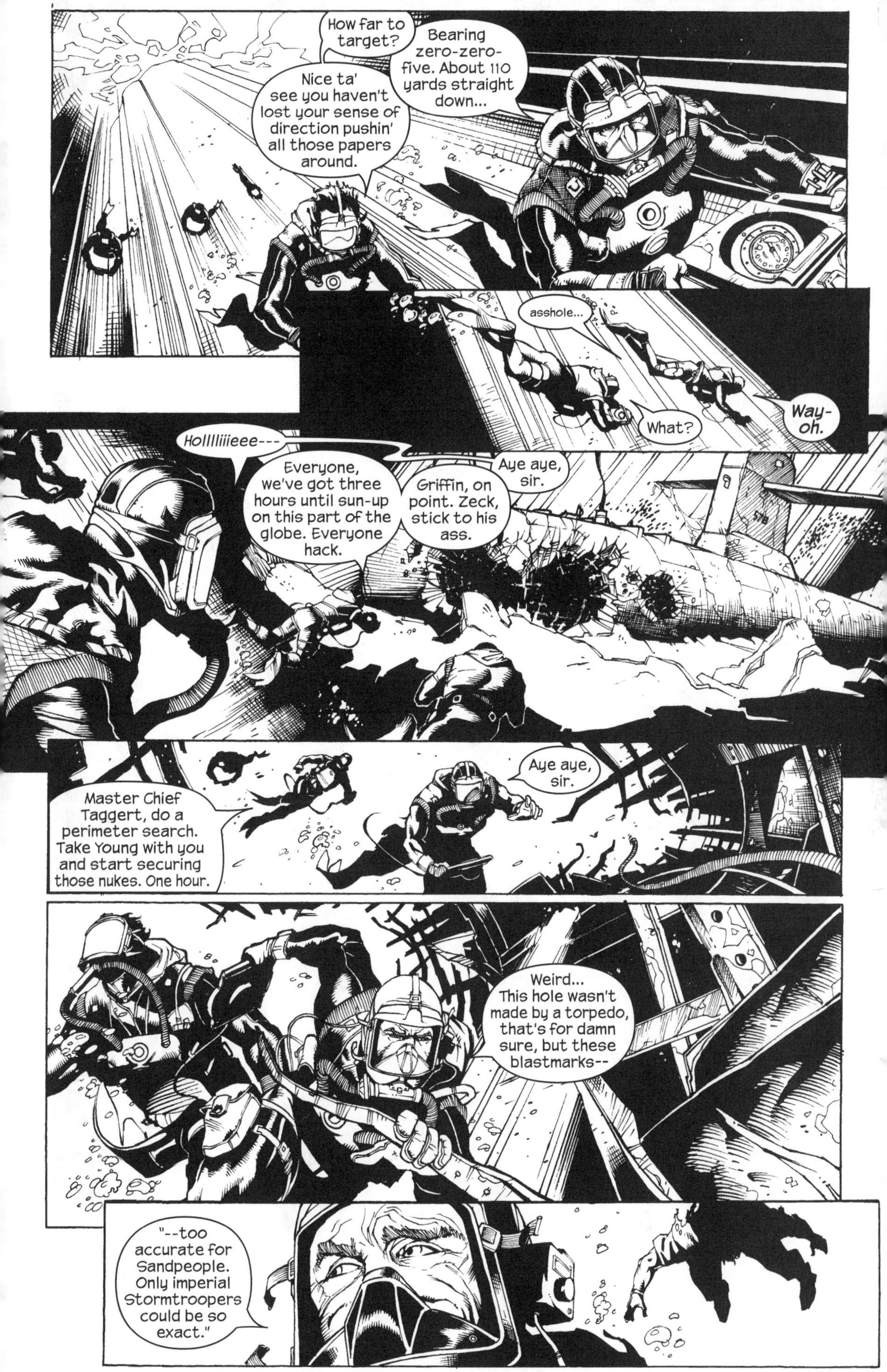
How far to target?
Bearing zero-zero-five. About 110 yards straight down...
Nice ta' see you haven't lost your sense of direction pushin' all those papers around.
asshole...
What?
Way-oh.
Hollllliiieee---
Everyone, we've got three hours until sun-up on this part of the globe. Everyone hack.
Griffin, on point. Zeck, stick to his ass.
Aye aye, sir.
Master Chief Taggert, do a perimeter search. Take Young with you and start securing those nukes. One hour.
Aye aye, sir.
Weird... This hole wasn't made by a torpedo, that's for damn sure, but these blastmarks--
"--too accurate for Sandpeople. Only imperial Stormtroopers could be so exact."

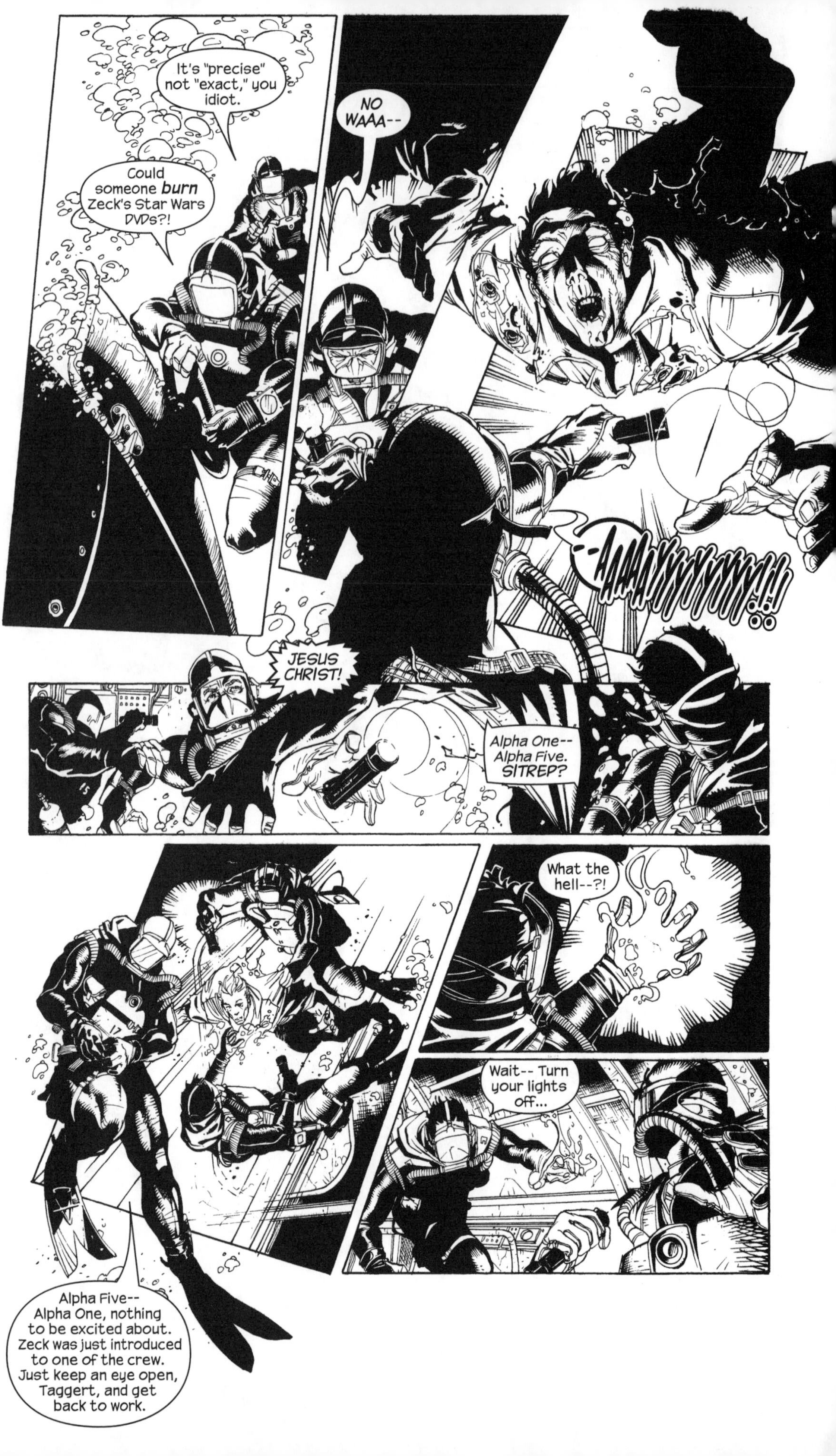
It's "precise" not "exact," you idiot.
Could someone burn Zeck's Star Wars DVDs?!
NO WAAA--
AAAAAYYYYYYYY!!!
JESUS CHRIST!
Alpha One-- Alpha Five. SITREP?
What the hell--?!
Wait-- Turn your lights off...
Alpha Five-- Alpha One, nothing to be excited about. Zeck was just introduced to one of the crew. Just keep an eye open, Taggert, and get back to work.

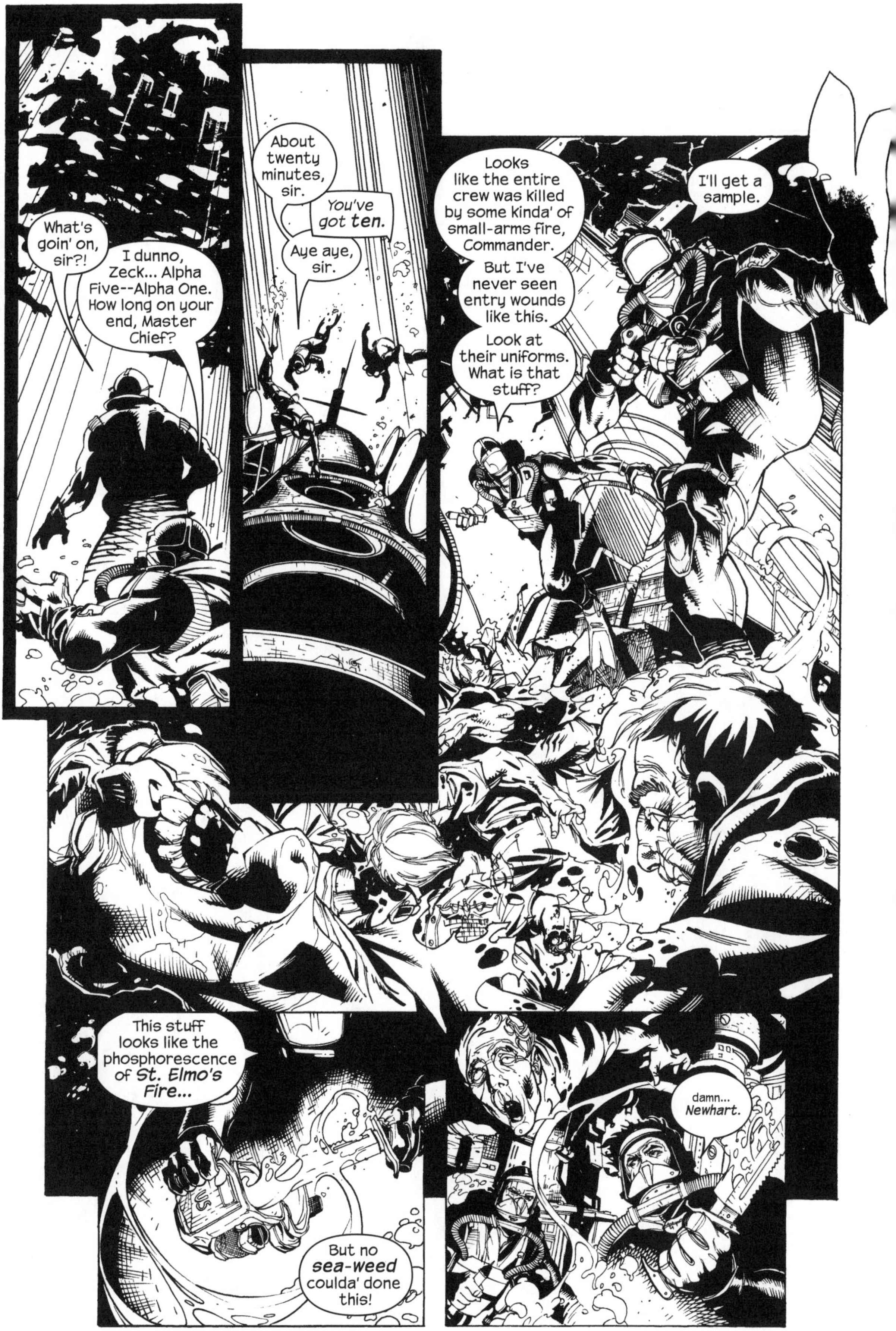
What's goin' on, sir?!
I dunno, Zeck... Alpha Five--Alpha One. How long on your end, Master Chief?
About twenty minutes, sir.
You've got ten.
Aye aye, sir.
Looks like the entire crew was killed by some kinda' of small-arms fire, Commander.
But I've never seen entry wounds like this.
Look at their uniforms. What is that stuff?
I'll get a sample.
This stuff looks like the phosphorescence of St. Elmo's Fire...
But no sea-weed coulda' done this!
damn... Newhart.

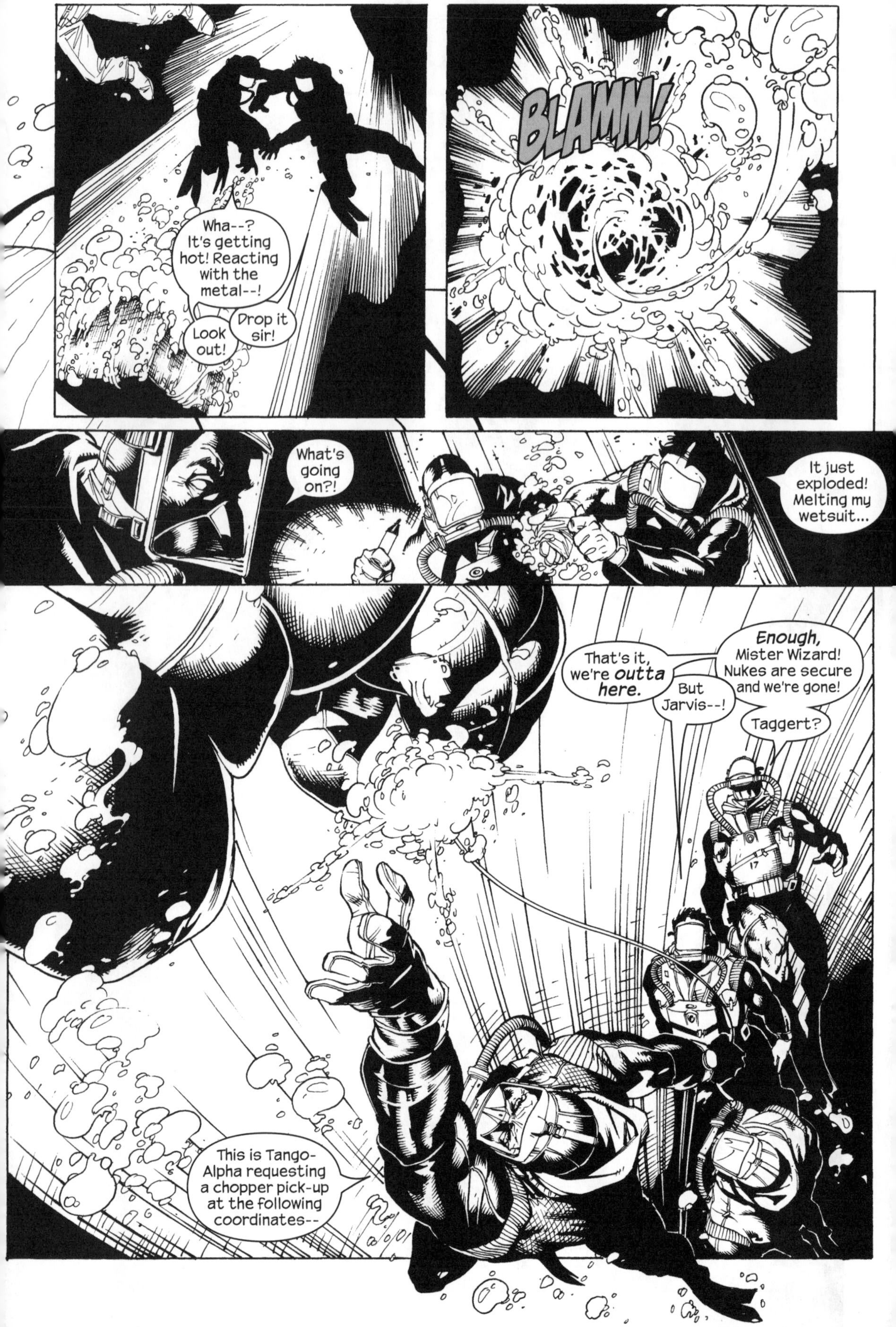
Wha--? It's getting hot! Reacting with the metal--!
Look out!
Drop it sir!
BLAMM!
What's going on?!
It just exploded! Melting my wetsuit...
That's it, we're *outta here.*
Enough, Mister Wizard! Nukes are secure and we're gone!
But Jarvis--!
Taggert?
This is Tango-Alpha requesting a chopper pick-up at the following coordinates--

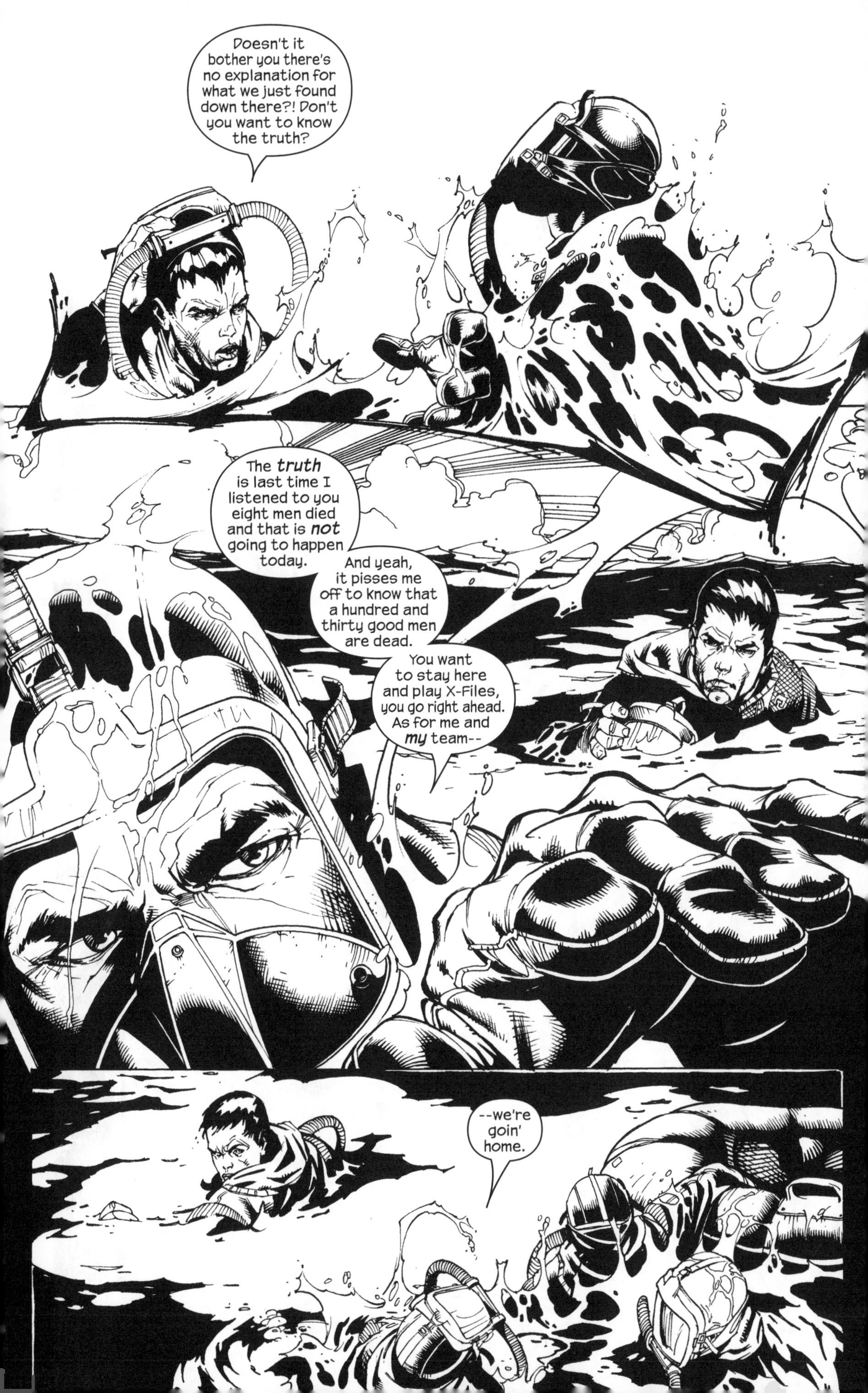
Doesn't it bother you there's no explanation for what we just found down there?! Don't you want to know the truth?
The *truth* is last time I listened to you eight men died and that is *not* going to happen today.
And yeah, it pisses me off to know that a hundred and thirty good men are dead.
You want to stay here and play X-Files, you go right ahead. As for me and *my* team--
--we're goin' home.

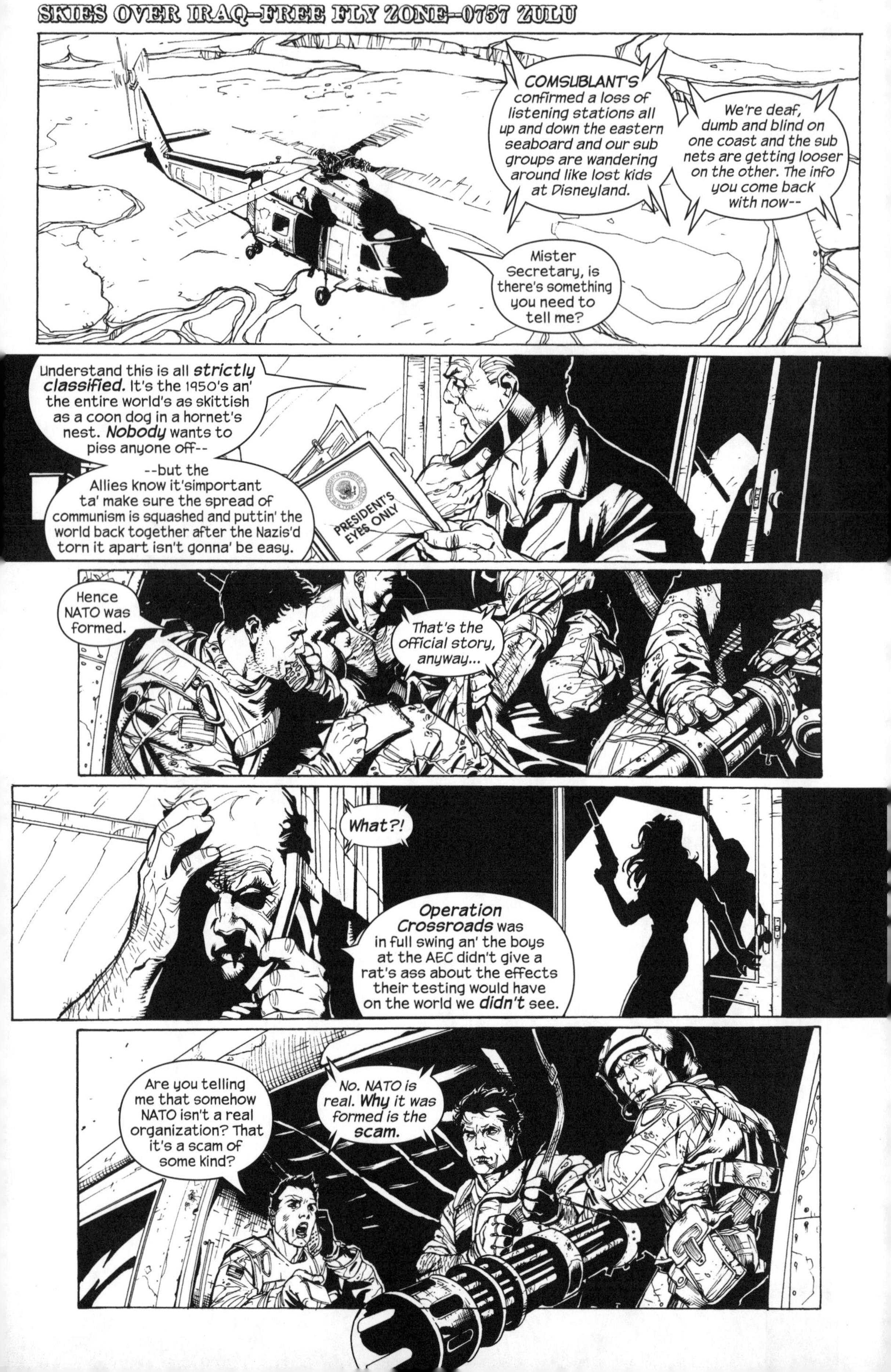
SKIES OVER IRAQ--FREE FLY ZONE--0757 ZULU
COMSUBLANT'S confirmed a loss of listening stations all up and down the eastern seaboard and our sub groups are wandering around like lost kids at Disneyland.
We're deaf, dumb and blind on one coast and the sub nets are getting looser on the other. The info you come back with now--
Mister Secretary, is there's something you need to tell me?
Understand this is all strictly classified. It's the 1950's an' the entire world's as skittish as a coon dog in a hornet's nest. Nobody wants to piss anyone off--
--but the Allies know it'simportant ta' make sure the spread of communism is squashed and puttin' the world back together after the Nazis'd torn it apart isn't gonna' be easy.
PRESIDENT'S EYES ONLY
Hence NATO was formed.
That's the official story, anyway...
What?!
Operation Crossroads was in full swing an' the boys at the AEC didn't give a rat's ass about the effects their testing would have on the world we didn't see.
Are you telling me that somehow NATO isn't a real organization? That it's a scam of some kind?
No. NATO is real. Why it was formed is the scam.

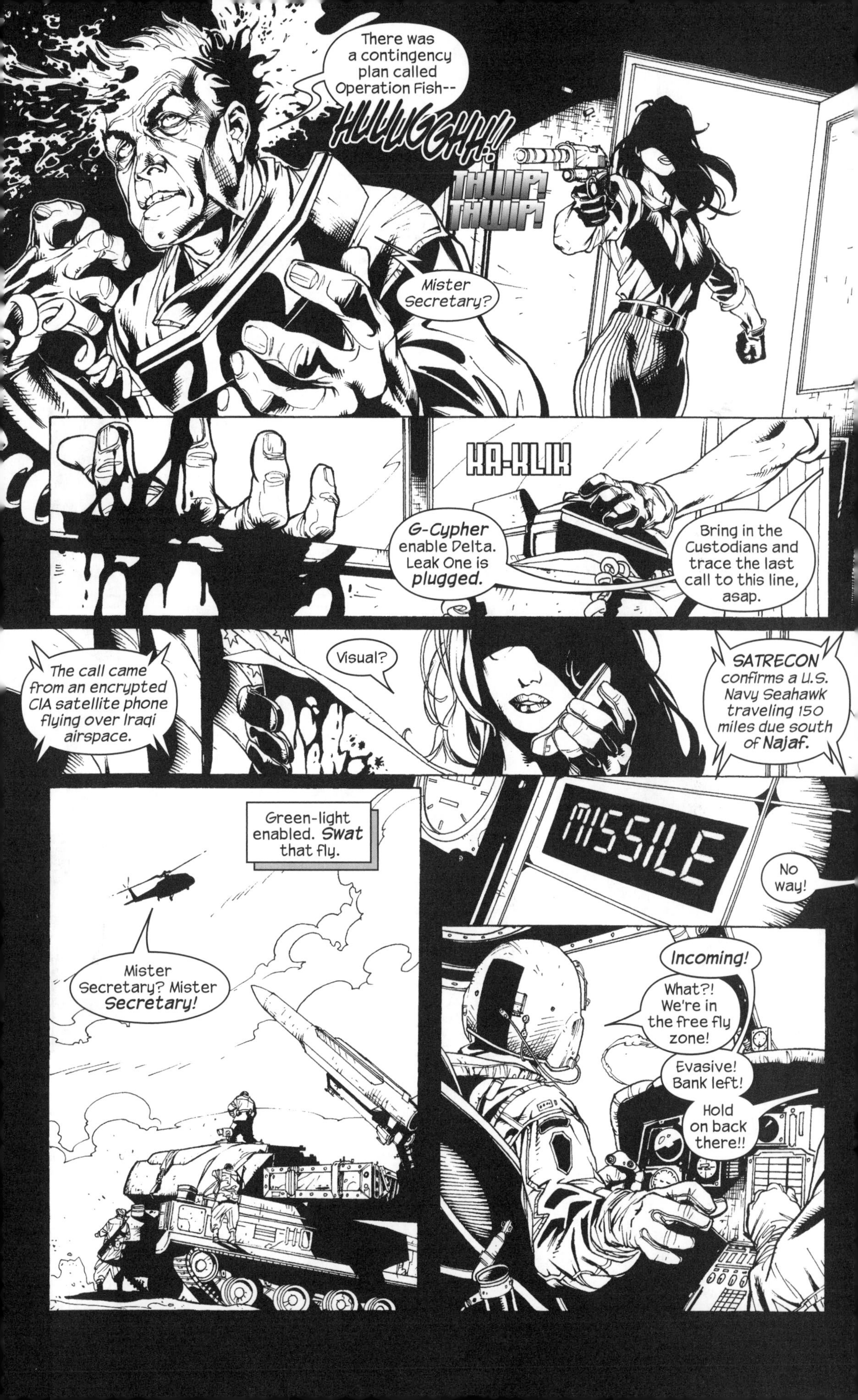
There was a contingency plan called Operation Fish--
HUUUGGHH!!
THWIP! THWIP!
Mister Secretary?
KA-KLIK
G-Cypher enable Delta. Leak One is plugged.
Bring in the Custodians and trace the last call to this line, asap.
The call came from an encrypted CIA satellite phone flying over Iraqi airspace.
Visual?
SATRECON confirms a U.S. Navy Seahawk traveling 150 miles due south of Najaf.
Green-light enabled. Swat that fly.
Mister Secretary? Mister Secretary!
MISSILE
No way!
Incoming!
What?! We're in the free fly zone!
Evasive! Bank left!
Hold on back there!!

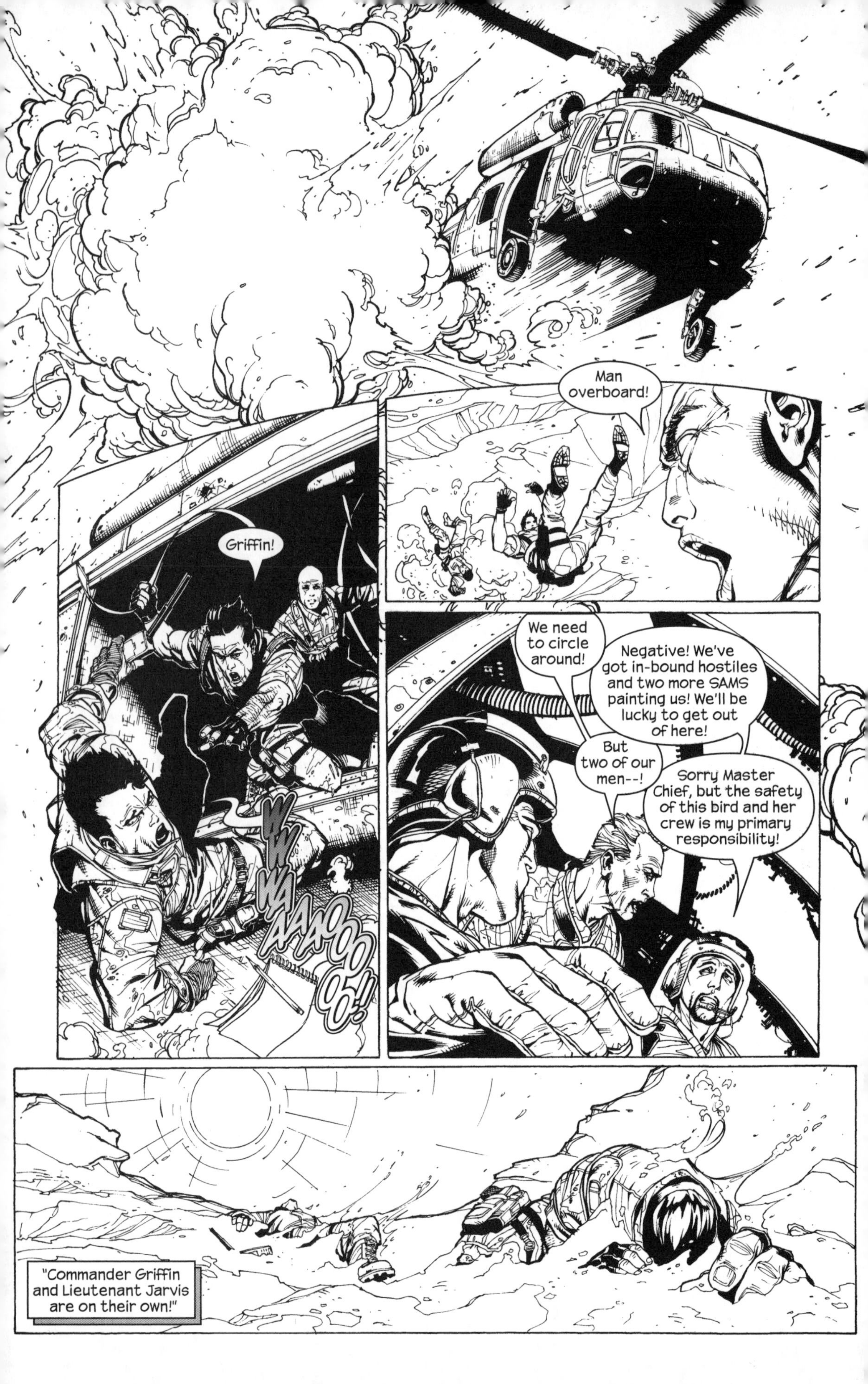
Griffin!
WWWAAAOOOO!!
Man overboard!
We need to circle around!
Negative! We've got in-bound hostiles and two more SAMS painting us! We'll be lucky to get out of here!
But two of our men--!
Sorry Master Chief, but the safety of this bird and her crew is my primary responsibility!
"Commander Griffin and Lieutenant Jarvis are on their own!"

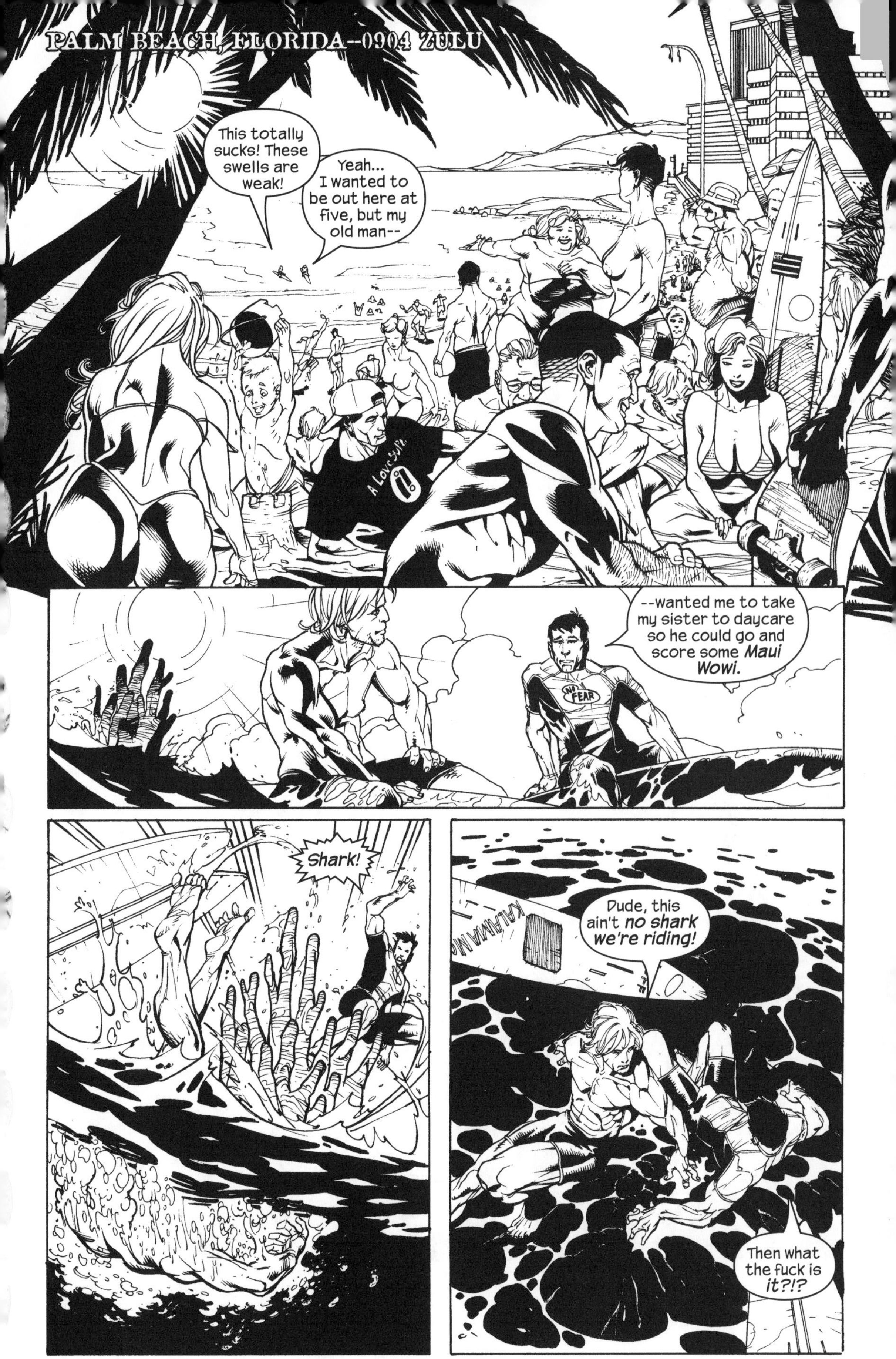
PALM BEACH, FLORIDA--0904 ZULU
This totally sucks! These swells are weak!
Yeah... I wanted to be out here at five, but my old man--
--wanted me to take my sister to daycare so he could go and score some Maui Wowi.
Shark!
Dude, this ain't no shark we're riding!
Then what the fuck is it?!?

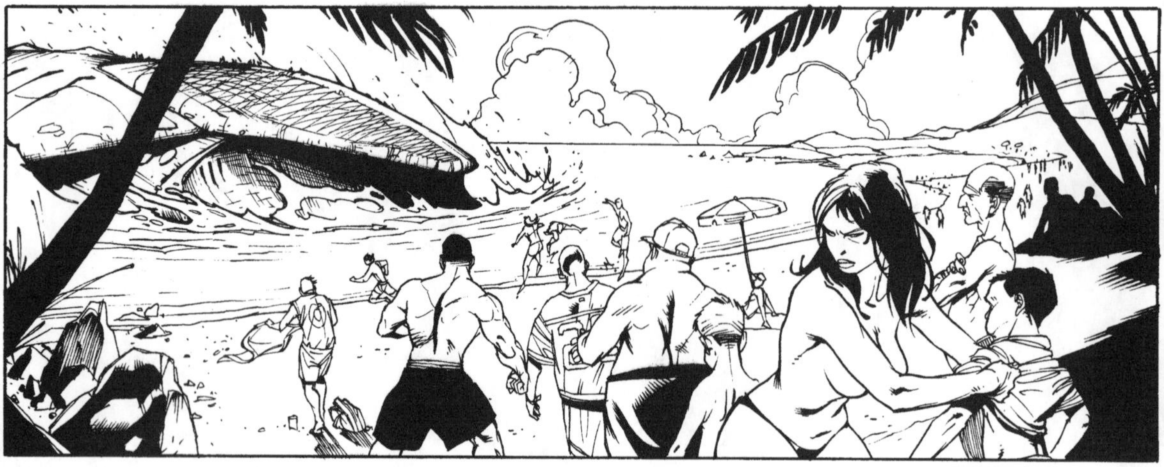

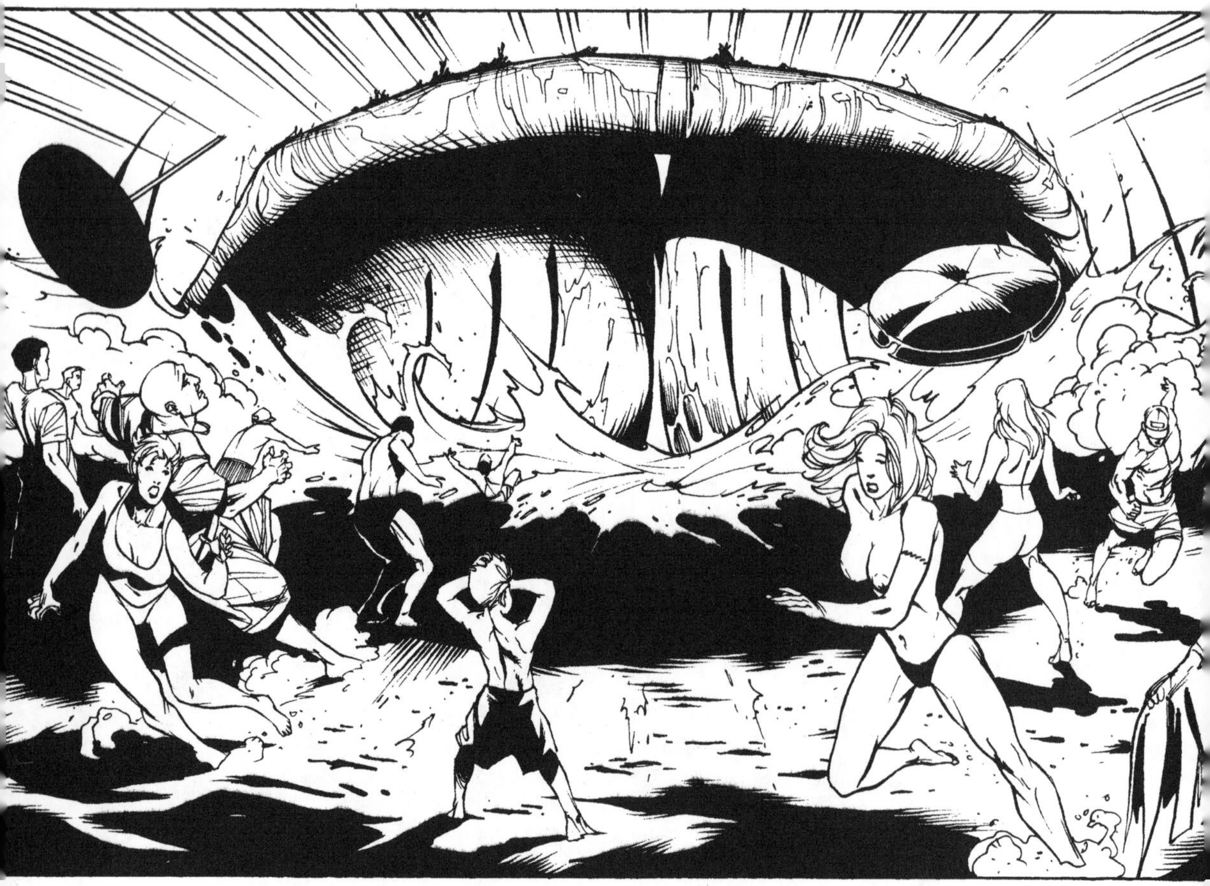

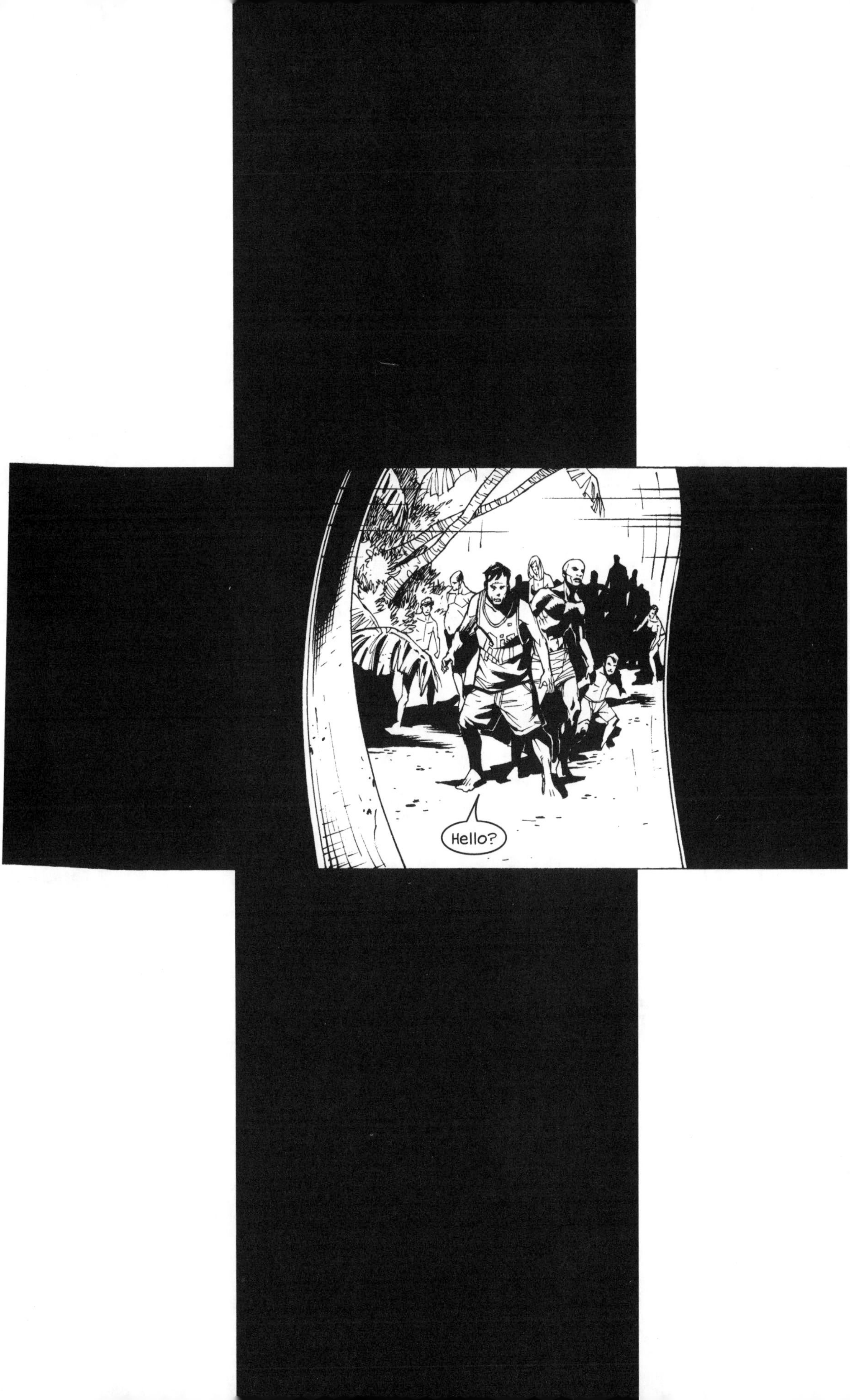
Hello?

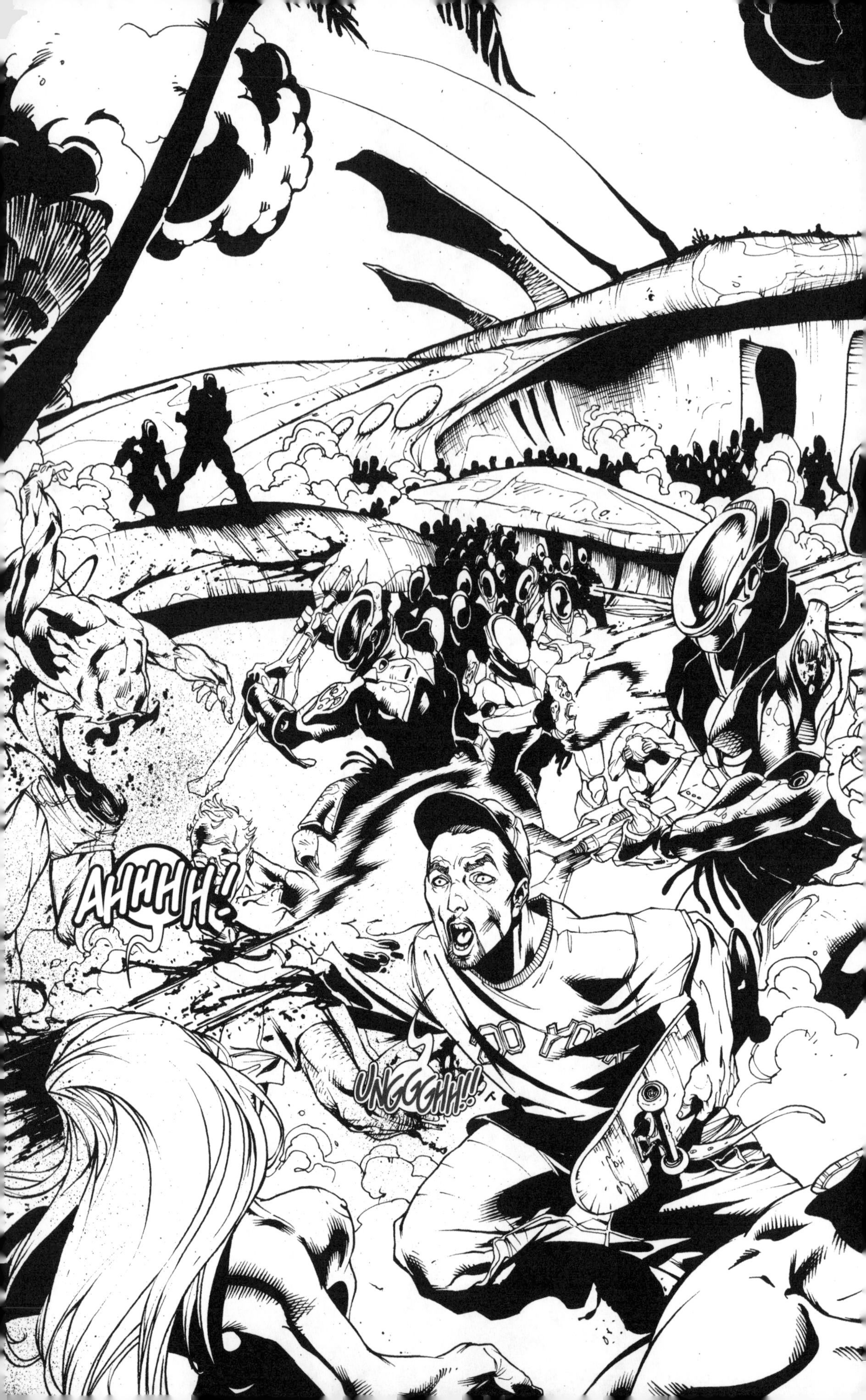
AHHHHH!
UNGGGHH!!

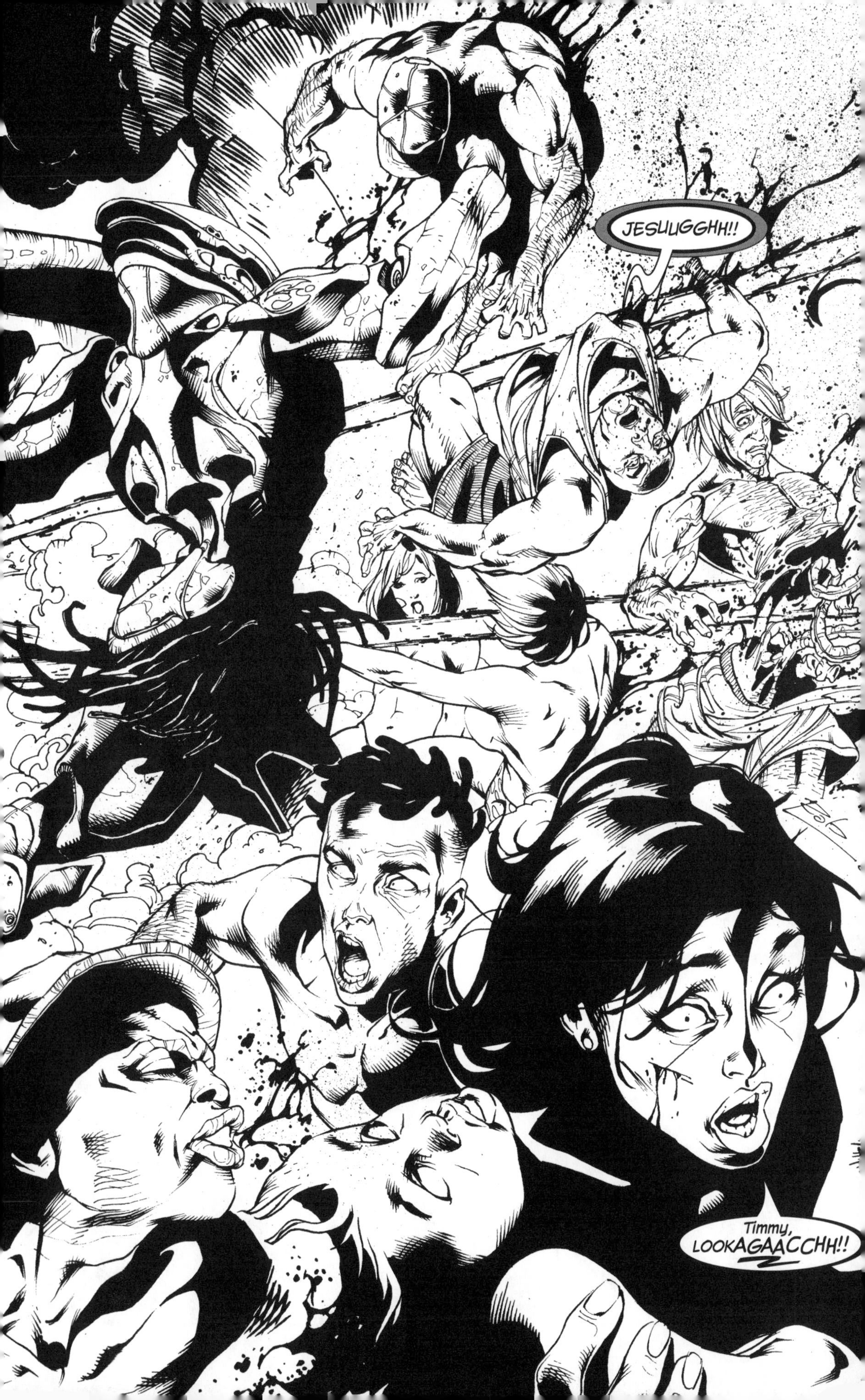
JESUUGGHH!!
Timmy, LOOKAGAACCHH!!

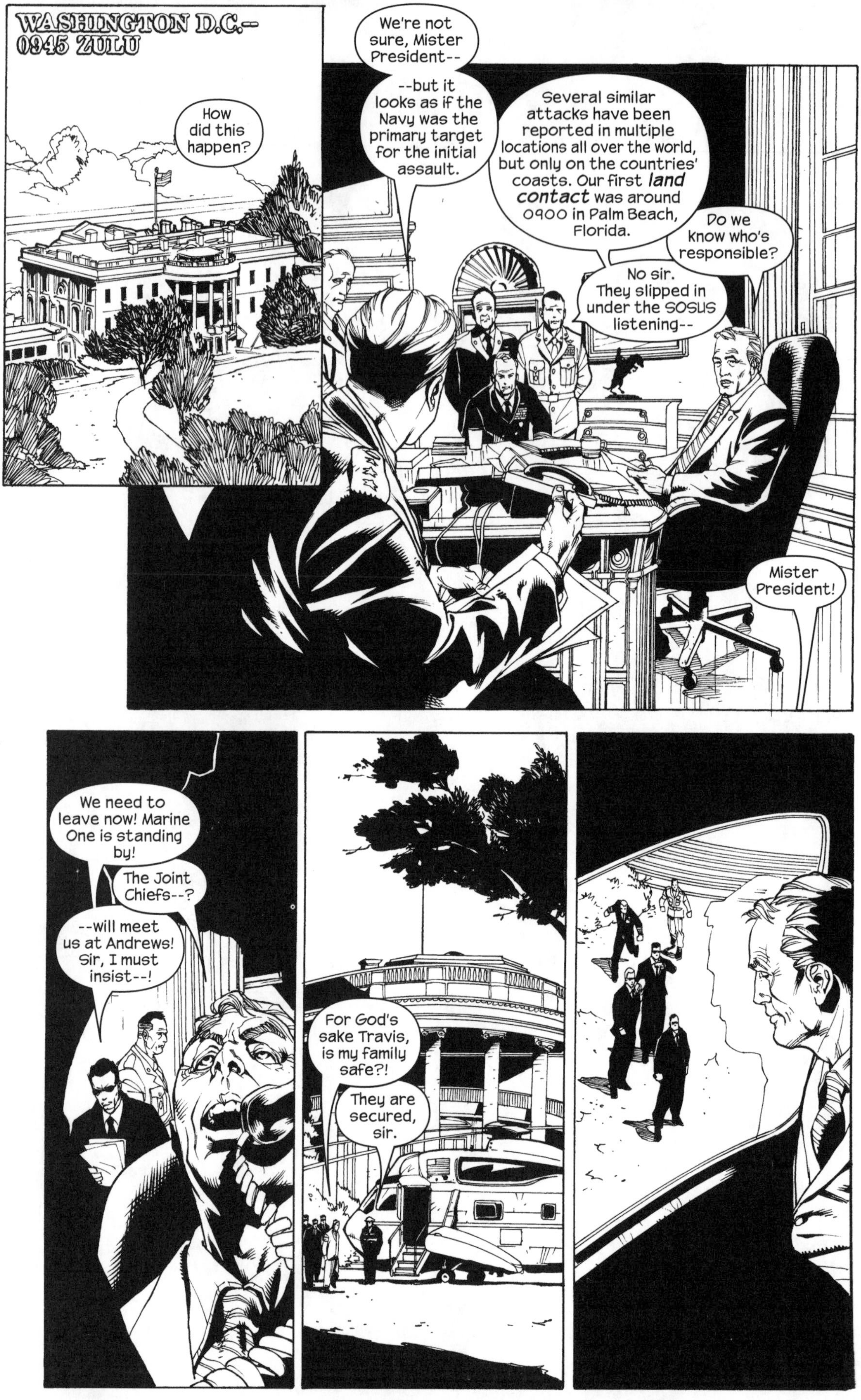
WASHINGTON D.C.--
0945 ZULU
How did this happen?
We're not sure, Mister President--
--but it looks as if the Navy was the primary target for the initial assault.
Several similar attacks have been reported in multiple locations all over the world, but only on the countries' coasts. Our first *land contact* was around 0900 in Palm Beach, Florida.
Do we know who's responsible?
No sir. They slipped in under the SOSUS listening--
Mister President!
We need to leave now! Marine One is standing by!
The Joint Chiefs--?
--will meet us at Andrews! Sir, I must insist--!
For God's sake Travis, is my family safe?!
They are secured, sir.

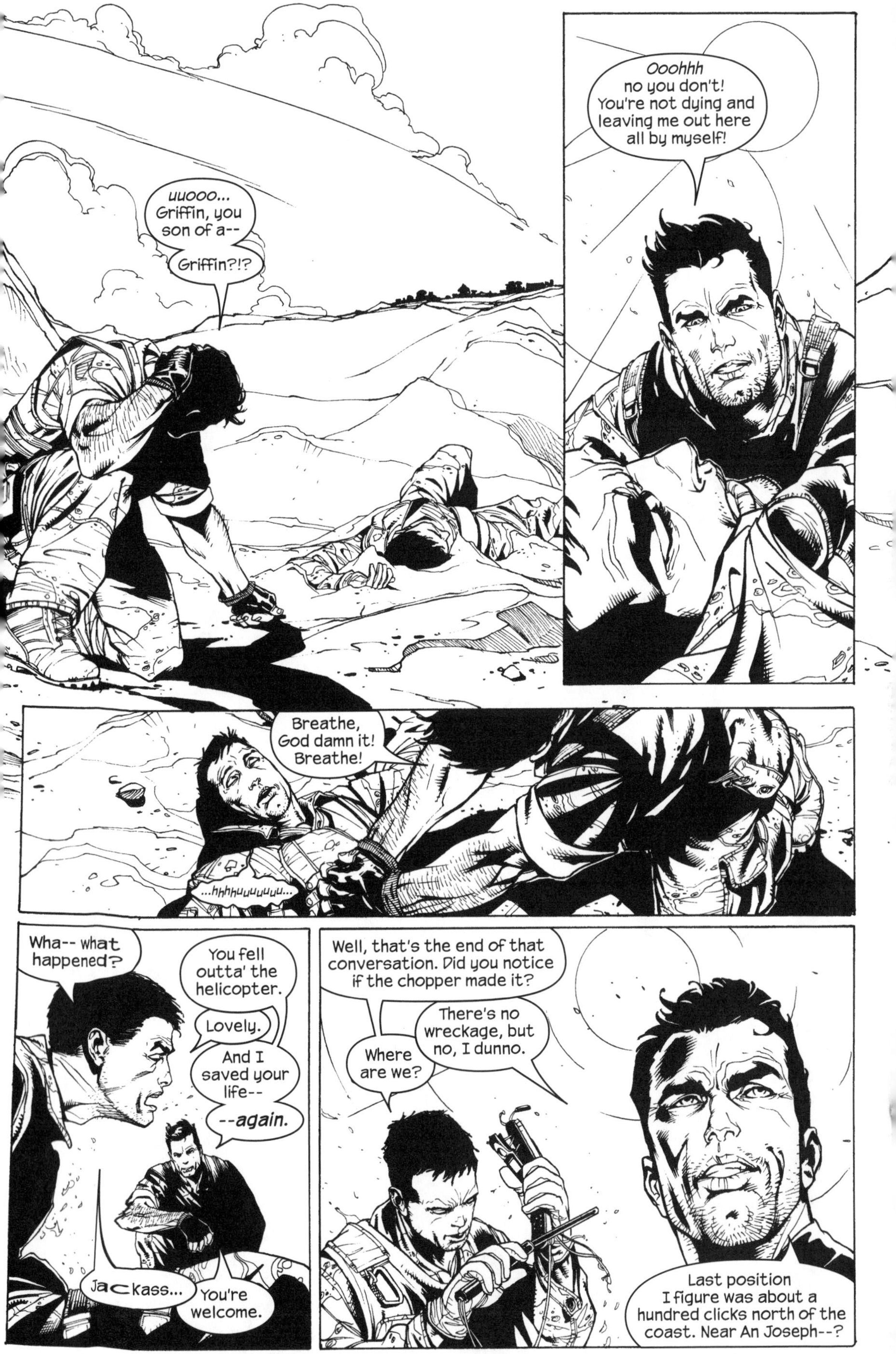
uuooo...
Griffin, you son of a--
Griffin?!?
Ooohhh no you don't! You're not dying and leaving me out here all by myself!
Breathe, God damn it! Breathe!
...hhhhuuuuuuu...
Wha-- what happened?
You fell outta' the helicopter.
Lovely.
And I saved your life--
--again.
Jackass...
You're welcome.
Well, that's the end of that conversation. Did you notice if the chopper made it?
Where are we?
There's no wreckage, but no, I dunno.
Last position I figure was about a hundred clicks north of the coast. Near An Joseph--?

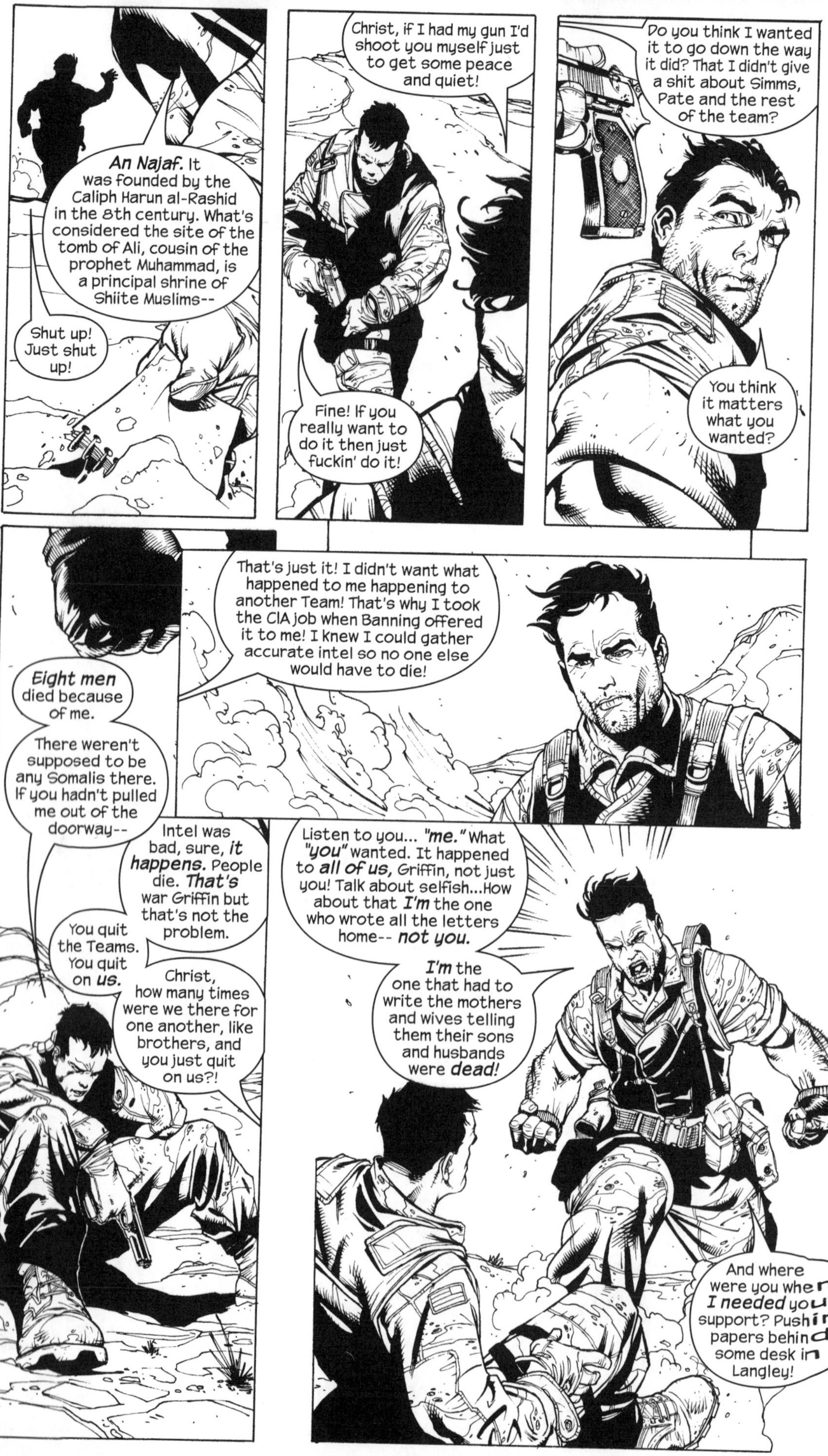
An Najaf. It was founded by the Caliph Harun al-Rashid in the 8th century. What's considered the site of the tomb of Ali, cousin of the prophet Muhammad, is a principal shrine of Shiite Muslims--
Shut up! Just shut up!
Christ, if I had my gun I'd shoot you myself just to get some peace and quiet!
Fine! If you really want to do it then just fuckin' do it!
Do you think I wanted it to go down the way it did? That I didn't give a shit about Simms, Pate and the rest of the team?
You think it matters what you wanted?
That's just it! I didn't want what happened to me happening to another Team! That's why I took the CIA job when Banning offered it to me! I knew I could gather accurate intel so no one else would have to die!
Eight men died because of me.
There weren't supposed to be any Somalis there. If you hadn't pulled me out of the doorway--
Intel was bad, sure, it happens. People die. That's war Griffin but that's not the problem.
You quit the Teams. You quit on us.
Christ, how many times were we there for one another, like brothers, and you just quit on us?!
Listen to you... "me." What "you" wanted. It happened to all of us, Griffin, not just you! Talk about selfish...How about that I'm the one who wrote all the letters home-- not you.
I'm the one that had to write the mothers and wives telling them their sons and husbands were dead!
And where were you when I needed your support? Pushing papers behind some desk in Langley!

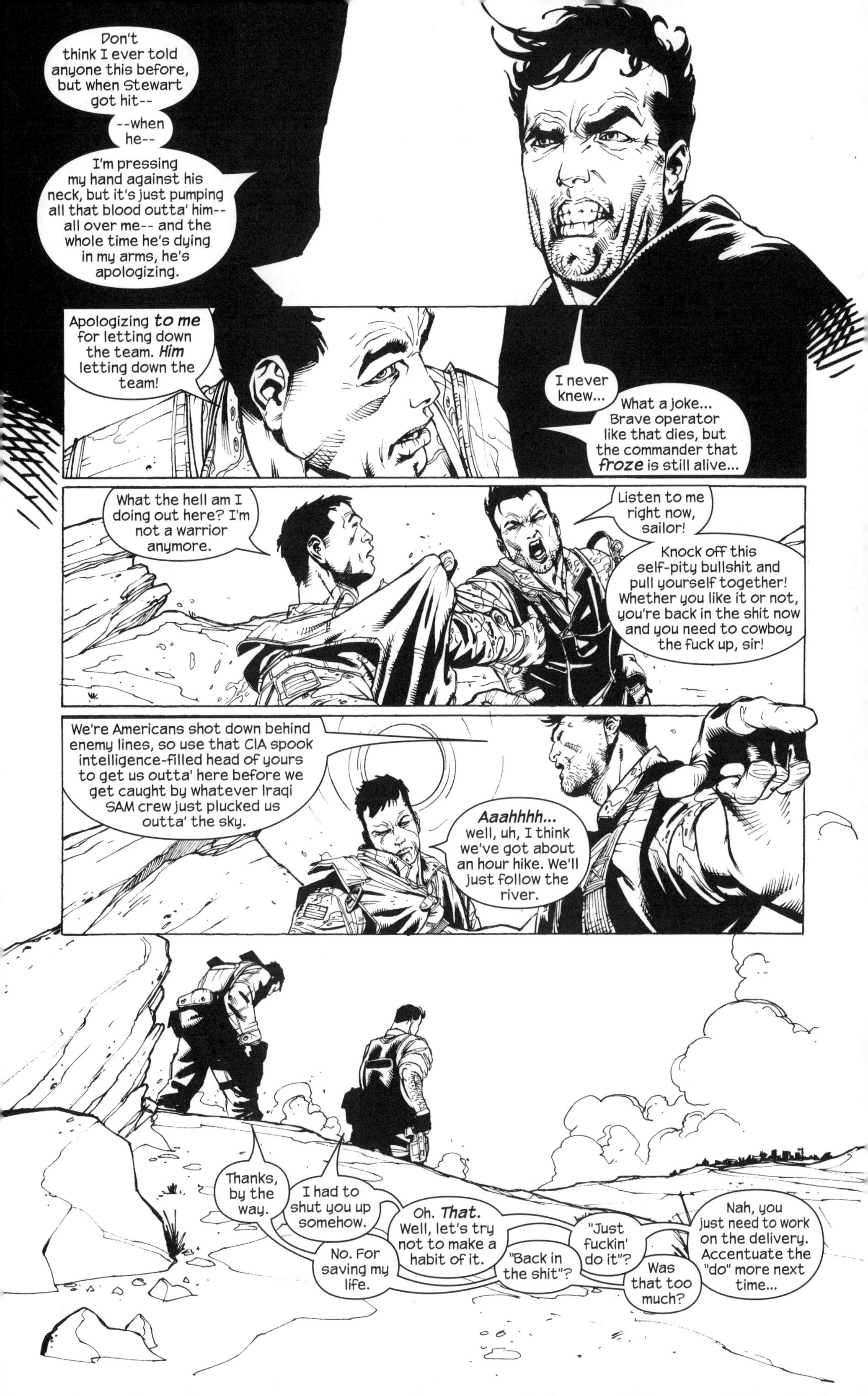
Don't think I ever told anyone this before, but when Stewart got hit--
--when he--
I'm pressing my hand against his neck, but it's just pumping all that blood outta' him-- all over me-- and the whole time he's dying in my arms, he's apologizing.
Apologizing *to me* for letting down the team. *Him* letting down the team!
I never knew...
What a joke... Brave operator like that dies, but the commander that *froze* is still alive...
What the hell am I doing out here? I'm not a warrior anymore.
Listen to me right now, sailor!
Knock off this self-pity bullshit and pull yourself together! Whether you like it or not, you're back in the shit now and you need to cowboy the fuck up, sir!
We're Americans shot down behind enemy lines, so use that CIA spook intelligence-filled head of yours to get us outta' here before we get caught by whatever Iraqi SAM crew just plucked us outta' the sky.
Aaahhhh... well, uh, I think we've got about an hour hike. We'll just follow the river.
Thanks, by the way.
I had to shut you up somehow.
No. For saving my life.
Oh. *That.* Well, let's try not to make a habit of it.
"Back in the shit"?
"Just fuckin' do it"?
Was that too much?
Nah, you just need to work on the delivery. Accentuate the "do" more next time...

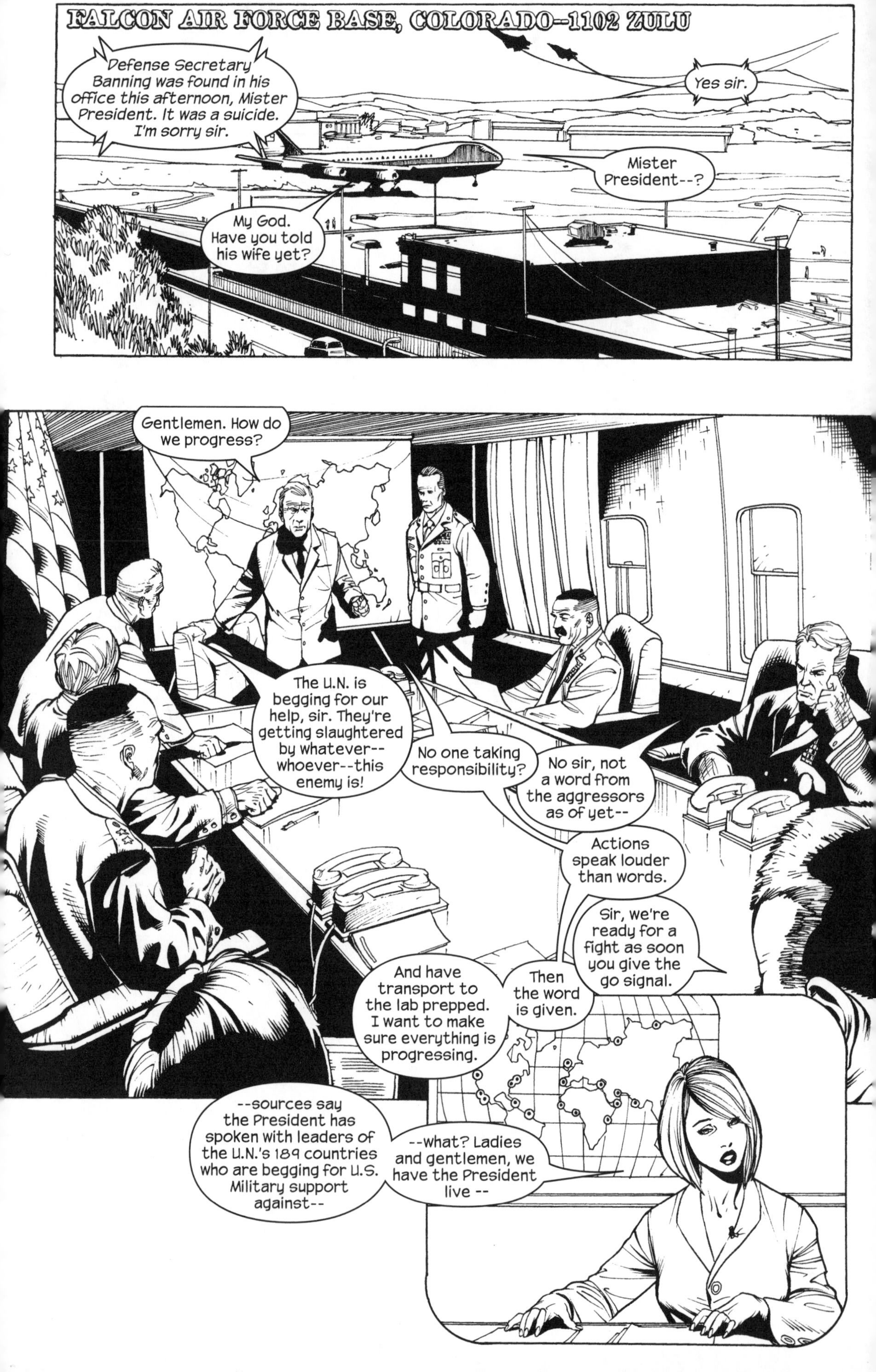

FALCON AIR FORCE BASE, COLORADO--1102 ZULU
Defense Secretary Banning was found in his office this afternoon, Mister President. It was a suicide. I'm sorry sir.
My God. Have you told his wife yet?
Yes sir.
Mister President--?
Gentlemen. How do we progress?
The U.N. is begging for our help, sir. They're getting slaughtered by whatever--whoever--this enemy is!
No one taking responsibility?
No sir, not a word from the aggressors as of yet--
Actions speak louder than words.
Sir, we're ready for a fight as soon you give the go signal.
Then the word is given.
And have transport to the lab prepped. I want to make sure everything is progressing.
--sources say the President has spoken with leaders of the U.N.'s 189 countries who are begging for U.S. Military support against--
--what? Ladies and gentlemen, we have the President live --

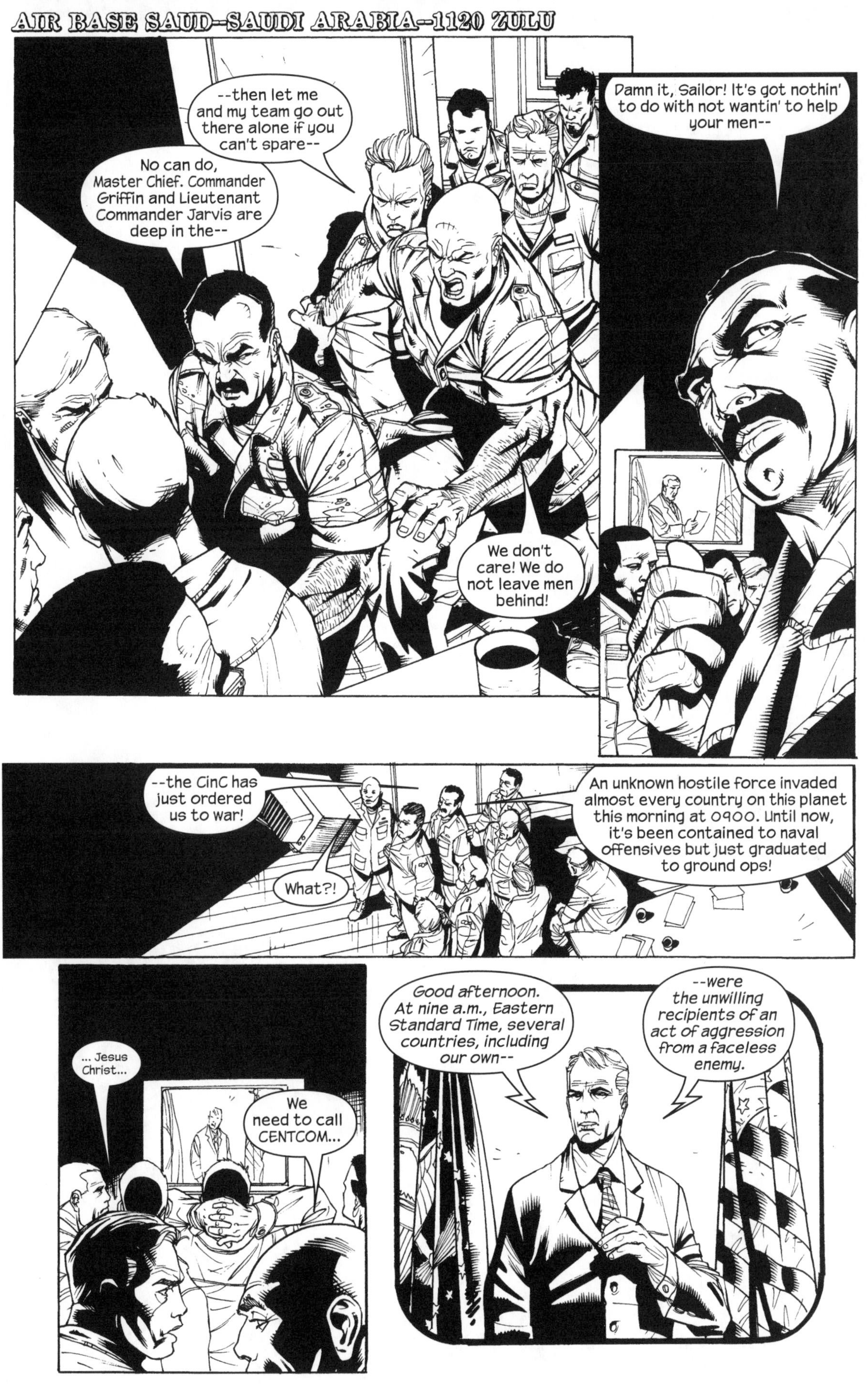
AIR BASE SAUD--SAUDI ARABIA--1120 ZULU
--then let me and my team go out there alone if you can't spare--
No can do, Master Chief. Commander Griffin and Lieutenant Commander Jarvis are deep in the--
We don't care! We do not leave men behind!
Damn it, Sailor! It's got nothin' to do with not wantin' to help your men--
--the CinC has just ordered us to war!
What?!
An unknown hostile force invaded almost every country on this planet this morning at 0900. Until now, it's been contained to naval offensives but just graduated to ground ops!
... Jesus Christ...
We need to call CENTCOM...
Good afternoon. At nine a.m., Eastern Standard Time, several countries, including our own--
--were the unwilling recipients of an act of aggression from a faceless enemy.

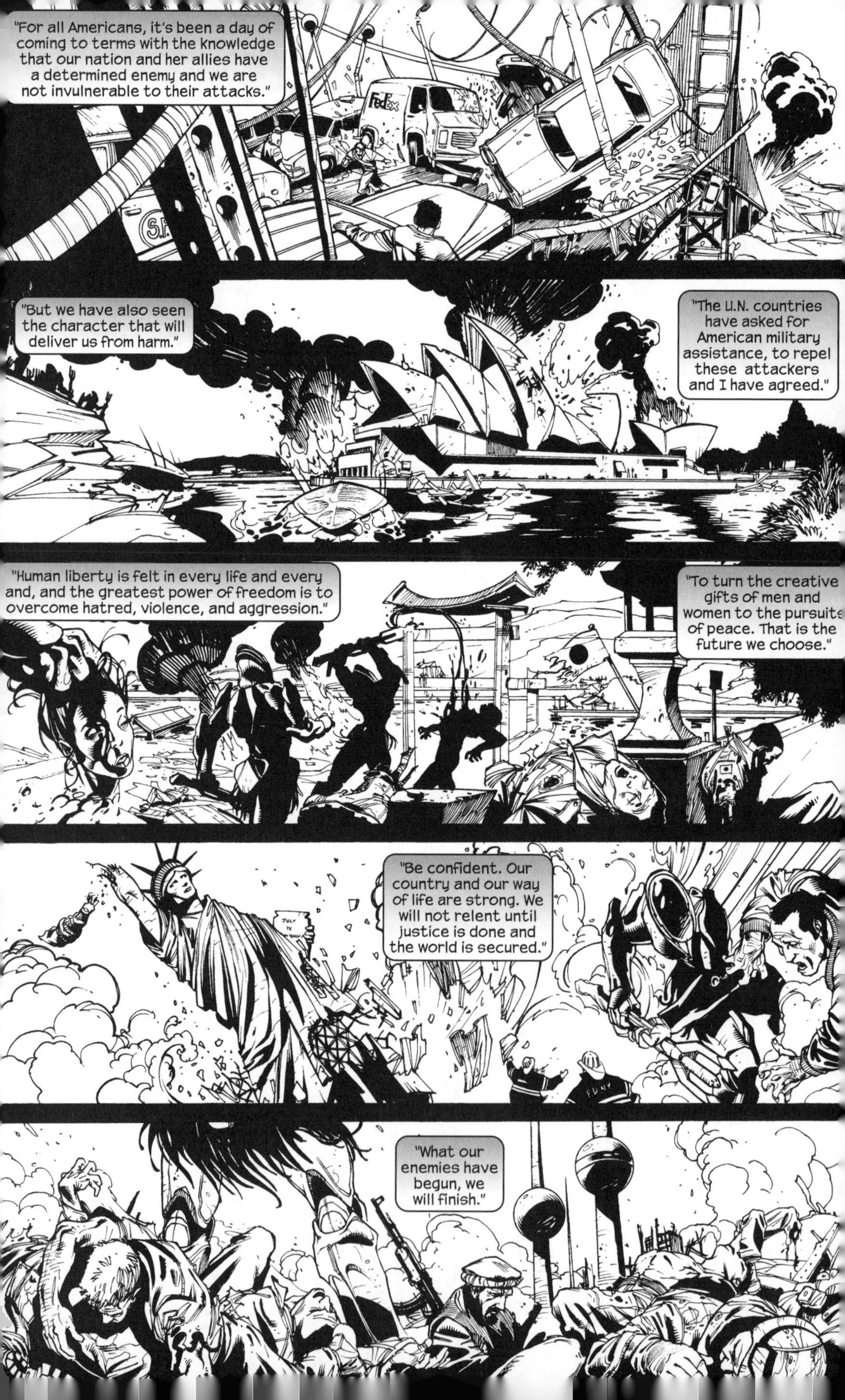
"For all Americans, it's been a day of coming to terms with the knowledge that our nation and her allies have a determined enemy and we are not invulnerable to their attacks."
FedEx
S.F.
"But we have also seen the character that will deliver us from harm."
"The U.N. countries have asked for American military assistance, to repel these attackers and I have agreed."
"Human liberty is felt in every life and every and, and the greatest power of freedom is to overcome hatred, violence, and aggression."
"To turn the creative gifts of men and women to the pursuits of peace. That is the future we choose."
"Be confident. Our country and our way of life are strong. We will not relent until justice is done and the world is secured."
"What our enemies have begun, we will finish."

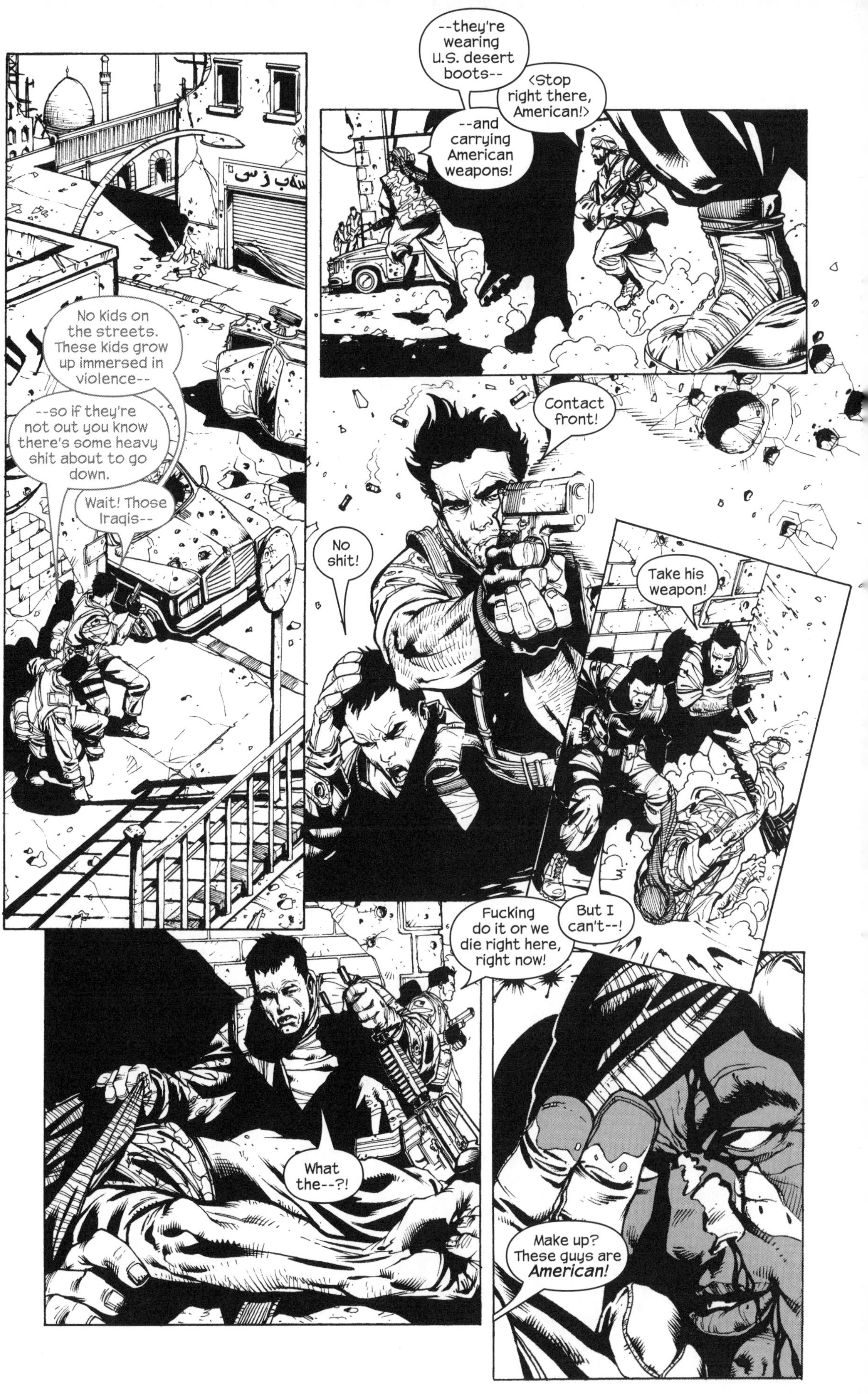
No kids on the streets. These kids grow up immersed in violence--
--so if they're not out you know there's some heavy shit about to go down.
Wait! Those Iraqis--
--they're wearing U.S. desert boots--
--and carrying American weapons!
<Stop right there, American!>
Contact front!
No shit!
Take his weapon!
But I can't--!
Fucking do it or we die right here, right now!
What the--?!
Make up? These guys are *American!*

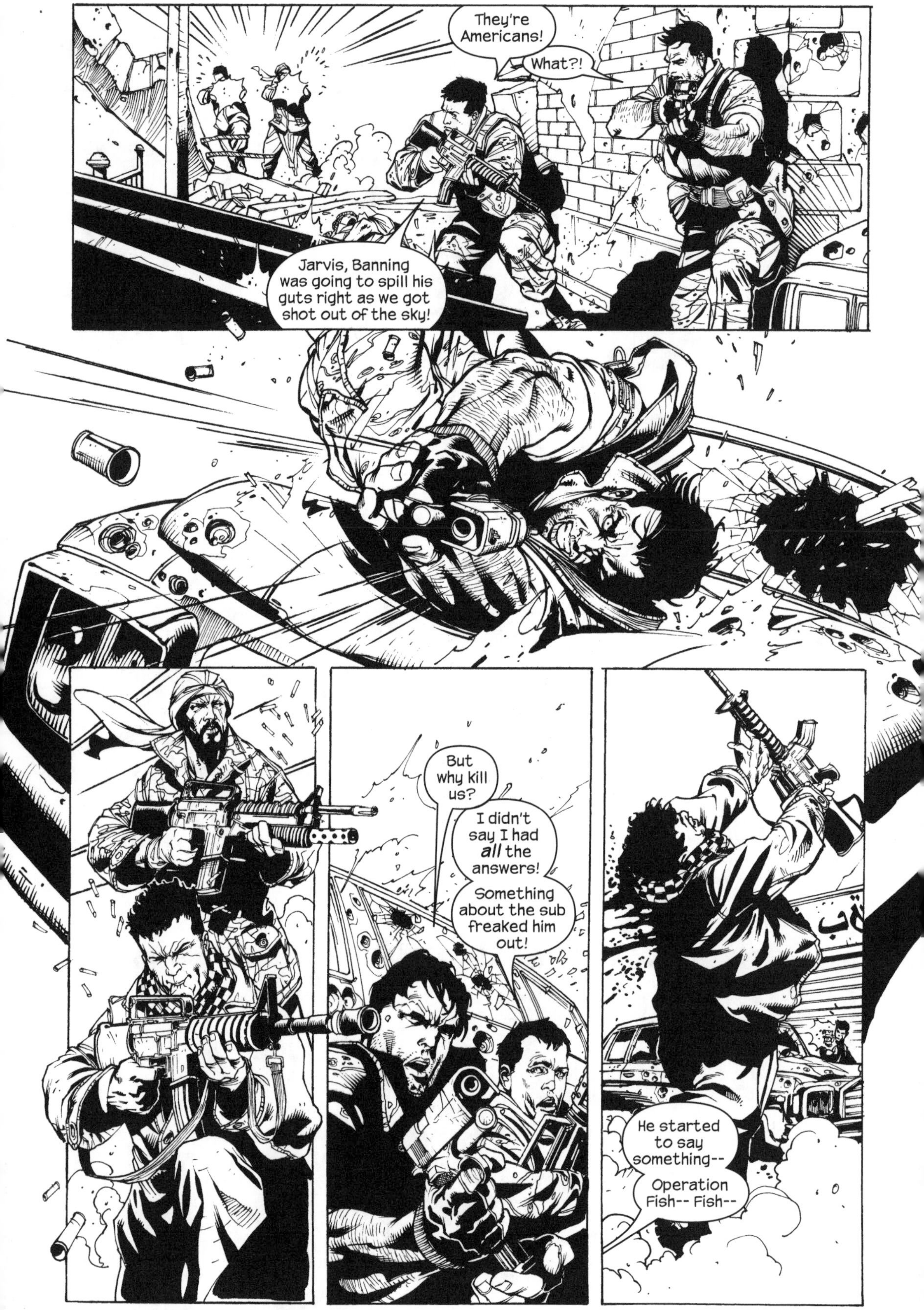
They're Americans!
What?!
Jarvis, Banning was going to spill his guts right as we got shot out of the sky!
But why kill us?
I didn't say I had *all* the answers!
Something about the sub freaked him out!
He started to say something--
Operation Fish-- Fish--

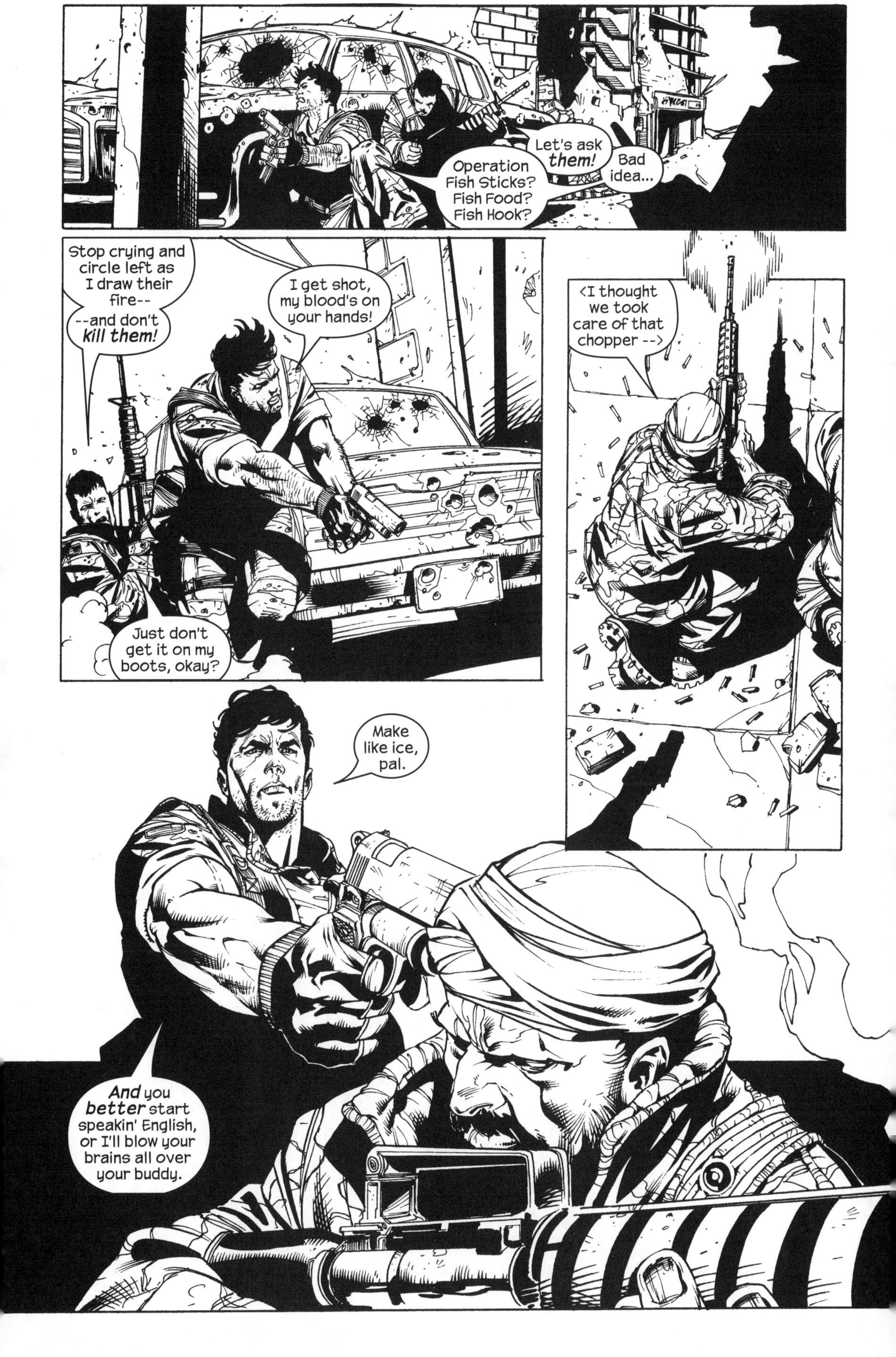
Operation Fish Sticks? Fish Food? Fish Hook?
Let's ask *them!*
Bad idea...
Stop crying and circle left as I draw their fire--
--and don't *kill them!*
I get shot, my blood's on your hands!
Just don't get it on my boots, okay?
<I thought we took care of that chopper -->
Make like ice, pal.
And you *better* start speakin' English, or I'll blow your brains all over your buddy.

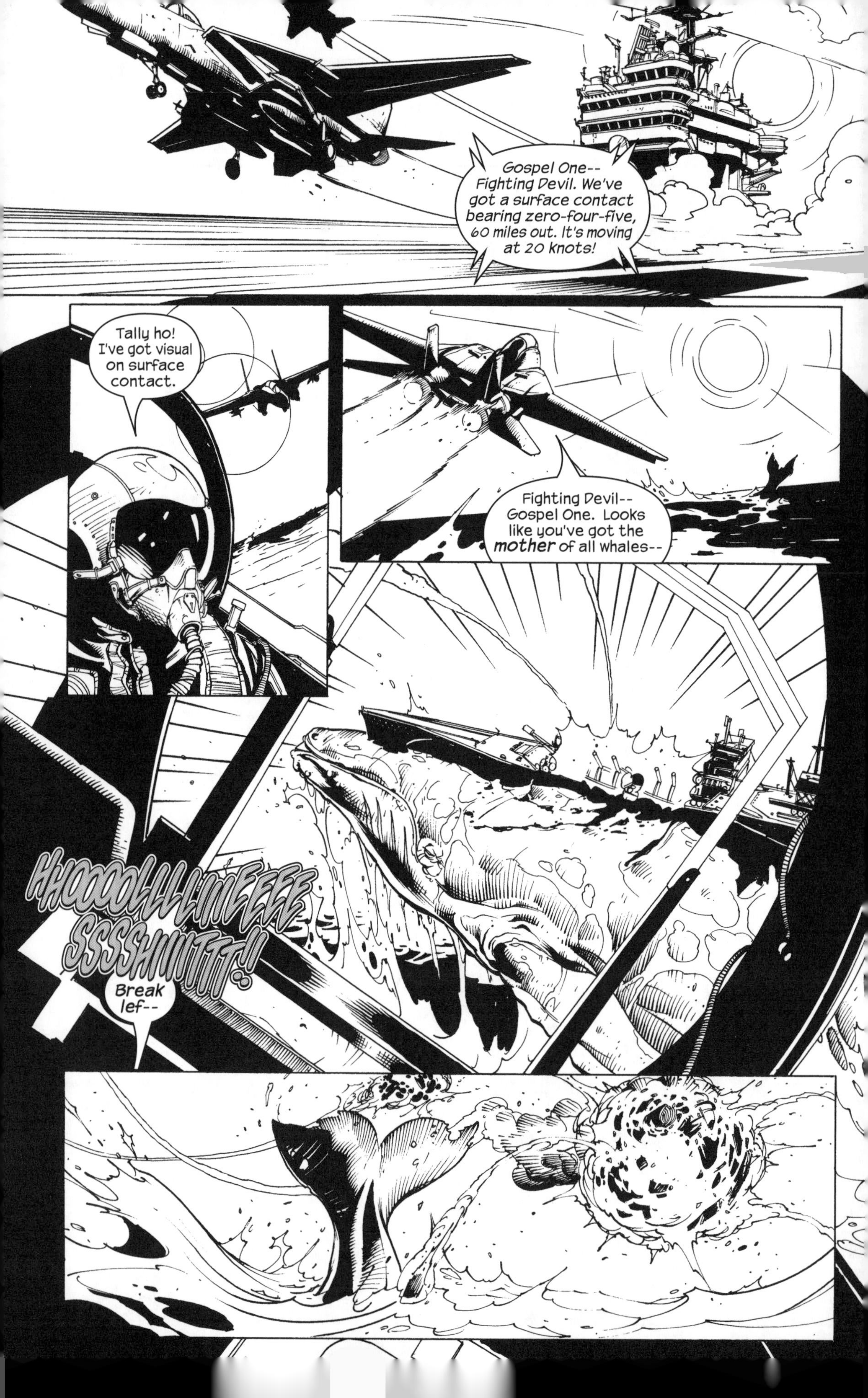
Gospel One-- Fighting Devil. We've got a surface contact bearing zero-four-five, 60 miles out. It's moving at 20 knots!
Tally ho! I've got visual on surface contact.
Fighting Devil-- Gospel One. Looks like you've got the *mother* of all whales--
HHOOOOLLLLIIIEEEE SSSSHHIIITTT!!
Break lef--

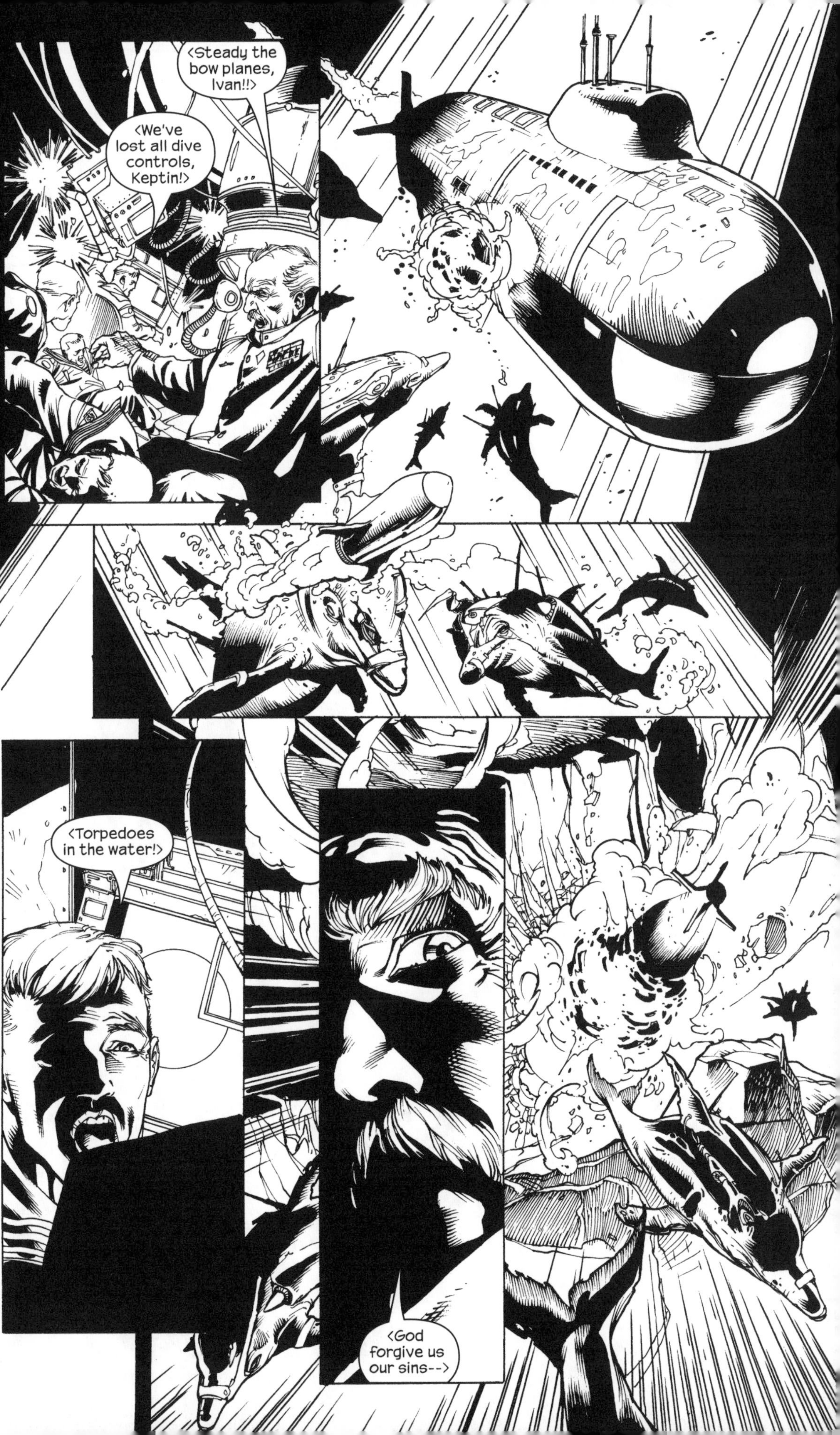
<Steady the bow planes, Ivan!!>
<We've lost all dive controls, Keptin!>
<Torpedoes in the water!>
<God forgive us our sins-->

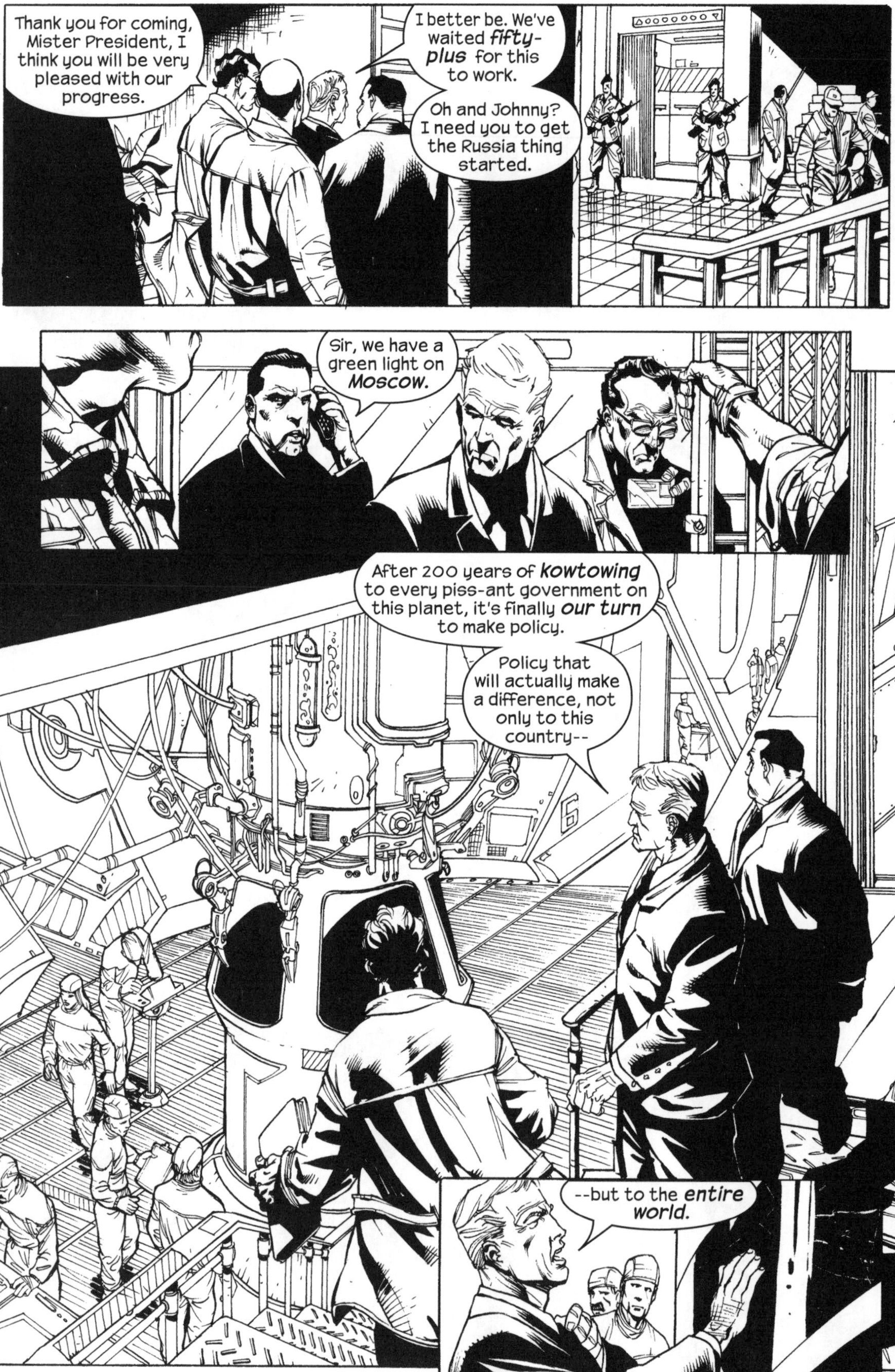

Thank you for coming, Mister President, I think you will be very pleased with our progress.
I better be. We've waited *fifty-plus* for this to work.
Oh and Johnny? I need you to get the Russia thing started.
Sir, we have a green light on *Moscow.*
After 200 years of *kowtowing* to every piss-ant government on this planet, it's finally *our turn* to make policy.
Policy that will actually make a difference, not only to this country--
--but to the *entire world.*

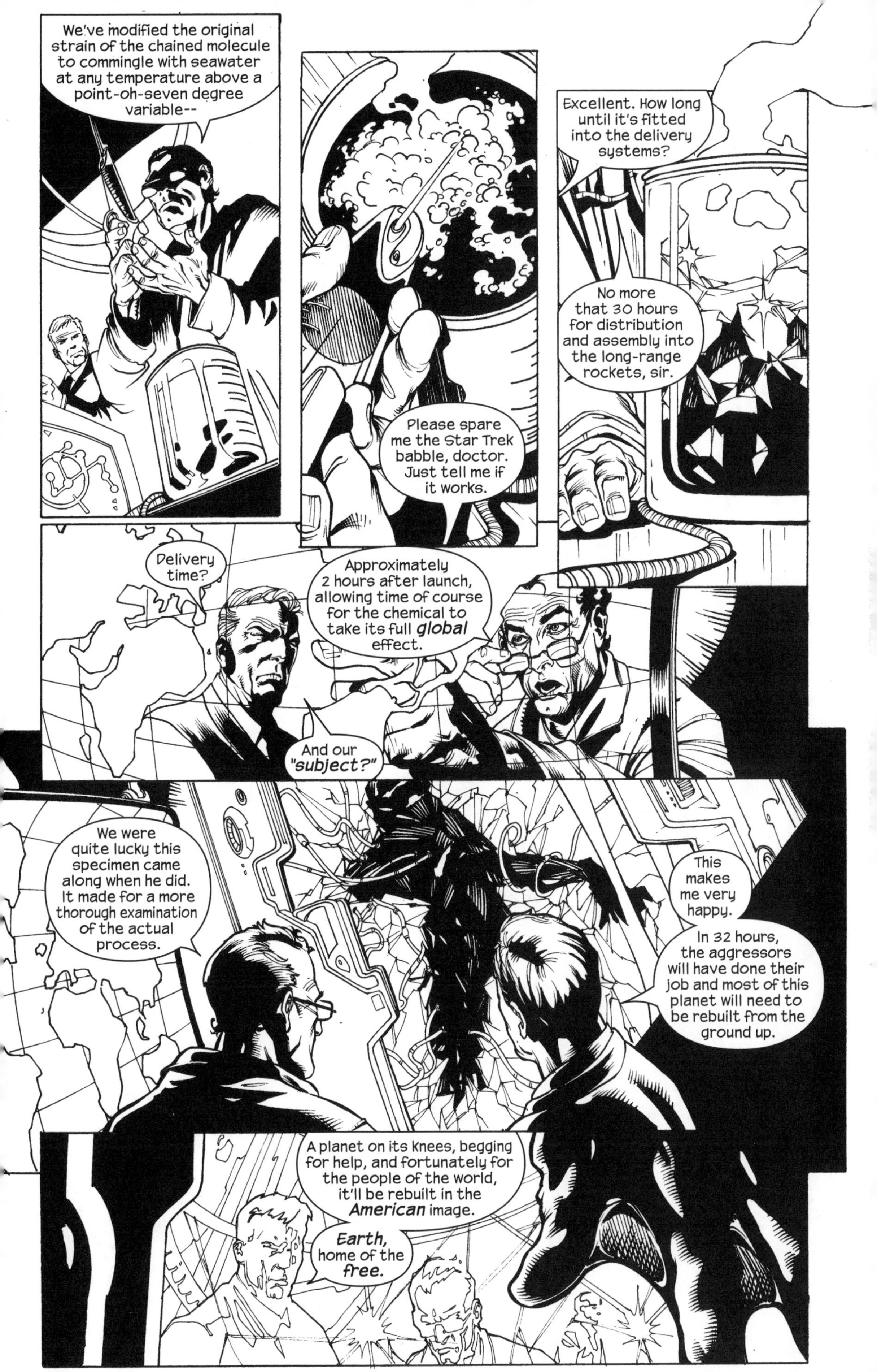
We've modified the original strain of the chained molecule to commingle with seawater at any temperature above a point-oh-seven degree variable--
Please spare me the Star Trek babble, doctor. Just tell me if it works.
Excellent. How long until it's fitted into the delivery systems?
No more that 30 hours for distribution and assembly into the long-range rockets, sir.
Delivery time?
Approximately 2 hours after launch, allowing time of course for the chemical to take its full *global* effect.
And our *"subject?"*
We were quite lucky this specimen came along when he did. It made for a more thorough examination of the actual process.
This makes me very happy.
In 32 hours, the aggressors will have done their job and most of this planet will need to be rebuilt from the ground up.
A planet on its knees, begging for help, and fortunately for the people of the world, it'll be rebuilt in the *American* image.
Earth, home of the *free.*

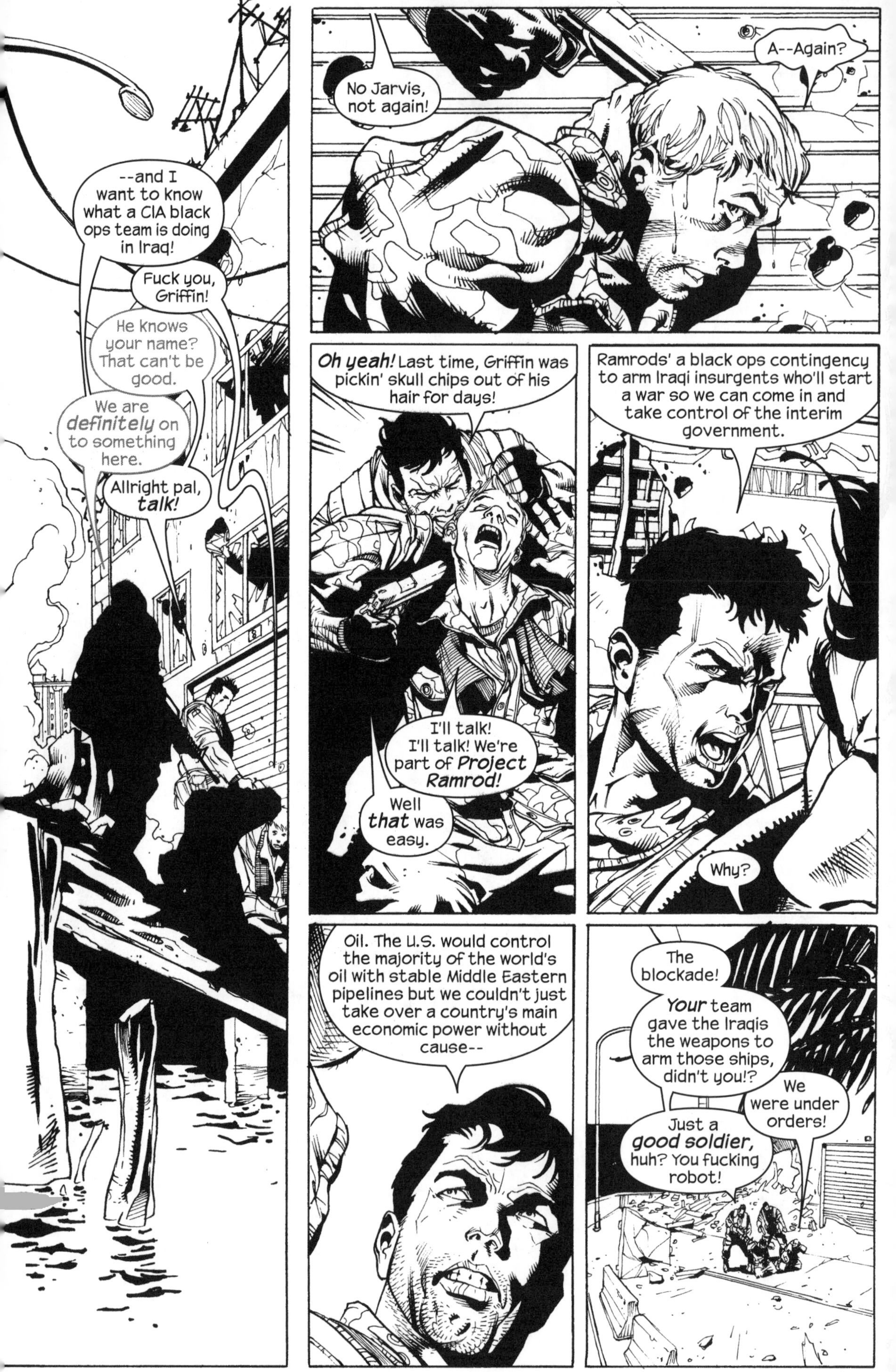
--and I want to know what a CIA black ops team is doing in Iraq!
Fuck you, Griffin!
He knows your name? That can't be good.
We are *definitely* on to something here.
Allright pal, *talk!*
No Jarvis, not again!
A--Again?
Oh yeah! Last time, Griffin was pickin' skull chips out of his hair for days!
I'll talk! I'll talk! We're part of *Project Ramrod!*
Well *that* was easy.
Ramrods' a black ops contingency to arm Iraqi insurgents who'll start a war so we can come in and take control of the interim government.
Why?
Oil. The U.S. would control the majority of the world's oil with stable Middle Eastern pipelines but we couldn't just take over a country's main economic power without cause--
The blockade!
Your team gave the Iraqis the weapons to arm those ships, didn't you!?
We were under orders!
Just a *good soldier,* huh? You fucking robot!

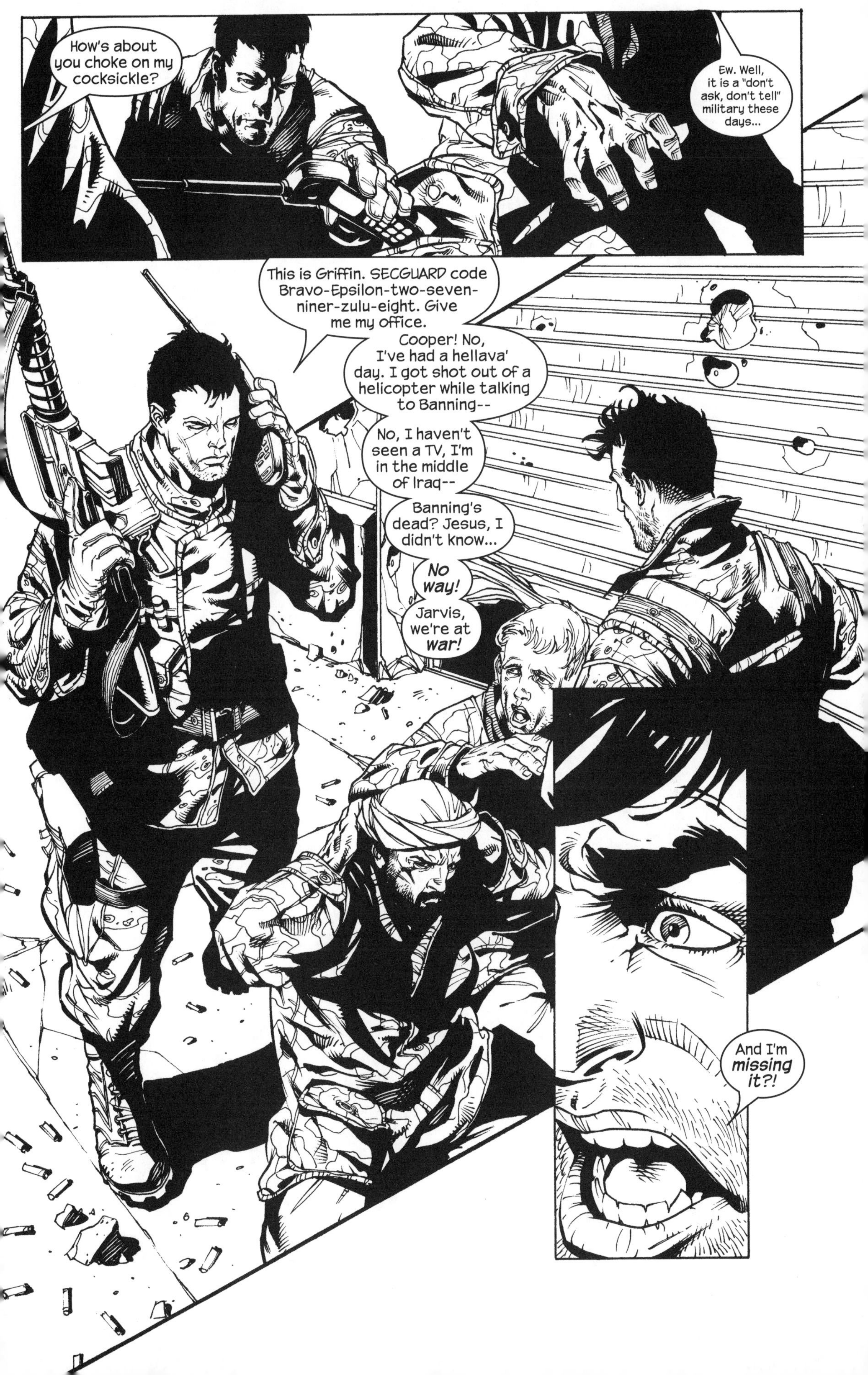
How's about you choke on my cocksickle?
Ew. Well, it is a "don't ask, don't tell" military these days...
This is Griffin. SECGUARD code Bravo-Epsilon-two-seven-niner-zulu-eight. Give me my office.
Cooper! No, I've had a hellava' day. I got shot out of a helicopter while talking to Banning--
No, I haven't seen a TV, I'm in the middle of Iraq--
Banning's dead? Jesus, I didn't know...
No way!
Jarvis, we're at *war!*
And I'm *missing it?!*

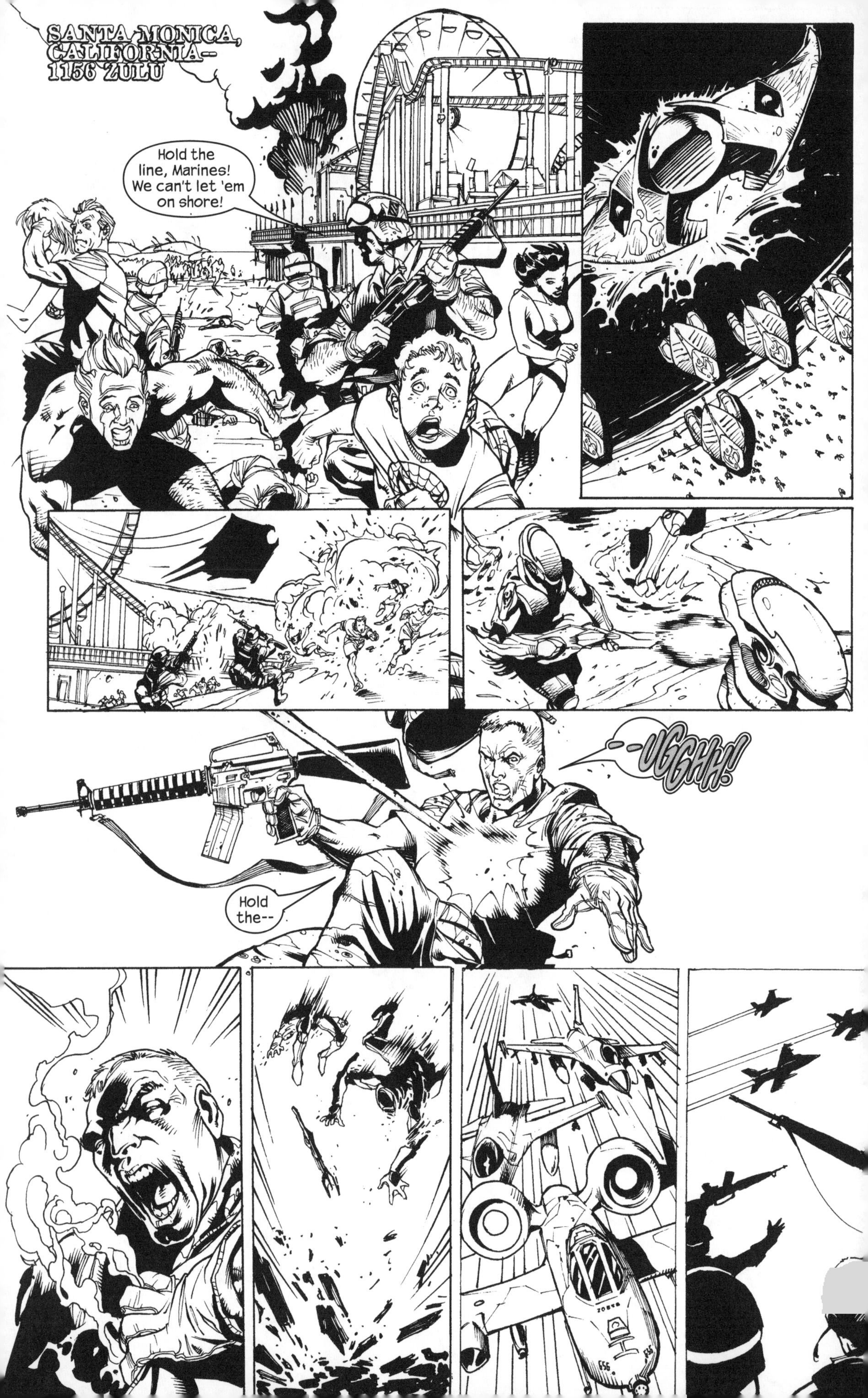
SANTA MONICA, CALIFORNIA-- 1156 ZULU
Hold the line, Marines! We can't let 'em on shore!
--UGGHH!
Hold the--

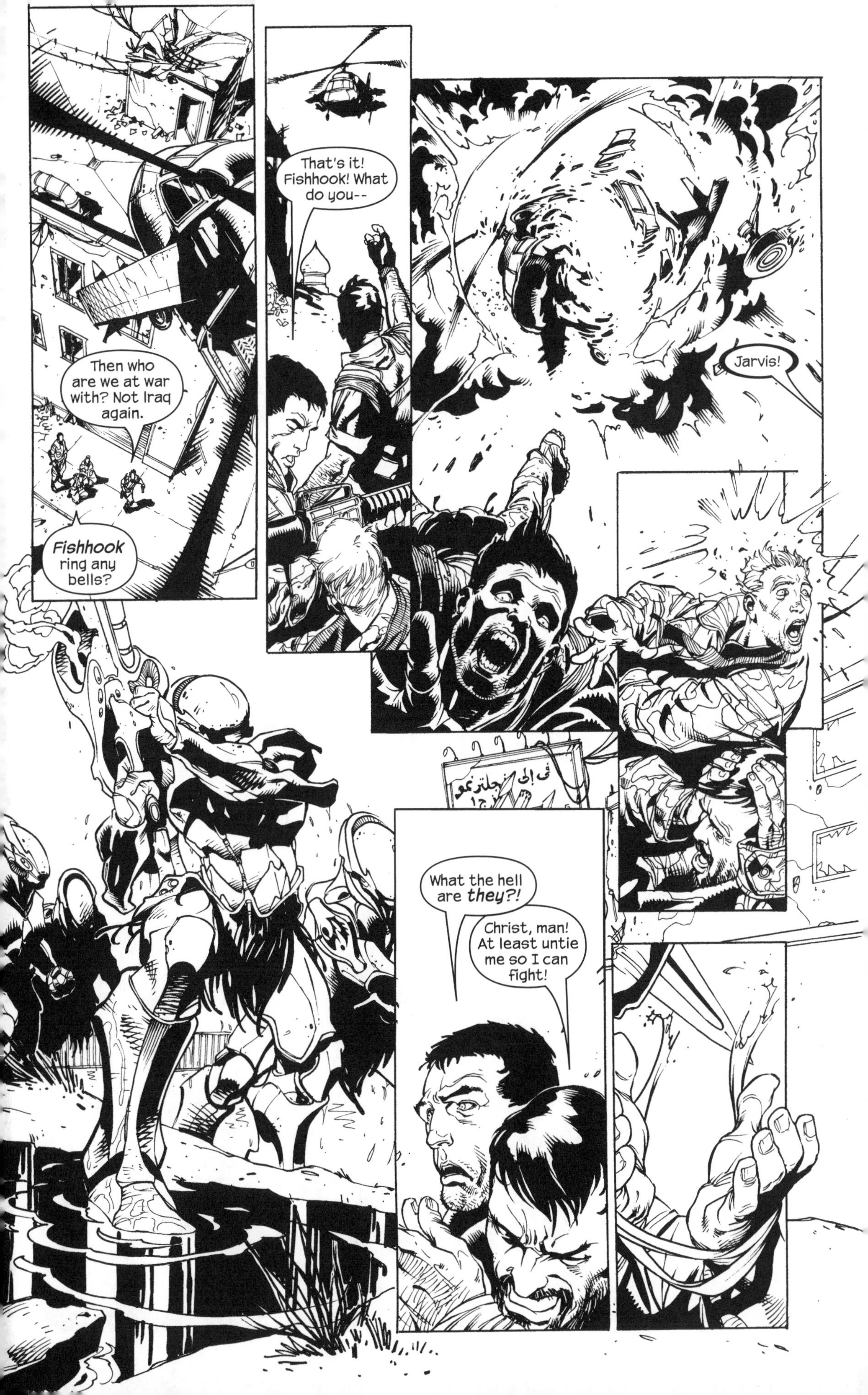
Then who are we at war with? Not Iraq again.
Fishhook ring any bells?
That's it! Fishhook! What do you--
Jarvis!
What the hell are *they*?!
Christ, man! At least untie me so I can fight!

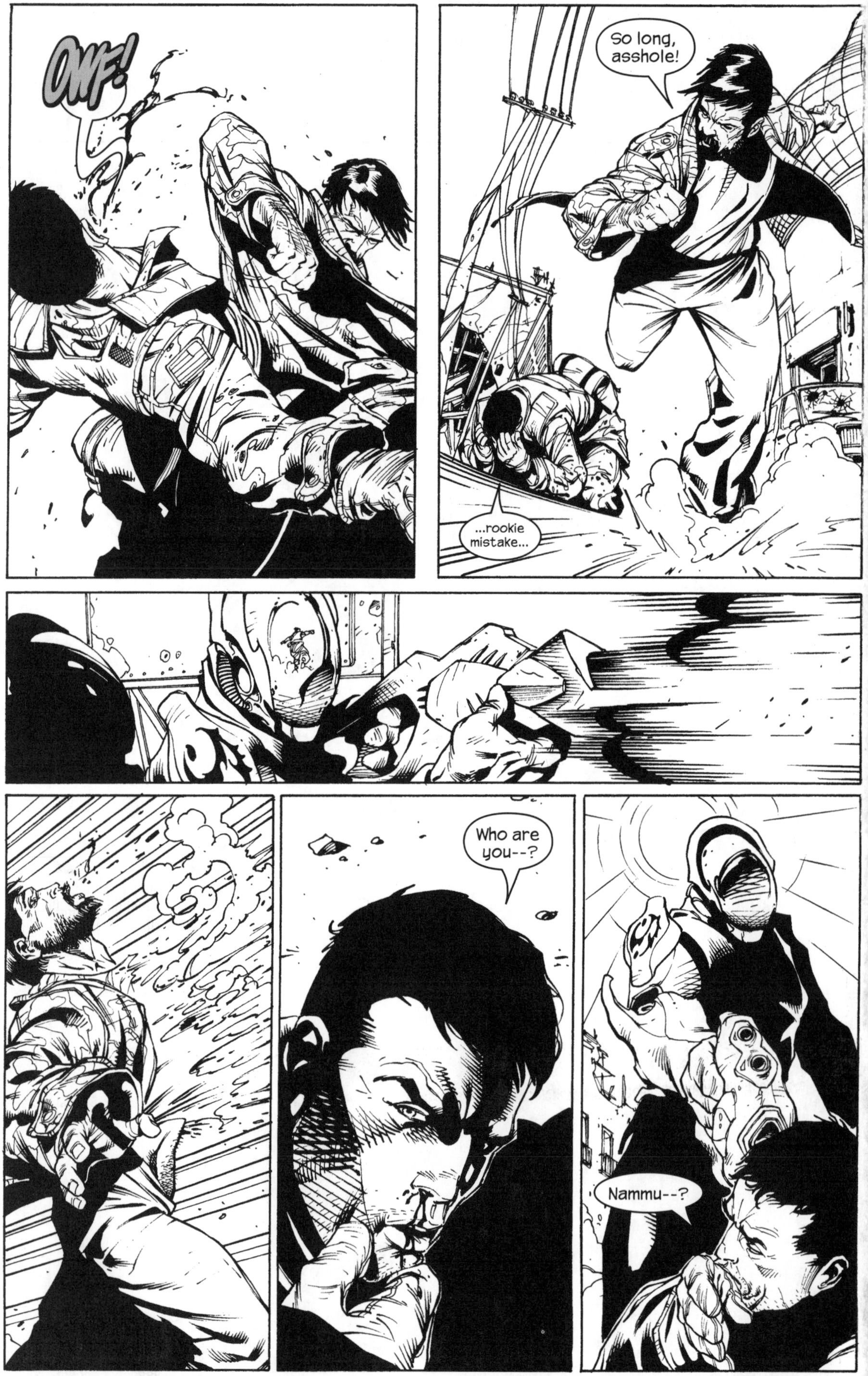
OWF!
So long, asshole!
...rookie mistake...
Who are you--?
Nammu--?

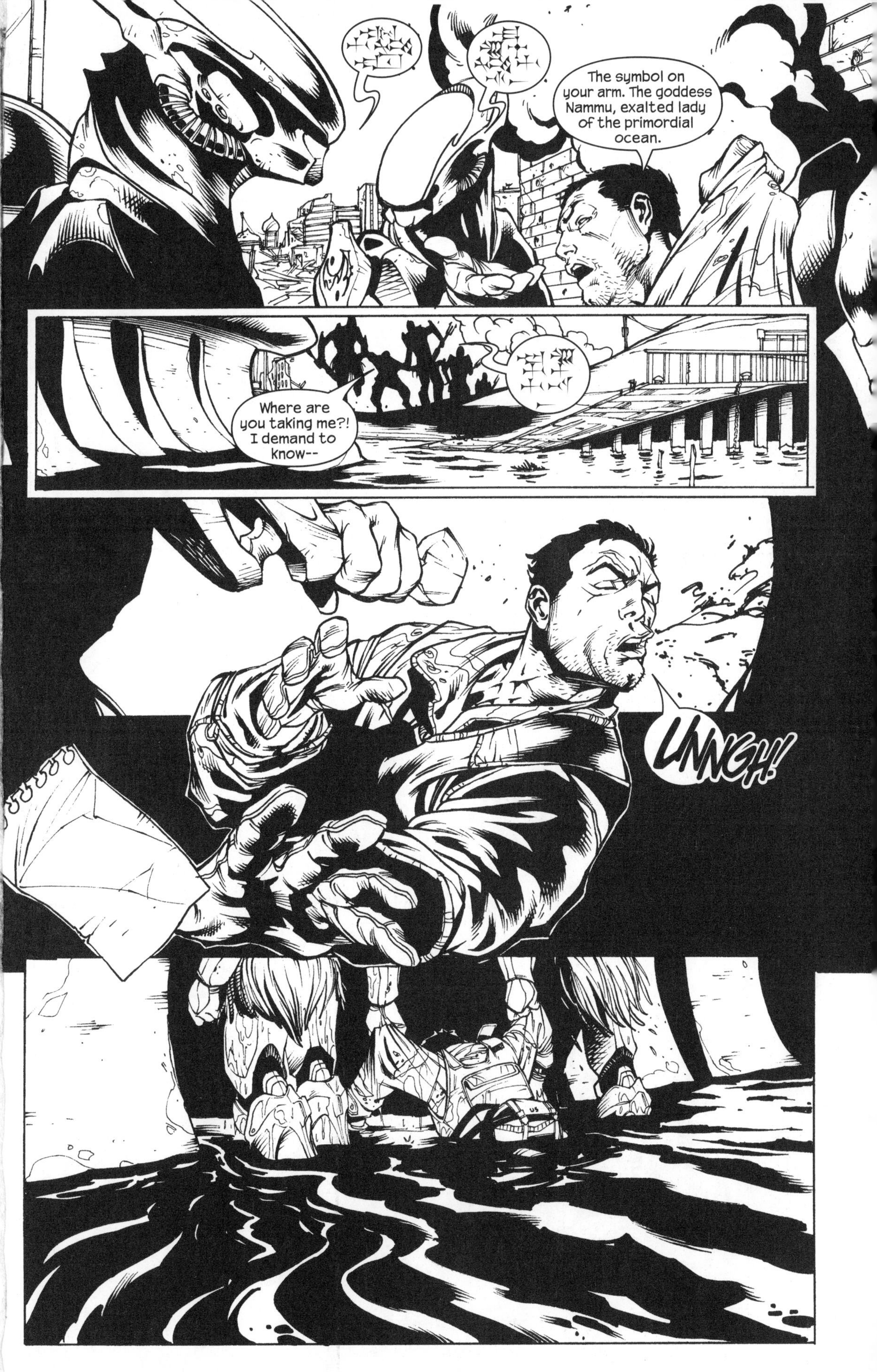
The symbol on your arm. The goddess Nammu, exalted lady of the primordial ocean.
Where are you taking me?! I demand to know--
UNNGH!

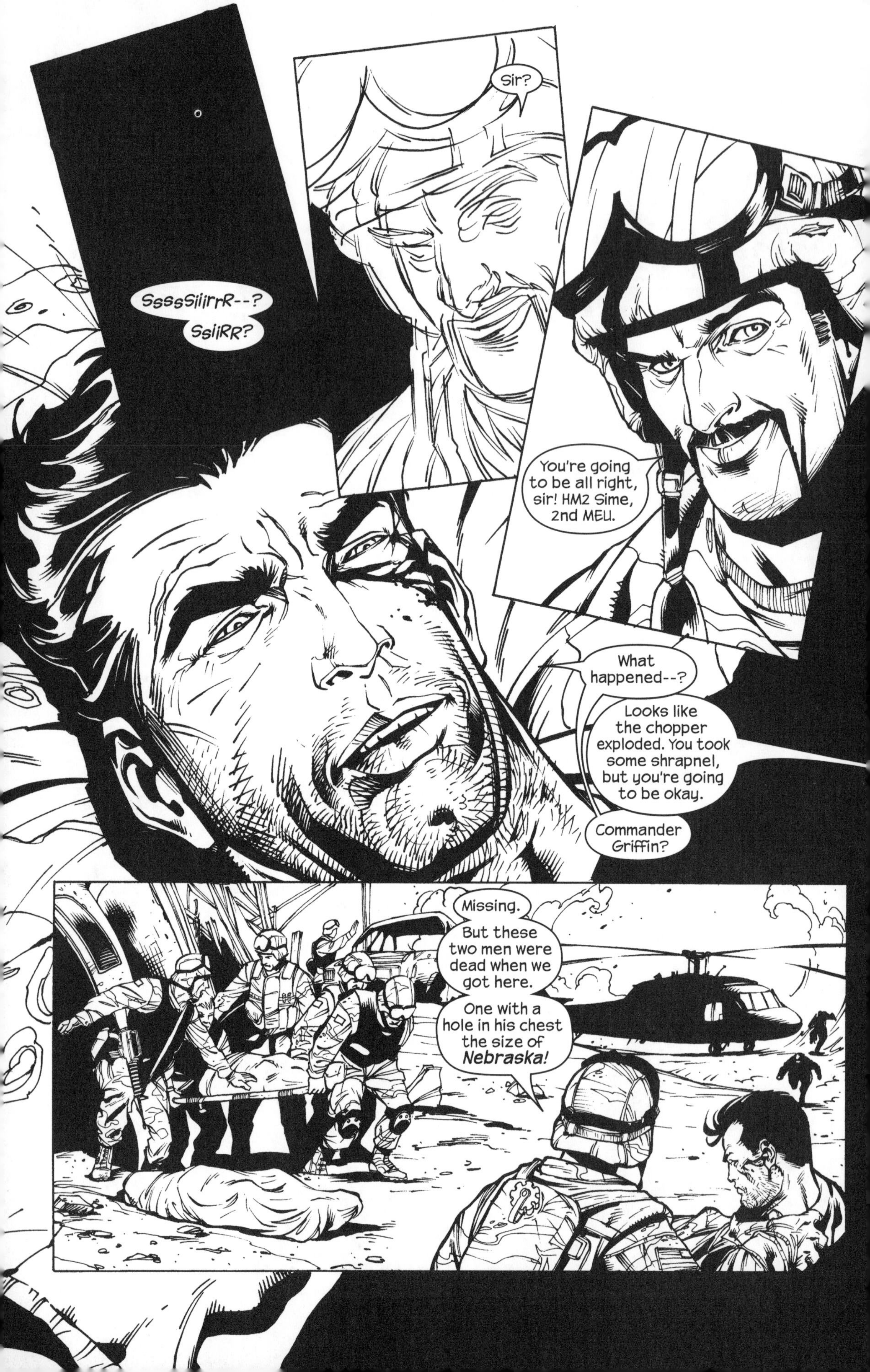
SsssSiiirrR--?
SsiiRR?
Sir?
You're going to be all right, sir! HM2 Sime, 2nd MEU.
What happened--?
Looks like the chopper exploded. You took some shrapnel, but you're going to be okay.
Commander Griffin?
Missing.
But these two men were dead when we got here.
One with a hole in his chest the size of *Nebraska!*

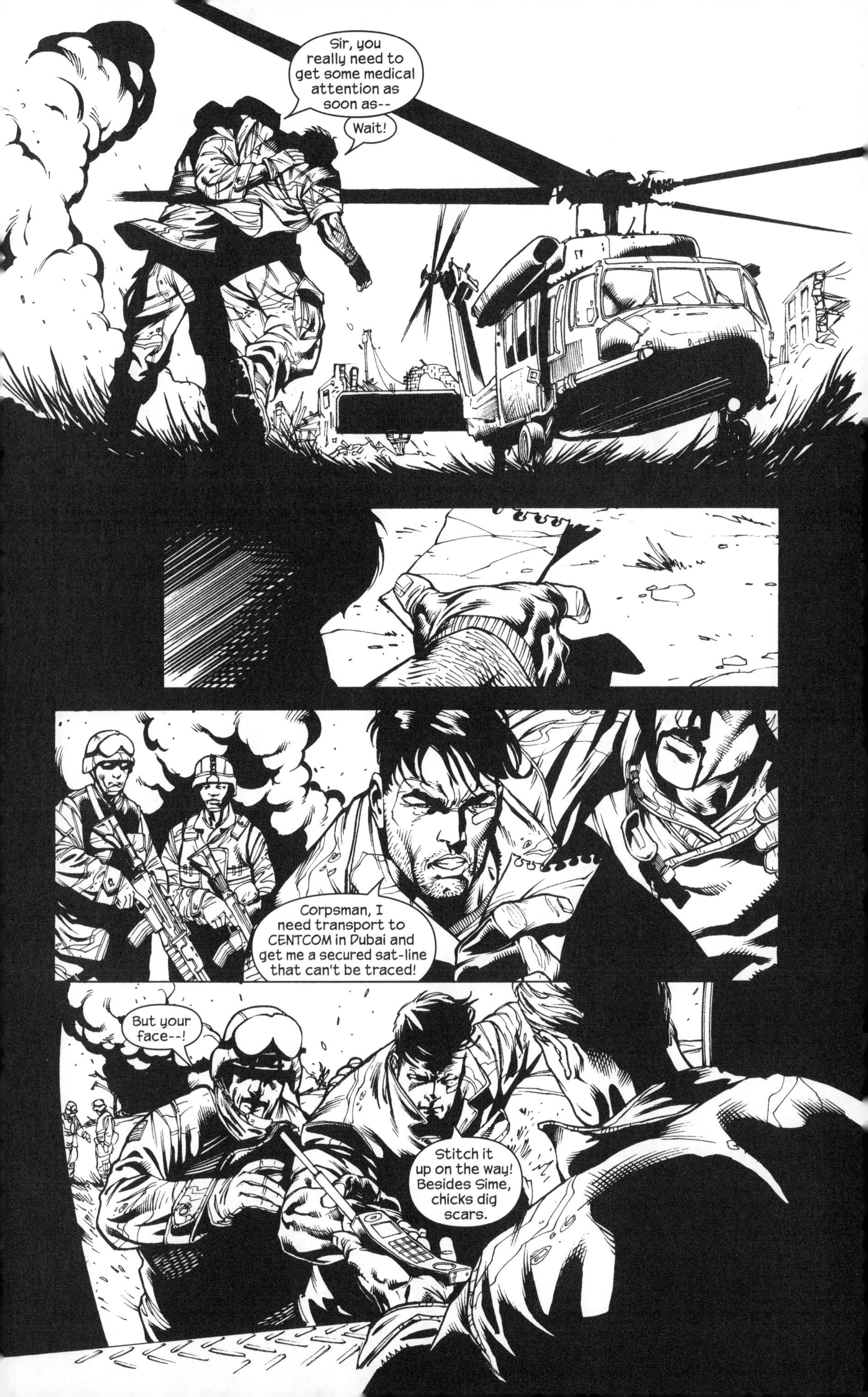
Sir, you really need to get some medical attention as soon as--
Wait!
Corpsman, I need transport to CENTCOM in Dubai and get me a secured sat-line that can't be traced!
But your face--!
Stitch it up on the way! Besides Sime, chicks dig scars.

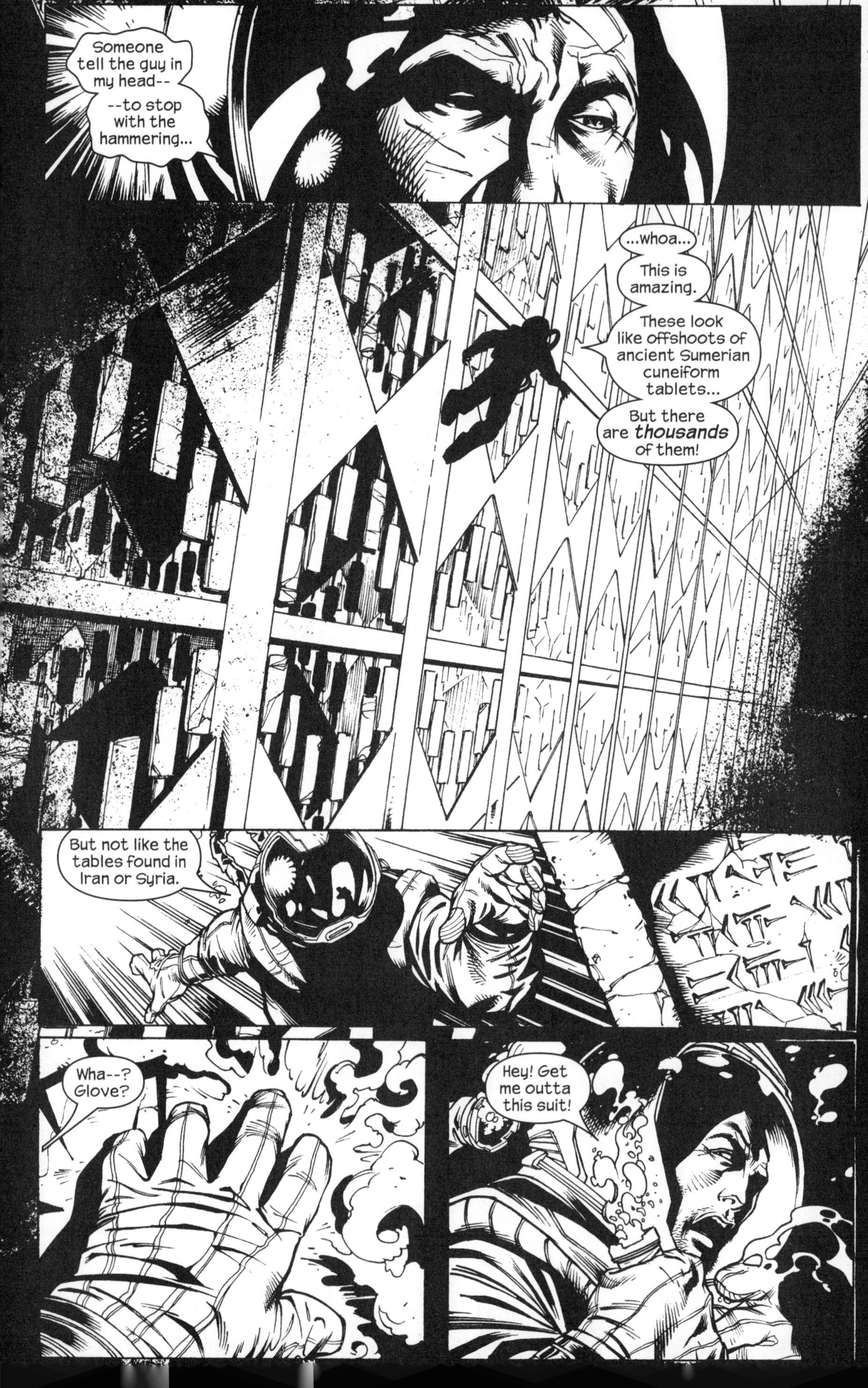
Someone tell the guy in my head--
--to stop with the hammering...
...whoa...
This is amazing.
These look like offshoots of ancient Sumerian cuneiform tablets...
But there are *thousands* of them!
But not like the tables found in Iran or Syria.
Wha--? Glove?
Hey! Get me outta this suit!

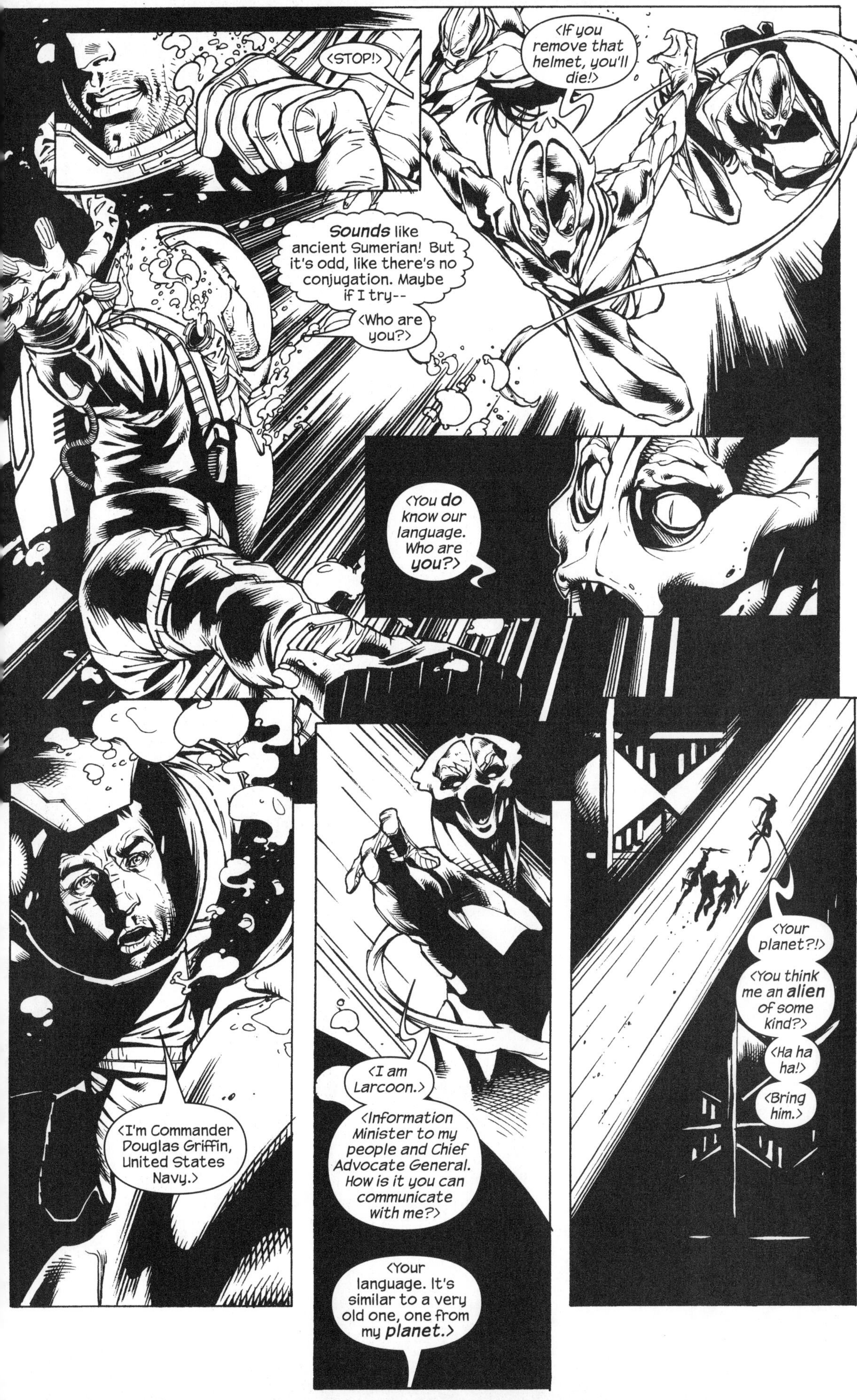
<STOP!>
<If you remove that helmet, you'll die!>
Sounds like ancient Sumerian! But it's odd, like there's no conjugation. Maybe if I try--
<Who are you?>
<You do know our language. Who are you?>
<I'm Commander Douglas Griffin, United States Navy.>
<I am Larcoon.>
<Information Minister to my people and Chief Advocate General. How is it you can communicate with me?>
<Your language. It's similar to a very old one, one from my planet.>
<Your planet?!>
<You think me an alien of some kind?>
<Ha ha ha!>
<Bring him.>

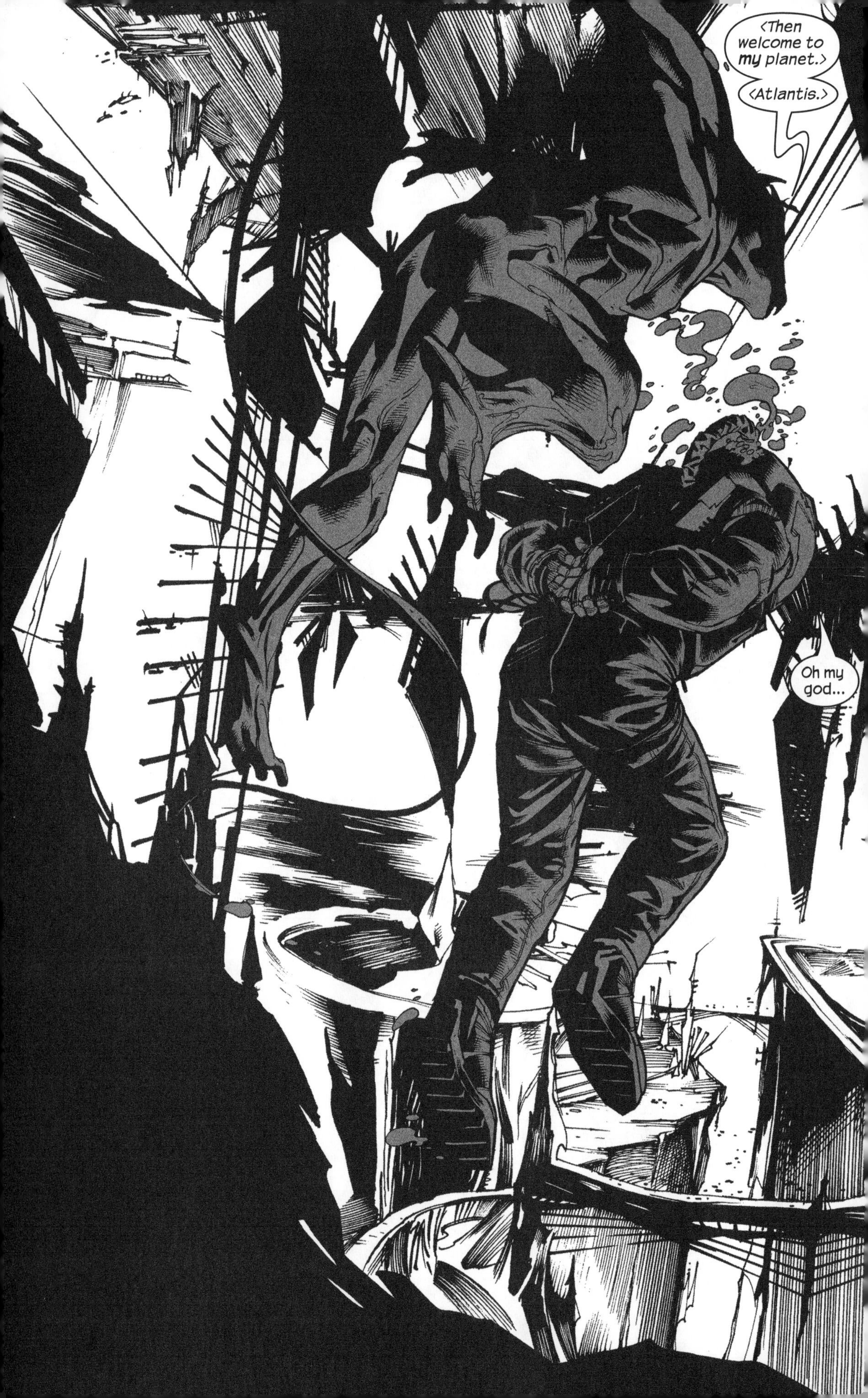
<Then welcome to my planet.>
<Atlantis.>
Oh my god...

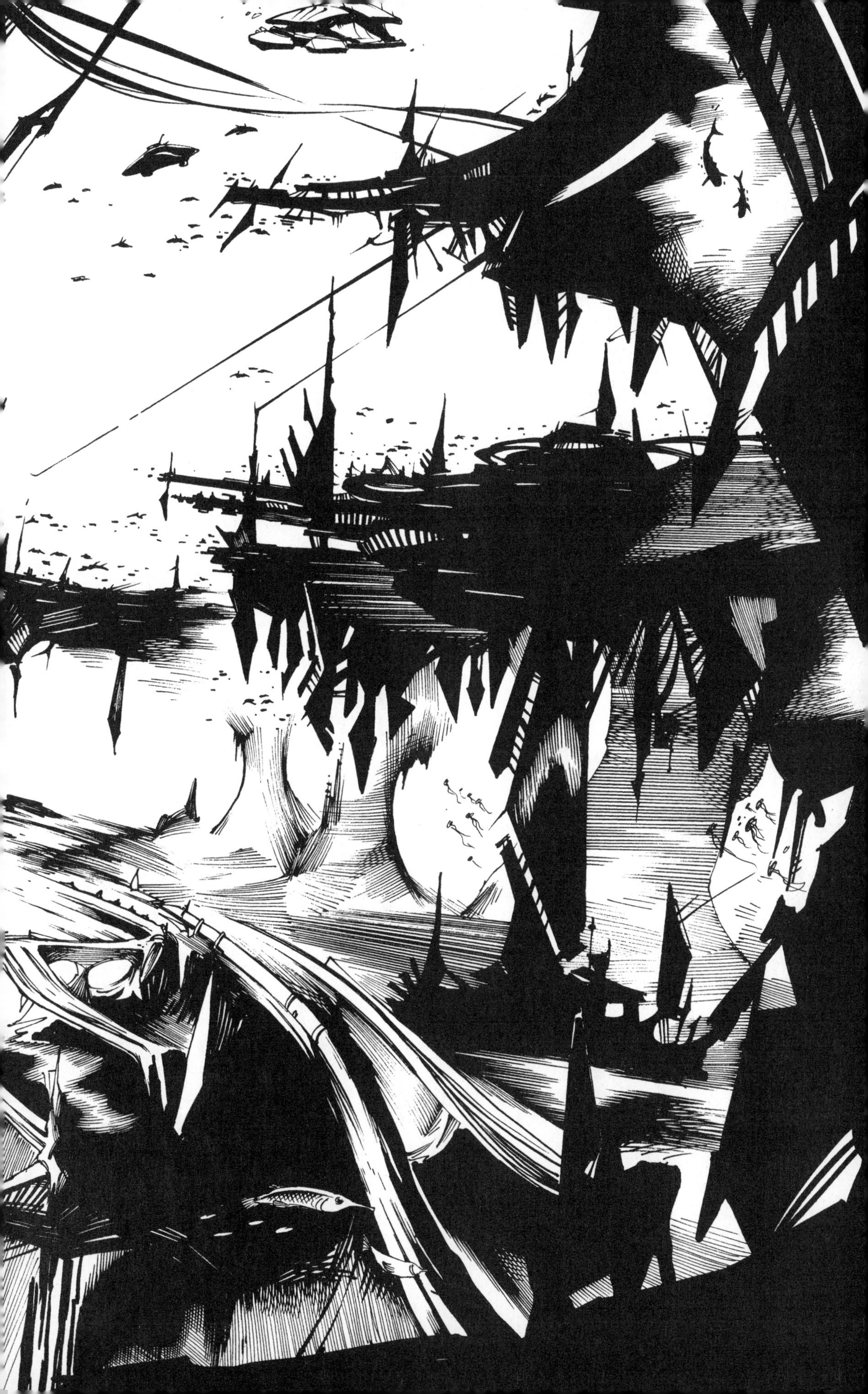

AIR SAUD--SAUDI ARABIA--1303 ZULU

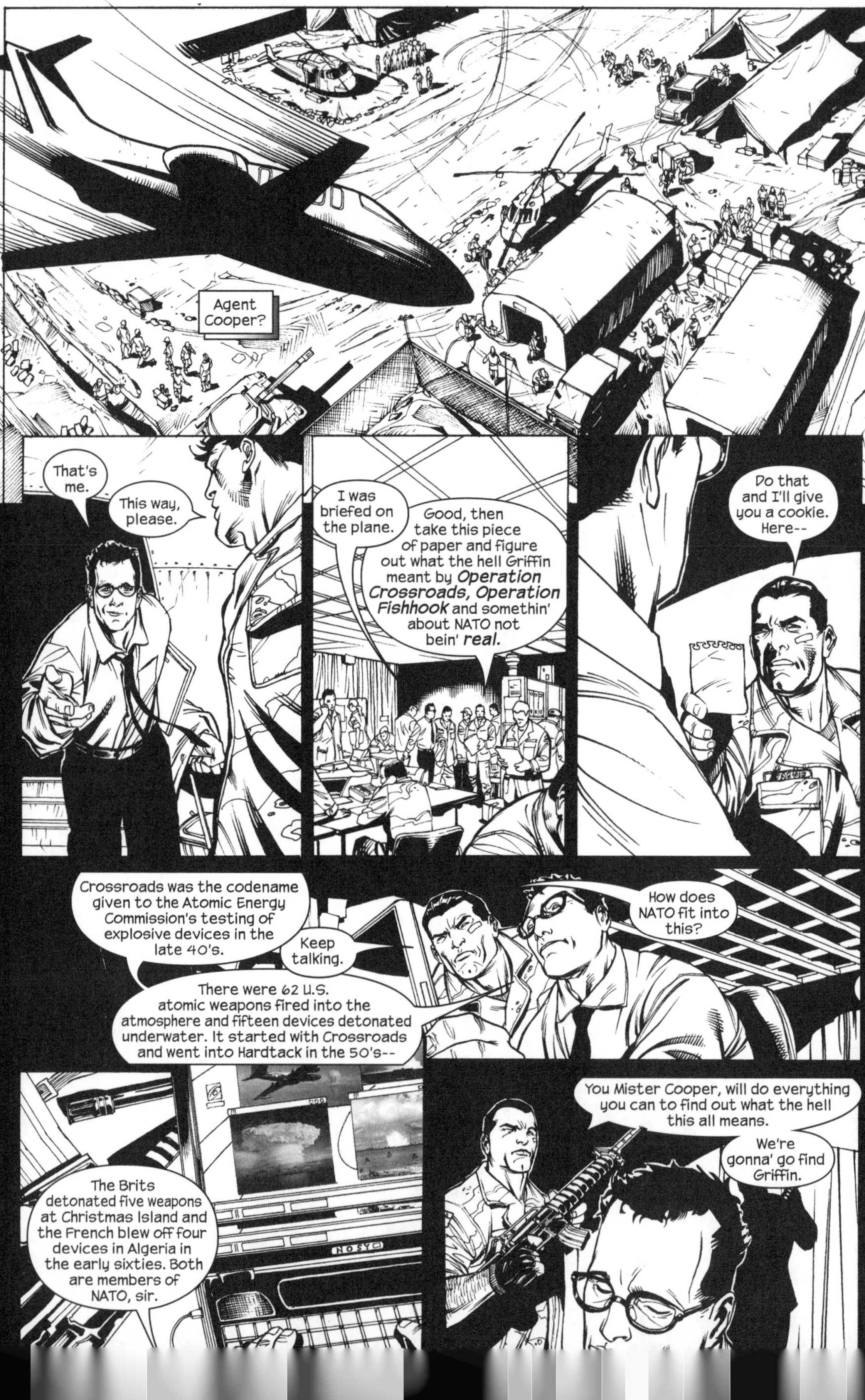
Agent Cooper?
That's me.
This way, please.
I was briefed on the plane.
Good, then take this piece of paper and figure out what the hell Griffin meant by *Operation Crossroads, Operation Fishhook* and somethin' about NATO not bein' *real.*
Do that and I'll give you a cookie. Here--
Crossroads was the codename given to the Atomic Energy Commission's testing of explosive devices in the late 40's.
Keep talking.
How does NATO fit into this?
There were 62 U.S. atomic weapons fired into the atmosphere and fifteen devices detonated underwater. It started with Crossroads and went into Hardtack in the 50's--
The Brits detonated five weapons at Christmas Island and the French blew off four devices in Algeria in the early sixties. Both are members of NATO, sir.
You Mister Cooper, will do everything you can to find out what the hell this all means.
We're gonna' go find Griffin.

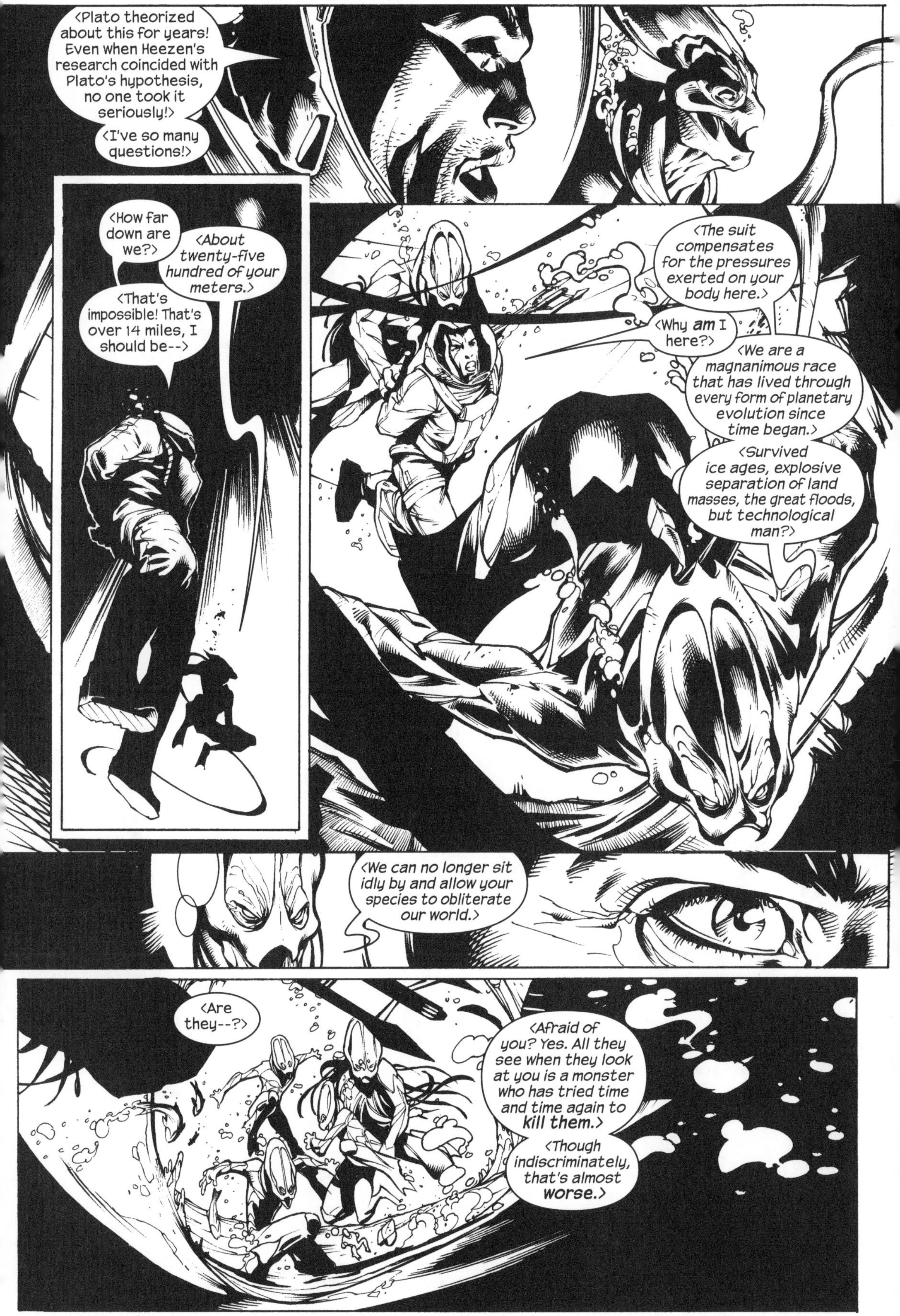
<Plato theorized about this for years! Even when Heezen's research coincided with Plato's hypothesis, no one took it seriously!>
<I've so many questions!>
<How far down are we?>
<About twenty-five hundred of your meters.>
<That's impossible! That's over 14 miles, I should be-->
<The suit compensates for the pressures exerted on your body here.>
<Why **am** I here?>
<We are a magnanimous race that has lived through every form of planetary evolution since time began.>
<Survived ice ages, explosive separation of land masses, the great floods, but technological man?>
<We can no longer sit idly by and allow your species to obliterate our world.>
<Are they--?>
<Afraid of you? Yes. All they see when they look at you is a monster who has tried time and time again to **kill them.**>
<Though indiscriminately, that's almost **worse.**>

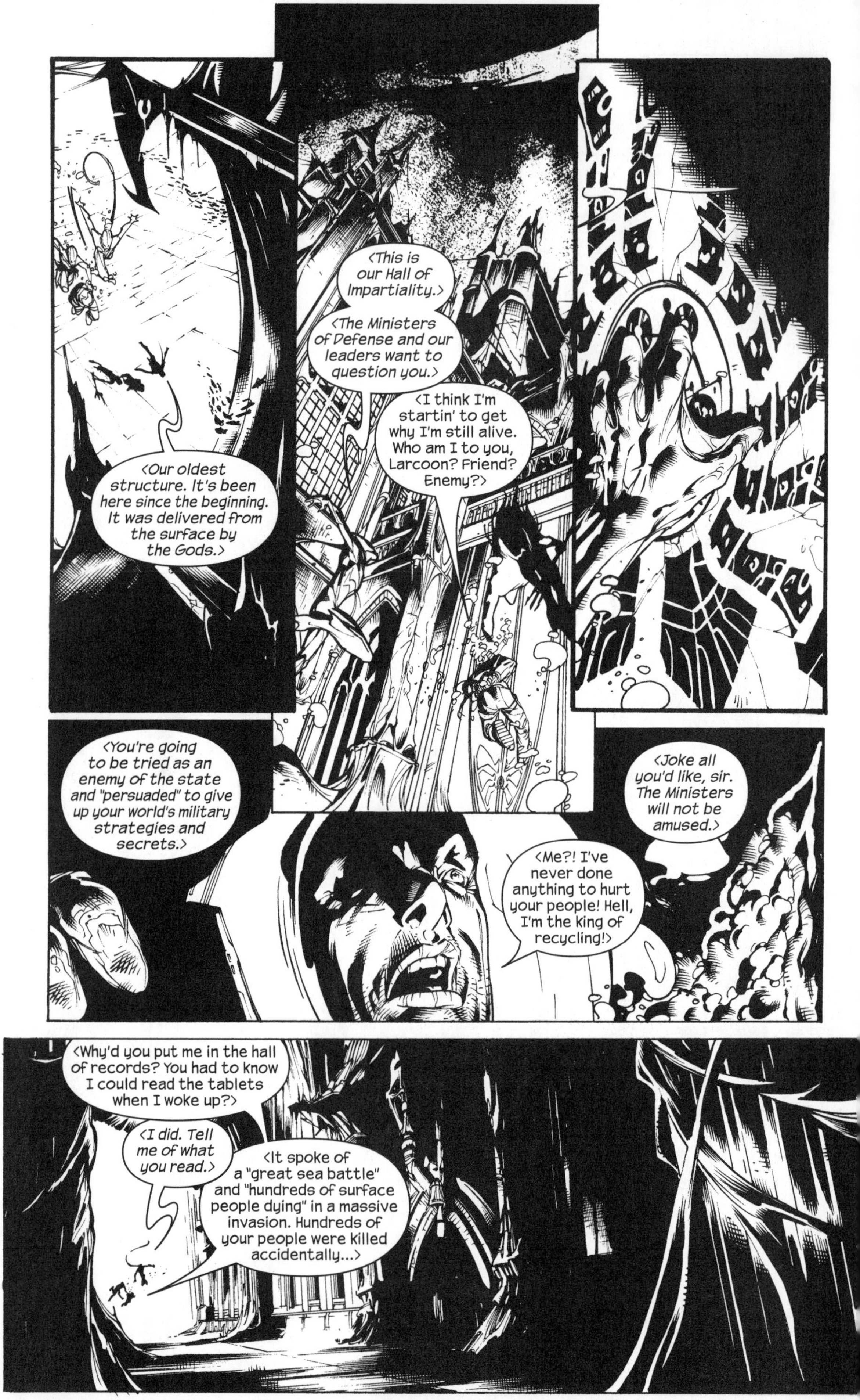
<Our oldest structure. It's been here since the beginning. It was delivered from the surface by the Gods.>
<This is our Hall of Impartiality.>
<The Ministers of Defense and our leaders want to question you.>
<I think I'm startin' to get why I'm still alive. Who am I to you, Larcoon? Friend? Enemy?>
<You're going to be tried as an enemy of the state and "persuaded" to give up your world's military strategies and secrets.>
<Me?! I've never done anything to hurt your people! Hell, I'm the king of recycling!>
<Joke all you'd like, sir. The Ministers will not be amused.>
<Why'd you put me in the hall of records? You had to know I could read the tablets when I woke up?>
<I did. Tell me of what you read.>
<It spoke of a "great sea battle" and "hundreds of surface people dying" in a massive invasion. Hundreds of your people were killed accidentally...>

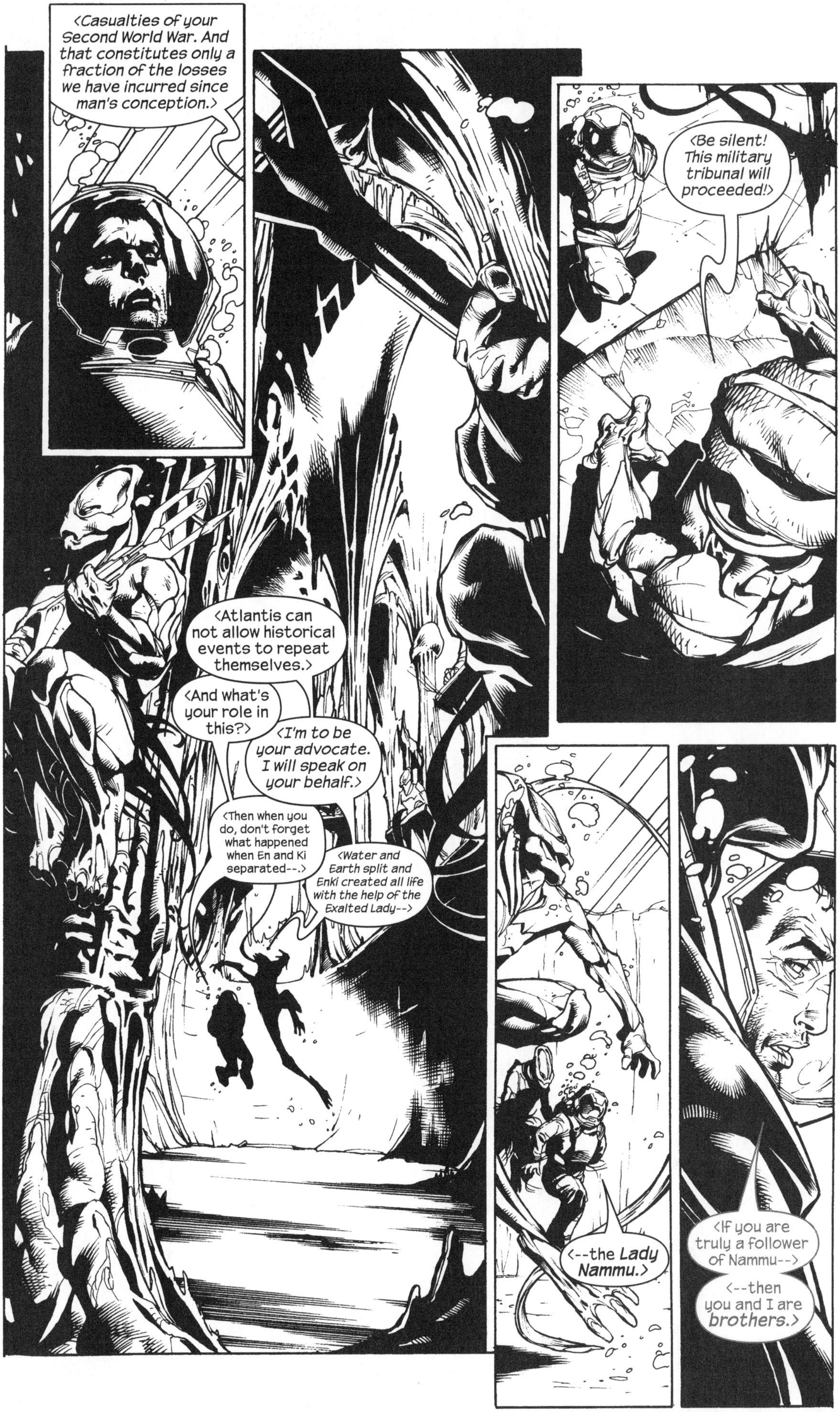

<Casualties of your Second World War. And that constitutes only a fraction of the losses we have incurred since man's conception.>
<Be silent! This military tribunal will proceeded!>
<Atlantis can not allow historical events to repeat themselves.>
<And what's your role in this?>
<I'm to be your advocate. I will speak on your behalf.>
<Then when you do, don't forget what happened when En and Ki separated-->
<Water and Earth split and Enki created all life with the help of the Exalted Lady-->
<--the Lady Nammu.>
<If you are truly a follower of Nammu-->
<--then you and I are brothers.>

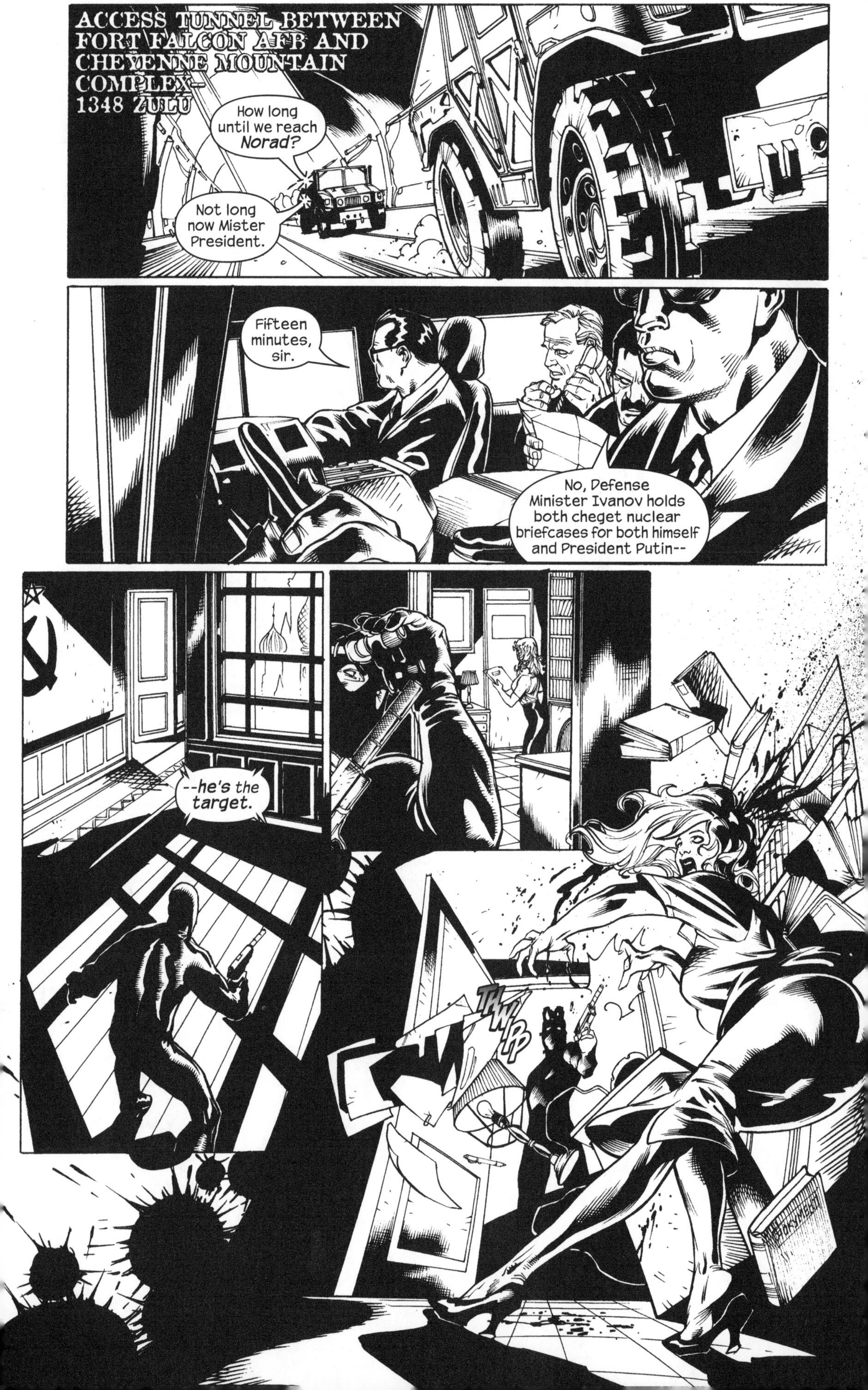
ACCESS TUNNEL BETWEEN FORT FALCON AFB AND CHEYENNE MOUNTAIN COMPLEX-
1348 ZULU
How long until we reach Norad?
Not long now Mister President.
Fifteen minutes, sir.
No, Defense Minister Ivanov holds both cheget nuclear briefcases for both himself and President Putin--
--he's the target.
THWIPP

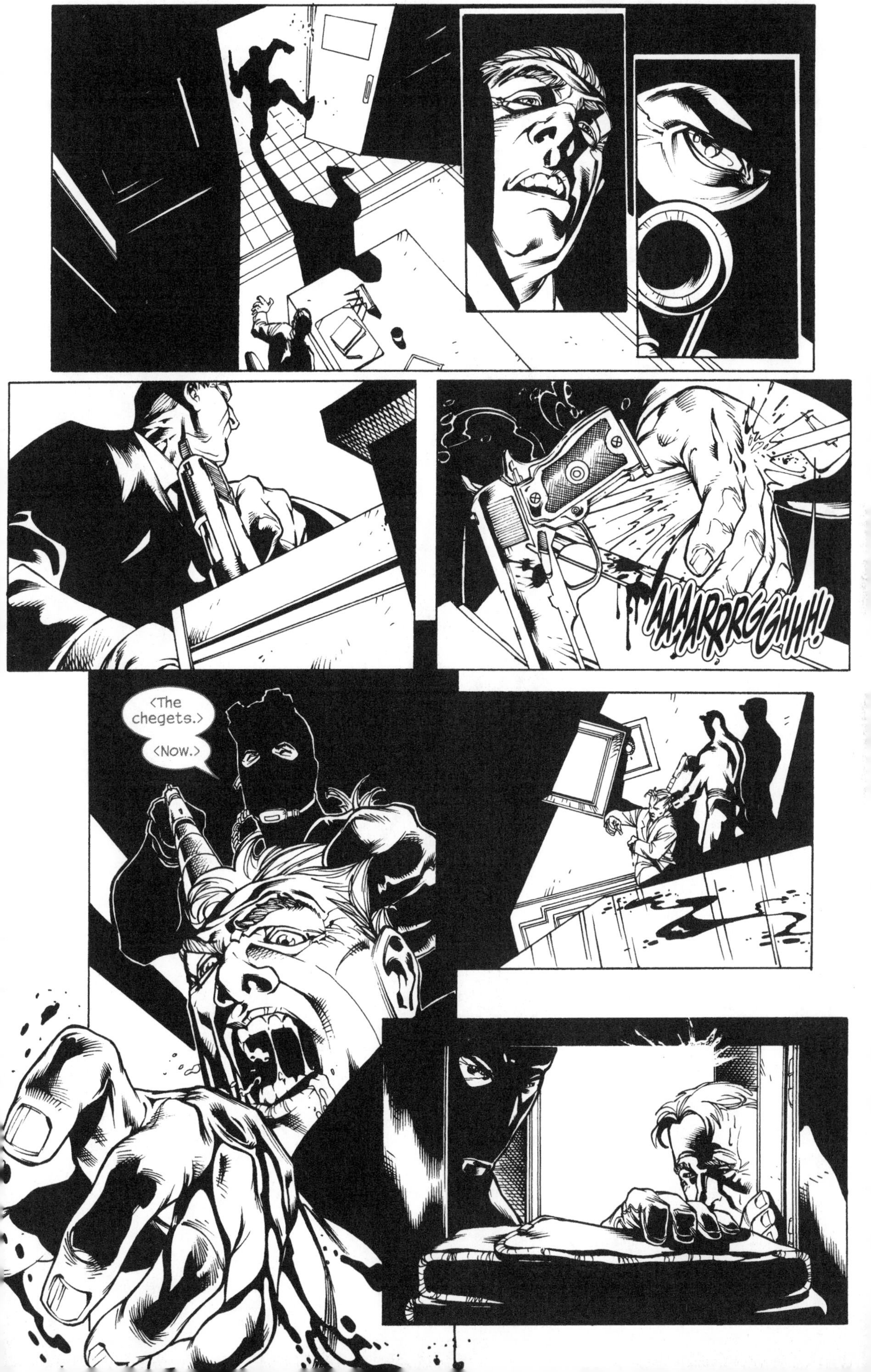
AAAARRRGGHHH!
<The chegets.>
<Now.>

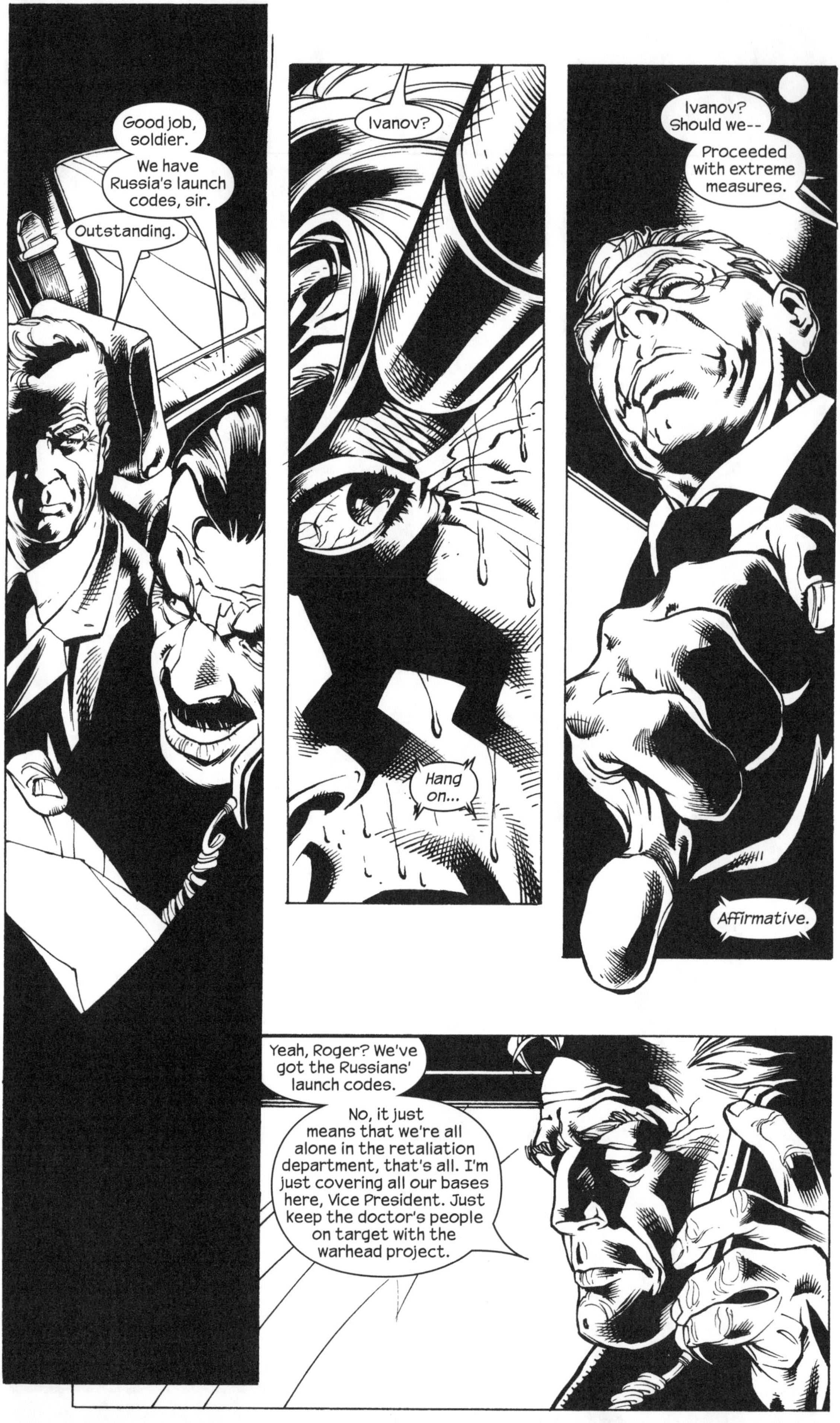
Good job, soldier.
We have Russia's launch codes, sir.
Outstanding.
Ivanov?
Hang on...
Ivanov? Should we--
Proceeded with extreme measures.
Affirmative.
Yeah, Roger? We've got the Russians' launch codes.
No, it just means that we're all alone in the retaliation department, that's all. I'm just covering all our bases here, Vice President. Just keep the doctor's people on target with the warhead project.

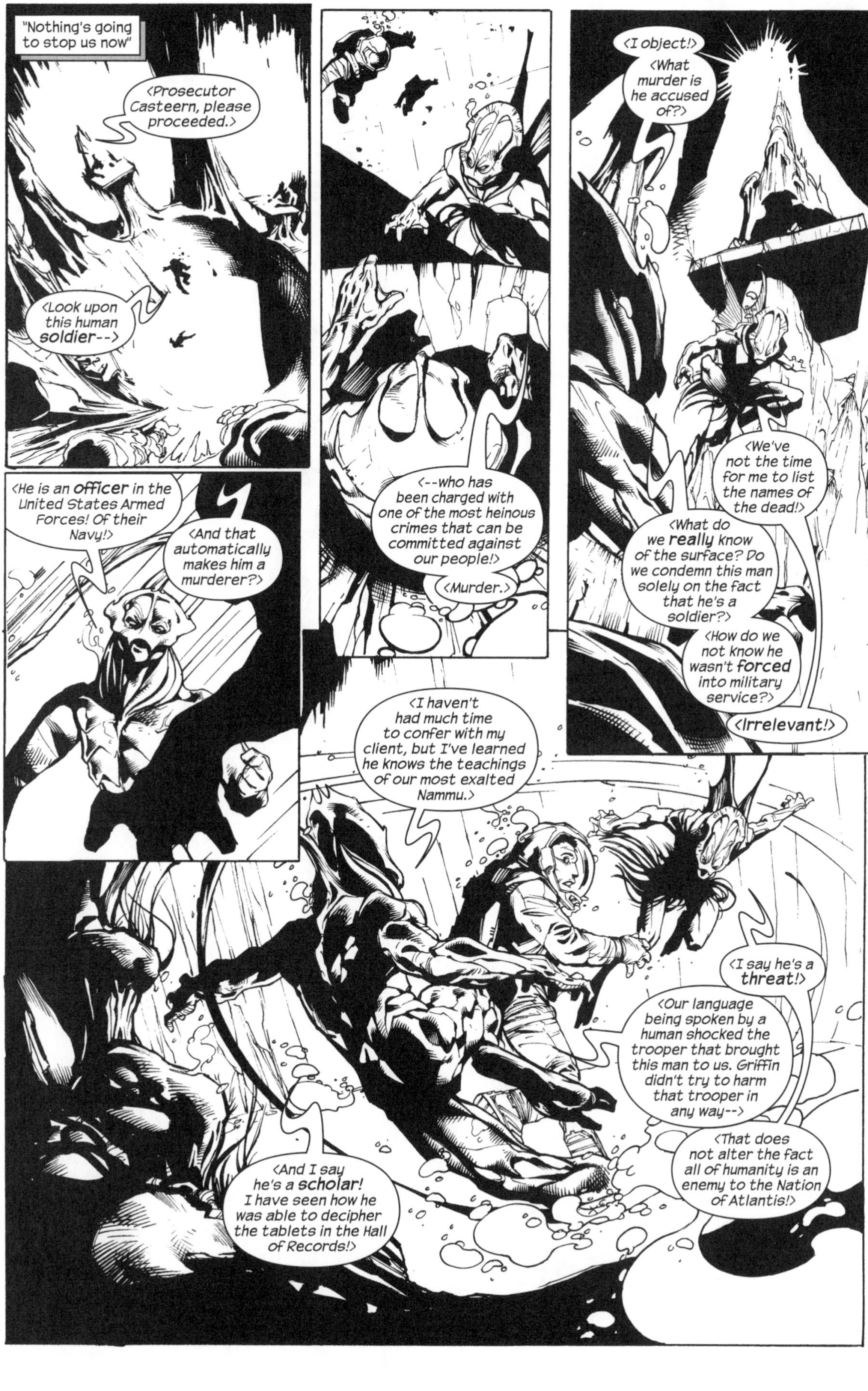
"Nothing's going to stop us now"
<Prosecutor Casteern, please proceeded.>
<Look upon this human soldier-->
<--who has been charged with one of the most heinous crimes that can be committed against our people!>
<Murder.>
<I object!>
<What murder is he accused of?>
<We've not the time for me to list the names of the dead!>
<He is an officer in the United States Armed Forces! Of their Navy!>
<And that automatically makes him a murderer?>
<What do we really know of the surface? Do we condemn this man solely on the fact that he's a soldier?>
<How do we not know he wasn't forced into military service?>
<Irrelevant!>
<I haven't had much time to confer with my client, but I've learned he knows the teachings of our most exalted Nammu.>
<I say he's a threat!>
<Our language being spoken by a human shocked the trooper that brought this man to us. Griffin didn't try to harm that trooper in any way-->
<That does not alter the fact all of humanity is an enemy to the Nation of Atlantis!>
<And I say he's a scholar! I have seen how he was able to decipher the tablets in the Hall of Records!>

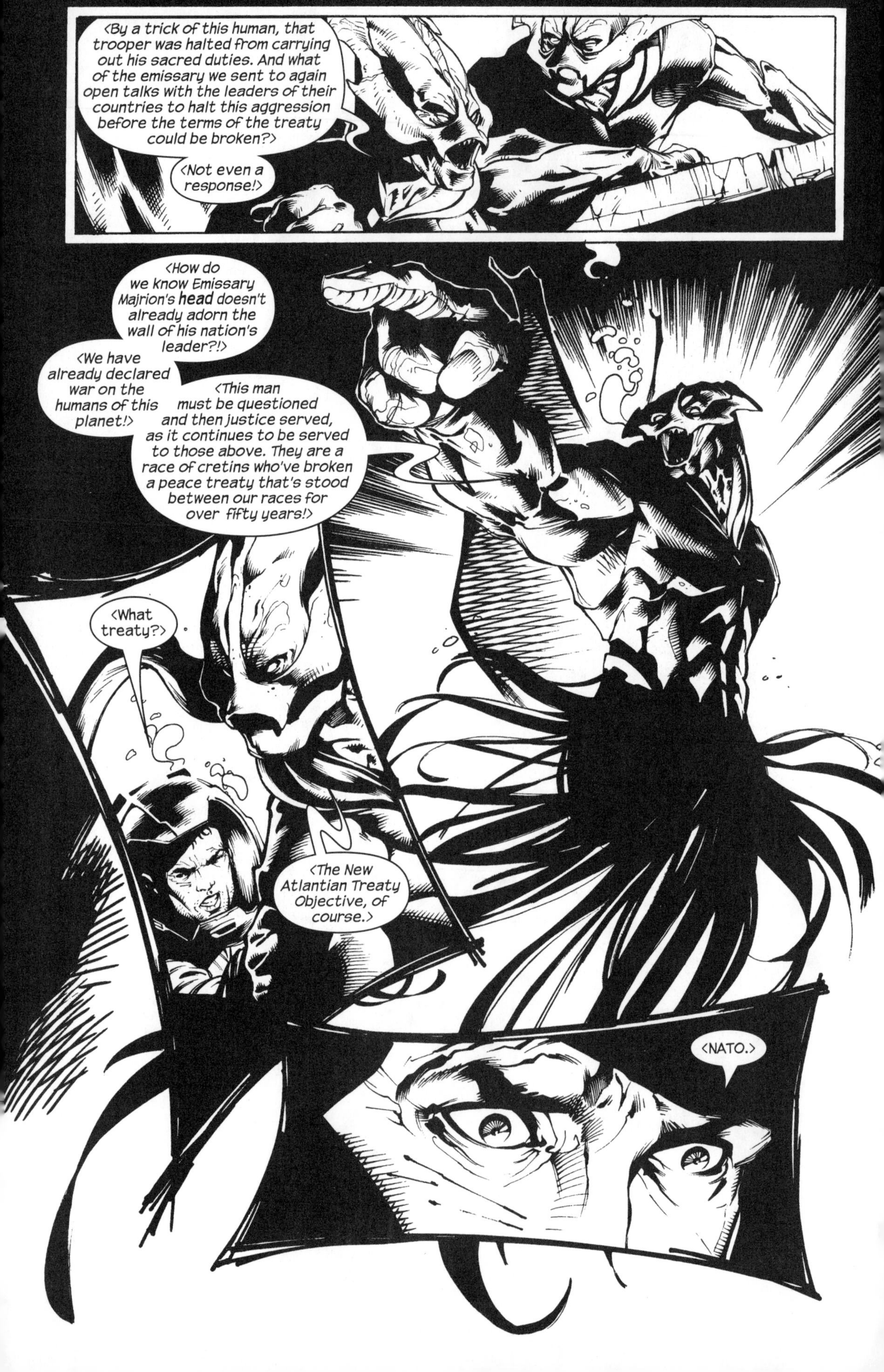
<By a trick of this human, that trooper was halted from carrying out his sacred duties. And what of the emissary we sent to again open talks with the leaders of their countries to halt this aggression before the terms of the treaty could be broken?>
<Not even a response!>
<How do we know Emissary Majrion's **head** doesn't already adorn the wall of his nation's leader?!>
<We have already declared war on the humans of this planet!>
<This man must be questioned and then justice served, as it continues to be served to those above. They are a race of cretins who've broken a peace treaty that's stood between our races for over fifty years!>
<What treaty?>
<The New Atlantian Treaty Objective, of course.>
<NATO.>

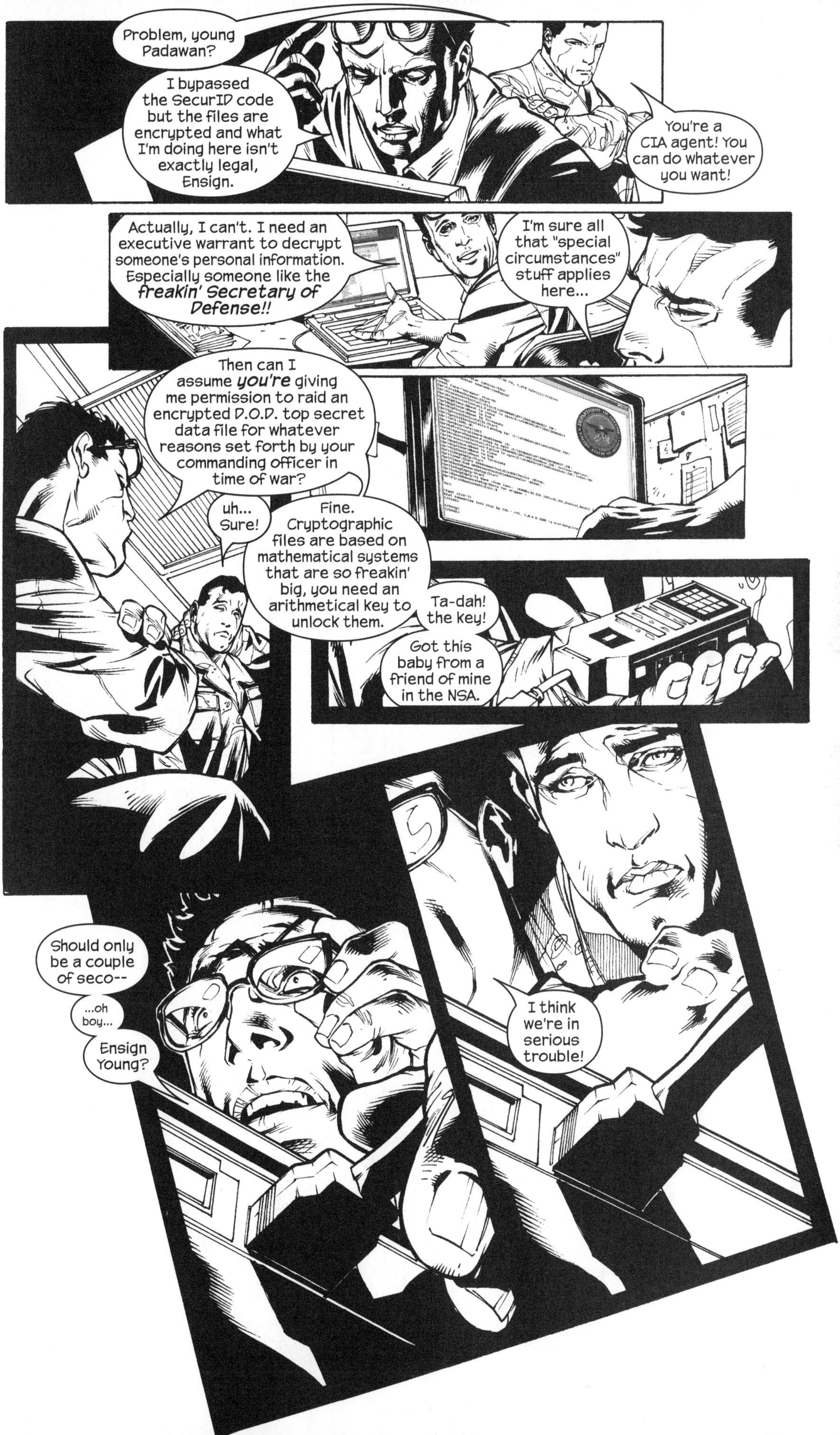
Problem, young Padawan?
I bypassed the SecurID code but the files are encrypted and what I'm doing here isn't exactly legal, Ensign.
You're a CIA agent! You can do whatever you want!
Actually, I can't. I need an executive warrant to decrypt someone's personal information. Especially someone like the *freakin' Secretary of Defense!!*
I'm sure all that "special circumstances" stuff applies here...
Then can I assume *you're* giving me permission to raid an encrypted D.O.D. top secret data file for whatever reasons set forth by your commanding officer in time of war?
uh... Sure!
Fine. Cryptographic files are based on mathematical systems that are so freakin' big, you need an arithmetical key to unlock them.
Ta-dah! the key!
Got this baby from a friend of mine in the NSA.
Should only be a couple of seco--
...oh boy...
Ensign Young?
I think we're in serious trouble!

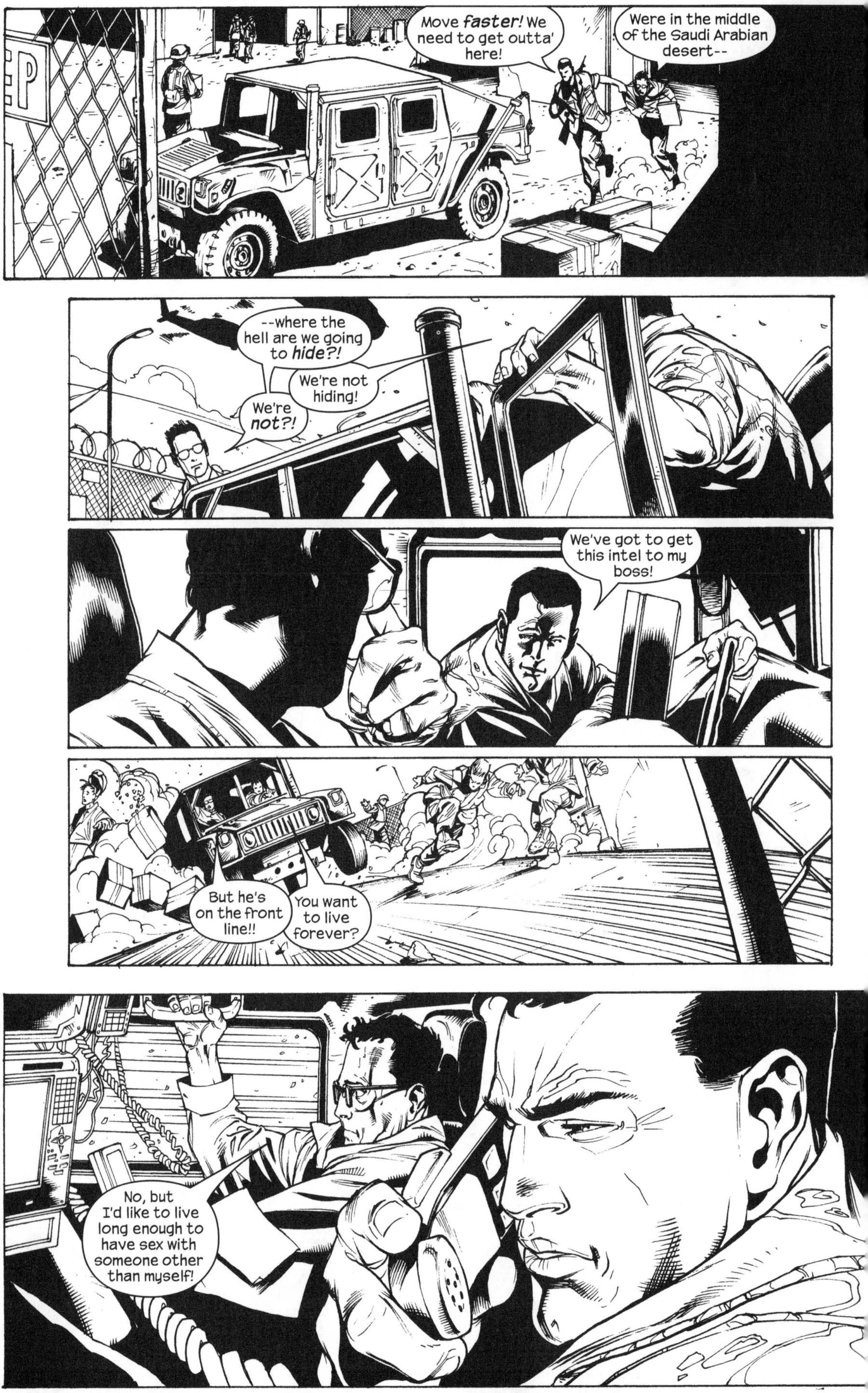

Move *faster!* We need to get outta' here!
Were in the middle of the Saudi Arabian desert--
--where the hell are we going to *hide?!*
We're not hiding!
We're *not?!*
We've got to get this intel to my boss!
But he's on the front line!!
You want to live forever?
No, but I'd like to live long enough to have sex with someone other than myself!

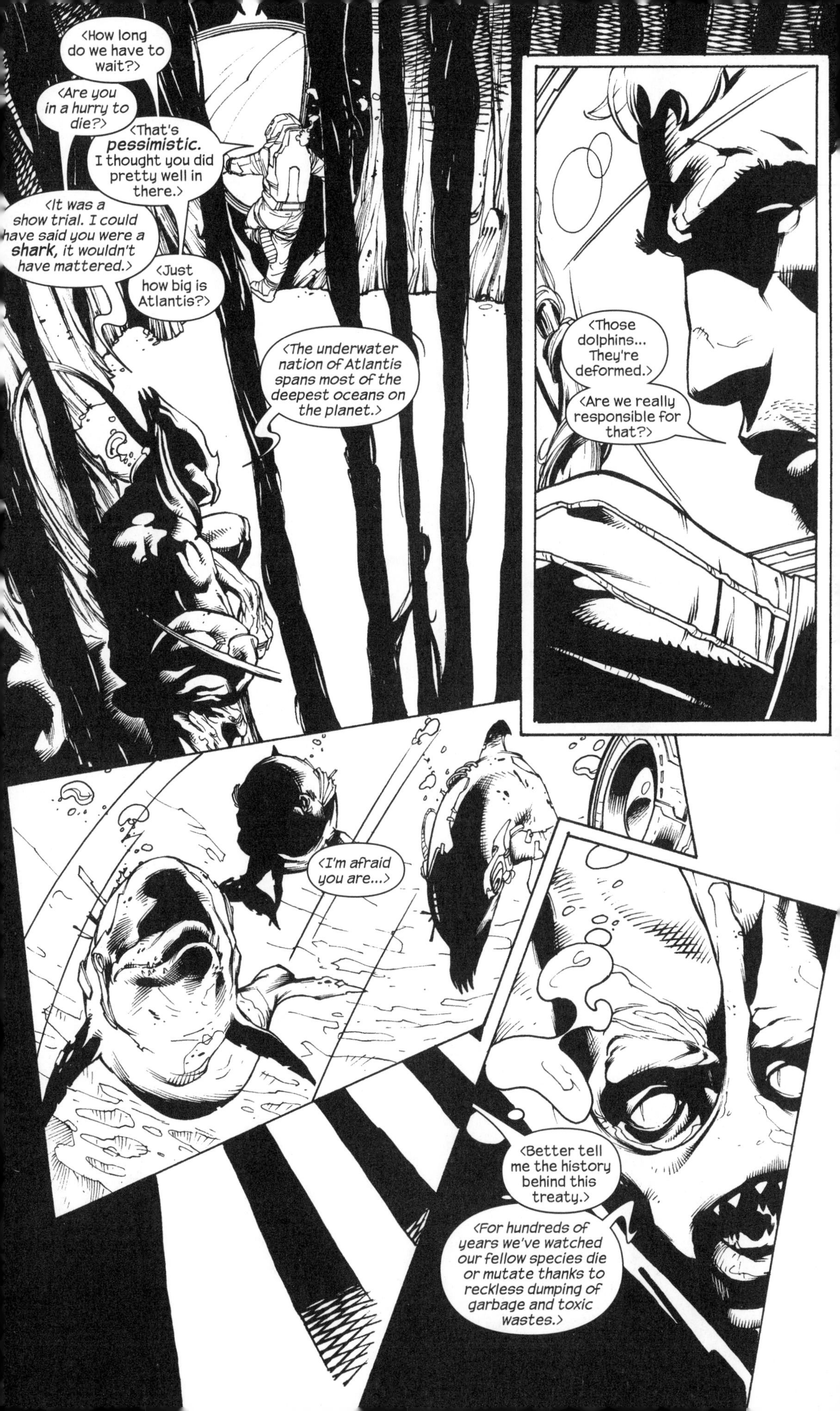

<How long do we have to wait?>
<Are you in a hurry to die?>
<That's pessimistic. I thought you did pretty well in there.>
<It was a show trial. I could have said you were a shark, it wouldn't have mattered.>
<Just how big is Atlantis?>
<The underwater nation of Atlantis spans most of the deepest oceans on the planet.>
<Those dolphins... They're deformed.>
<Are we really responsible for that?>
<I'm afraid you are...>
<Better tell me the history behind this treaty.>
<For hundreds of years we've watched our fellow species die or mutate thanks to reckless dumping of garbage and toxic wastes.>

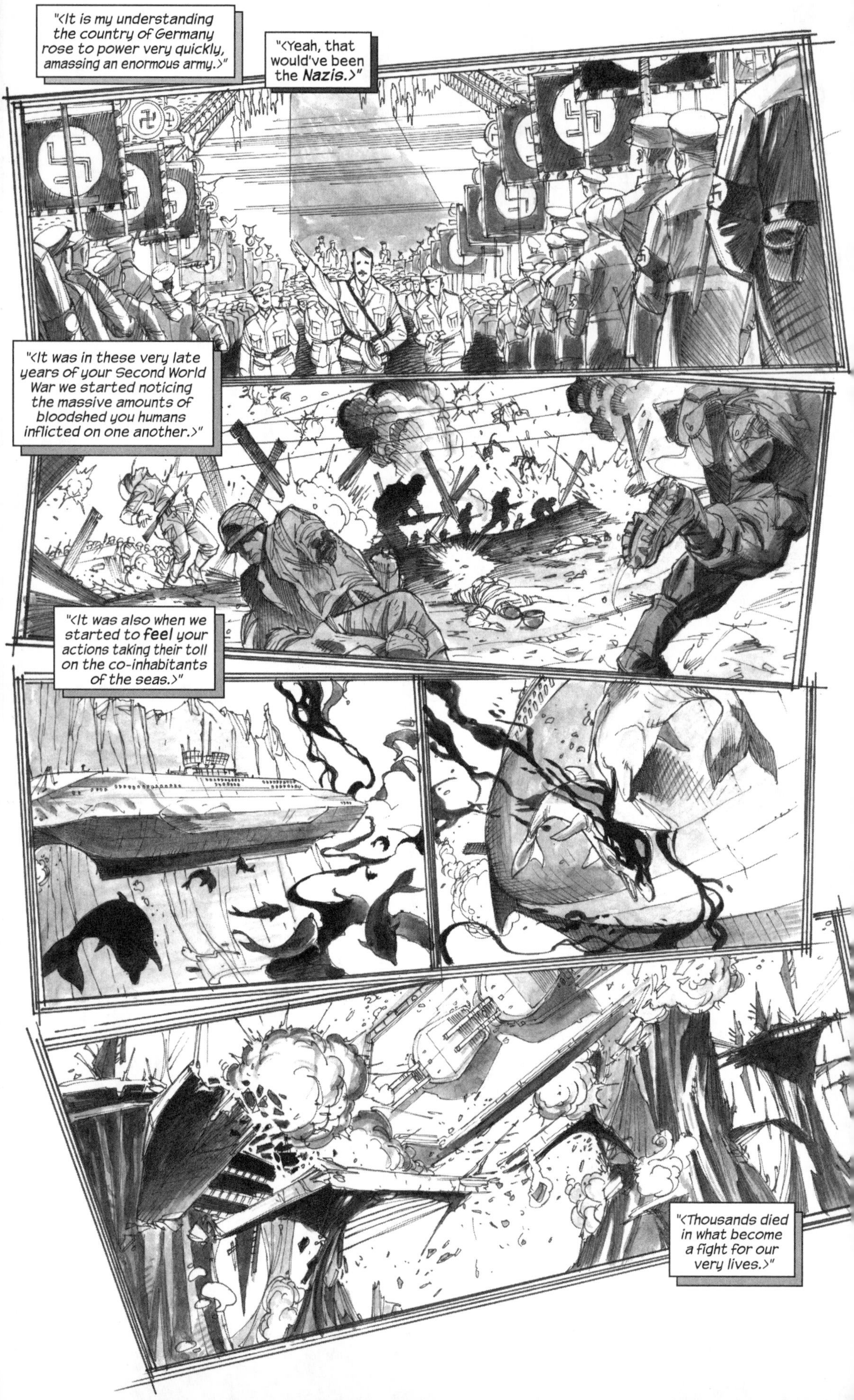
"<It is my understanding the country of Germany rose to power very quickly, amassing an enormous army.>"
"<Yeah, that would've been the *Nazis.*>"
"<It was in these very late years of your Second World War we started noticing the massive amounts of bloodshed you humans inflicted on one another.>"
"<It was also when we started to **feel** your actions taking their toll on the co-inhabitants of the seas.>"
"<Thousands died in what become a fight for our very lives.>"

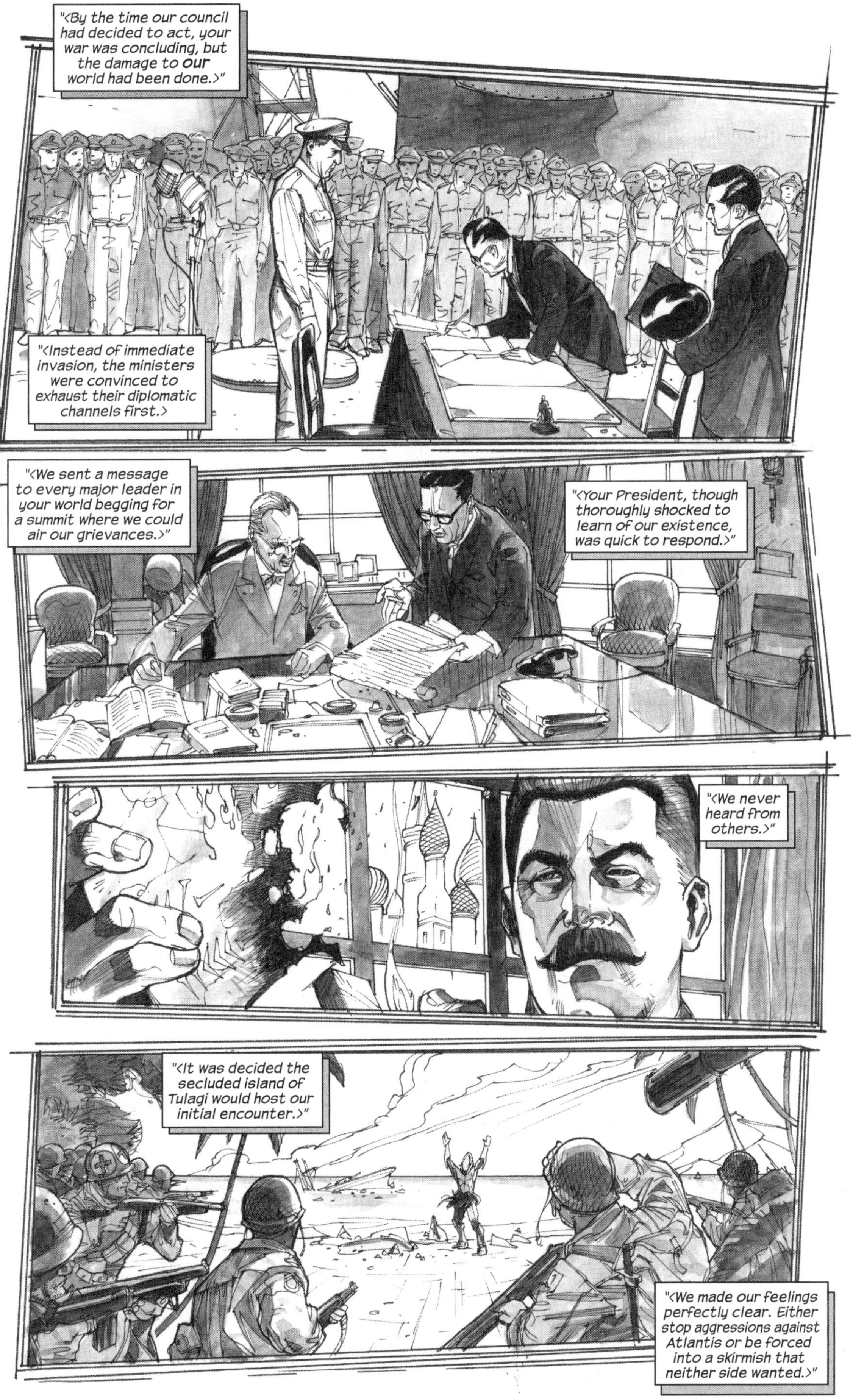
"<By the time our council had decided to act, your war was concluding, but the damage to **our** world had been done.>"
"<Instead of immediate invasion, the ministers were convinced to exhaust their diplomatic channels first.>
"<We sent a message to every major leader in your world begging for a summit where we could air our grievances.>"
"<Your President, though thoroughly shocked to learn of our existence, was quick to respond.>"
"<We never heard from others.>"
"<It was decided the secluded island of Tulagi would host our initial encounter.>"
"<We made our feelings perfectly clear. Either stop aggressions against Atlantis or be forced into a skirmish that neither side wanted.>"

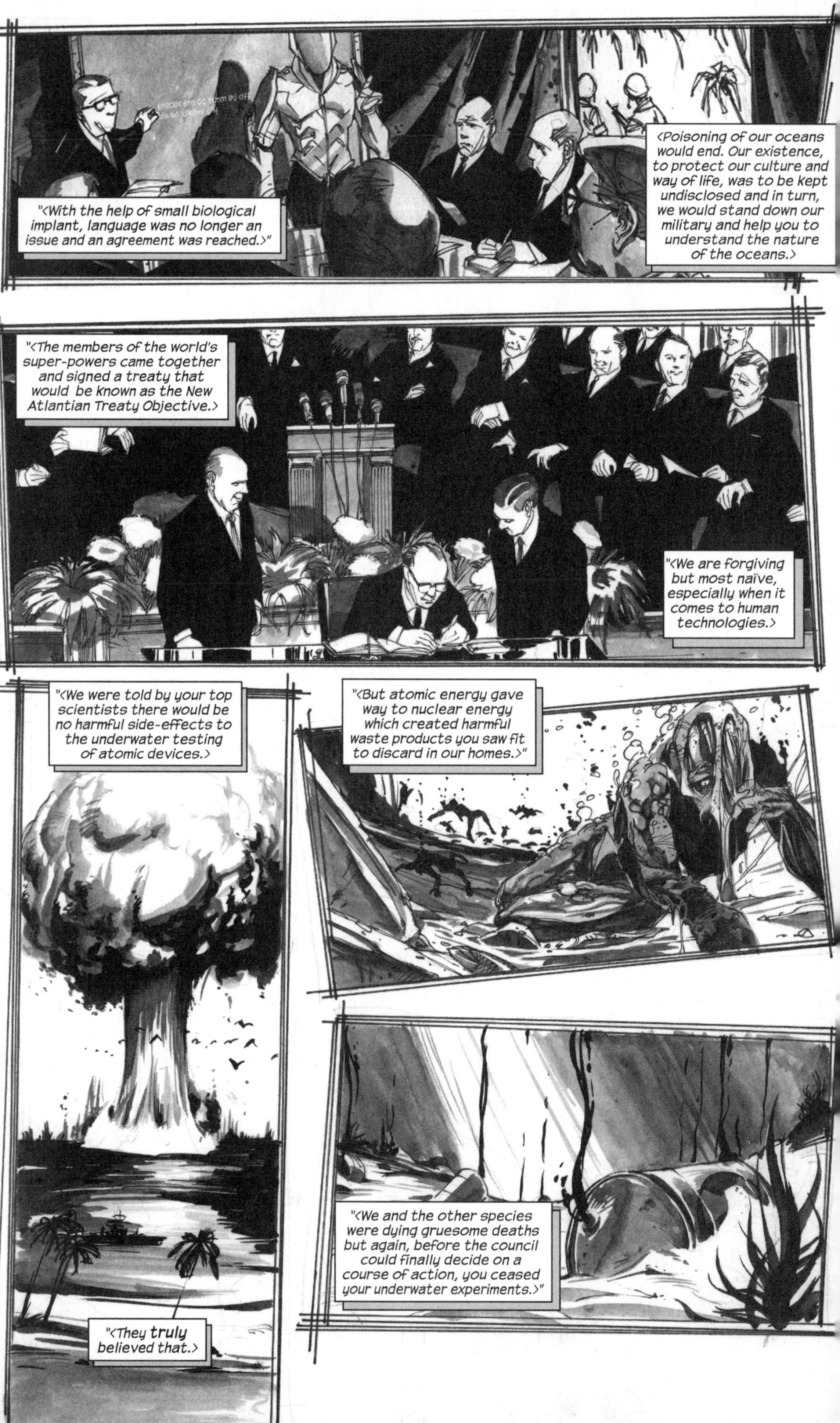
"<With the help of small biological implant, language was no longer an issue and an agreement was reached.>"
<Poisoning of our oceans would end. Our existence, to protect our culture and way of life, was to be kept undisclosed and in turn, we would stand down our military and help you to understand the nature of the oceans.>
"<The members of the world's super-powers came together and signed a treaty that would be known as the New Atlantian Treaty Objective.>
"<We are forgiving but most naïve, especially when it comes to human technologies.>
"<We were told by your top scientists there would be no harmful side-effects to the underwater testing of atomic devices.>
"<They **truly** believed that.>
"<But atomic energy gave way to nuclear energy which created harmful waste products you saw fit to discard in our homes.>"
"<We and the other species were dying gruesome deaths but again, before the council could finally decide on a course of action, you ceased your underwater experiments.>"

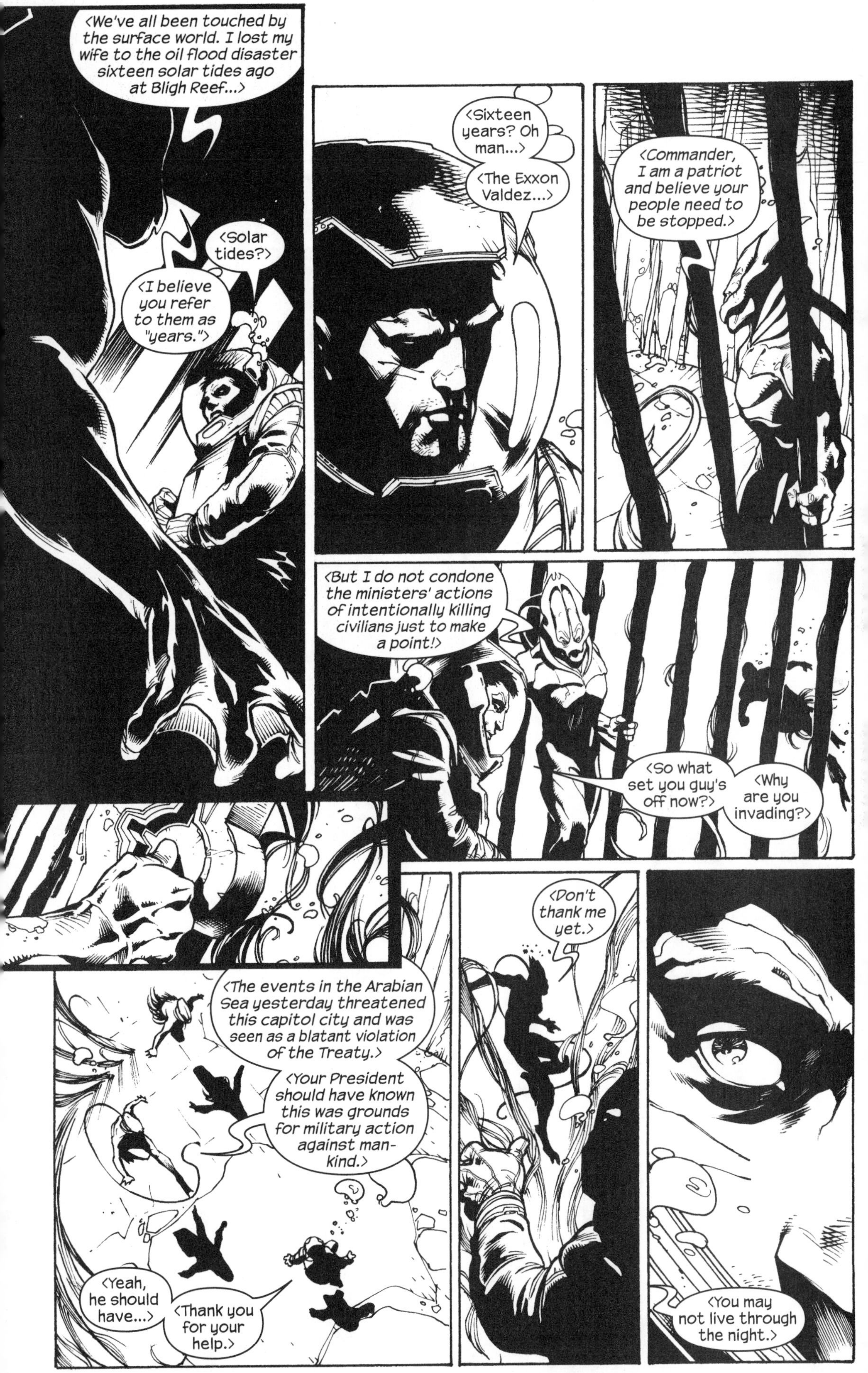
<We've all been touched by the surface world. I lost my wife to the oil flood disaster sixteen solar tides ago at Bligh Reef...>
<Solar tides?>
<I believe you refer to them as "years.">
<Sixteen years? Oh man...>
<The Exxon Valdez...>
<Commander, I am a patriot and believe your people need to be stopped.>
<But I do not condone the ministers' actions of intentionally killing civilians just to make a point!>
<So what set you guy's off now?>
<Why are you invading?>
<The events in the Arabian Sea yesterday threatened this capitol city and was seen as a blatant violation of the Treaty.>
<Your President should have known this was grounds for military action against man-kind.>
<Yeah, he should have...>
<Thank you for your help.>
<Don't thank me yet.>
<You may not live through the night.>

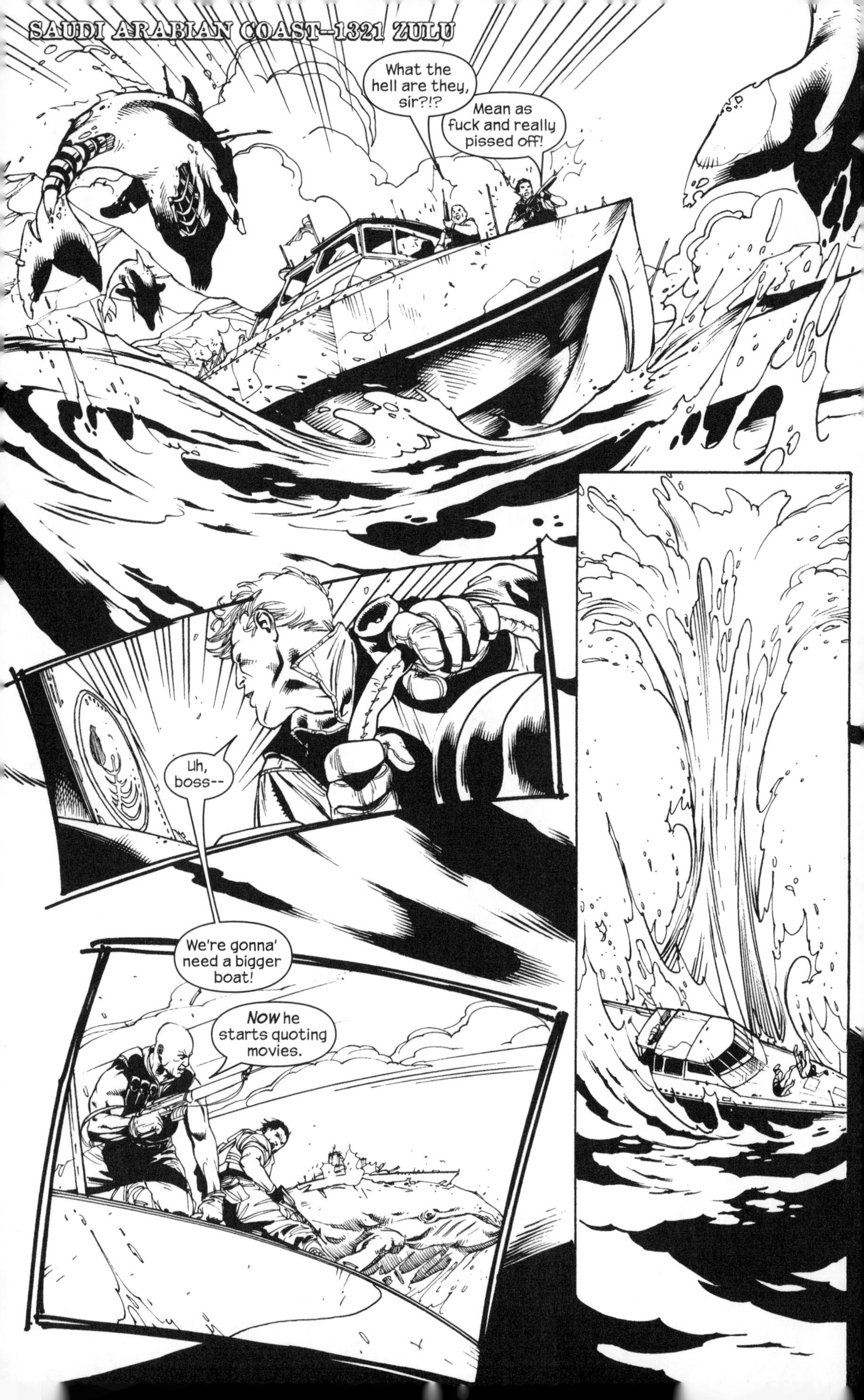
SAUDI ARABIAN COAST—1321 ZULU
What the hell are they, sir?!?
Mean as fuck and really pissed off!
Uh, boss--
We're gonna' need a bigger boat!
NOW he starts quoting movies.

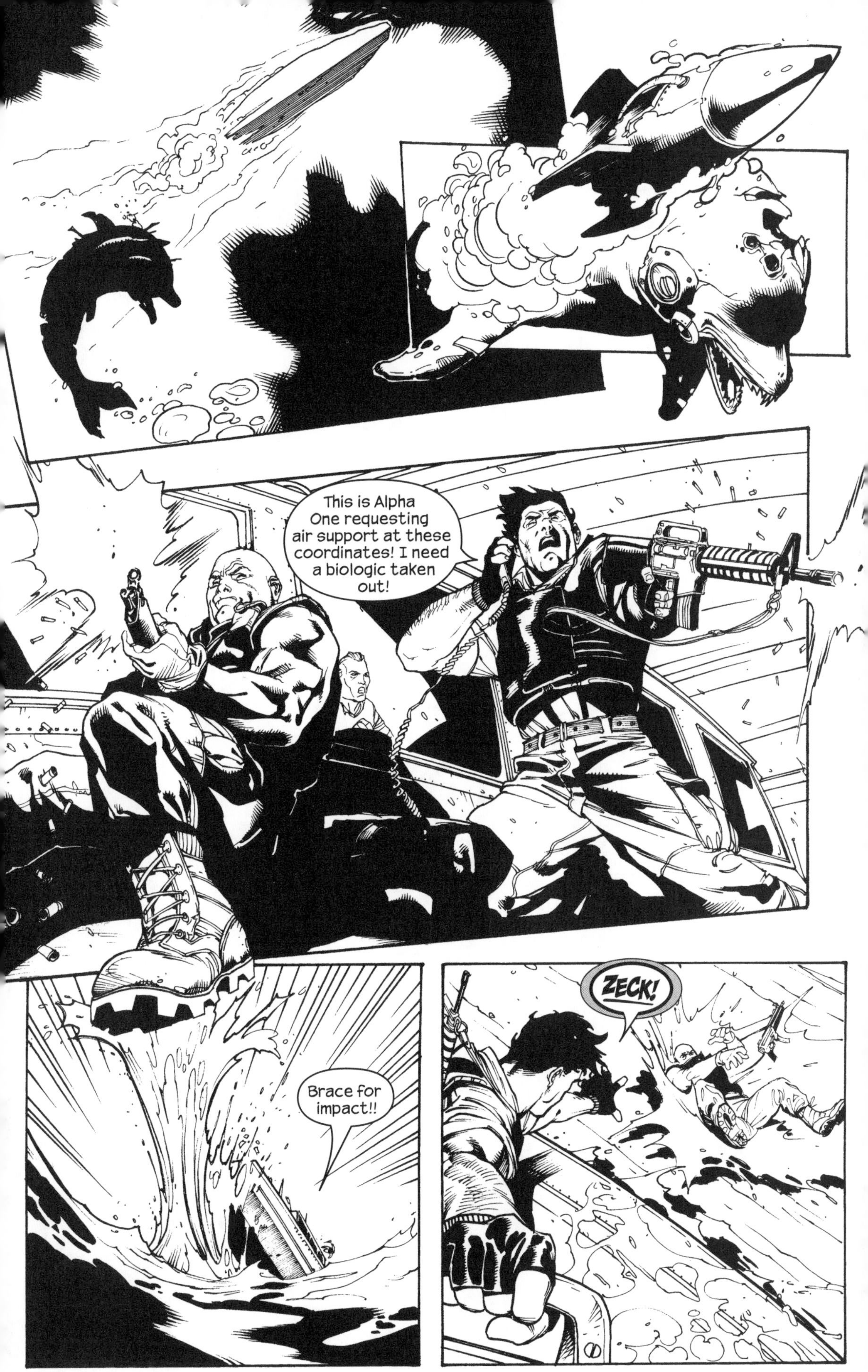
This is Alpha One requesting air support at these coordinates! I need a biologic taken out!
Brace for impact!!
ZECK!

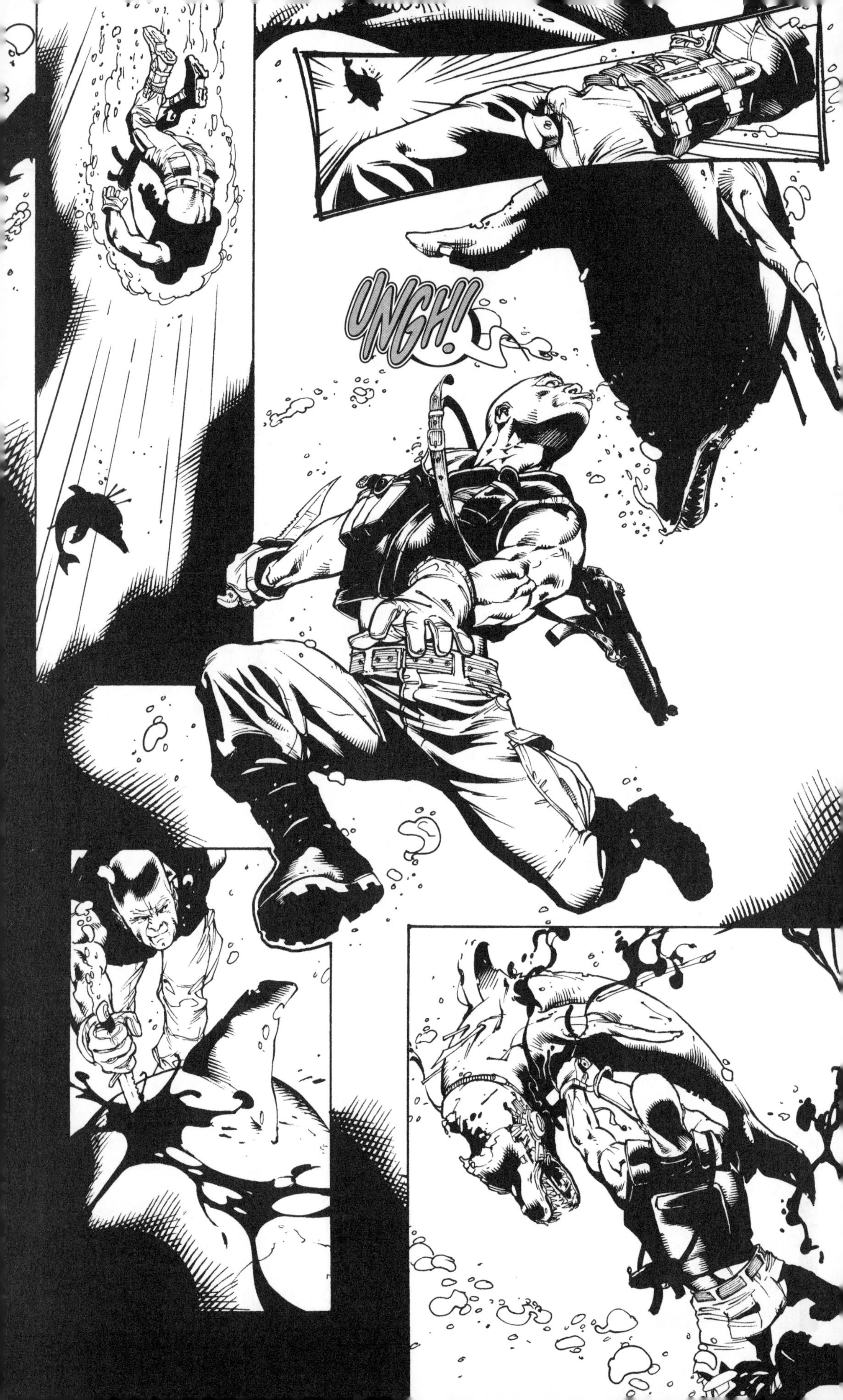
UNGH!

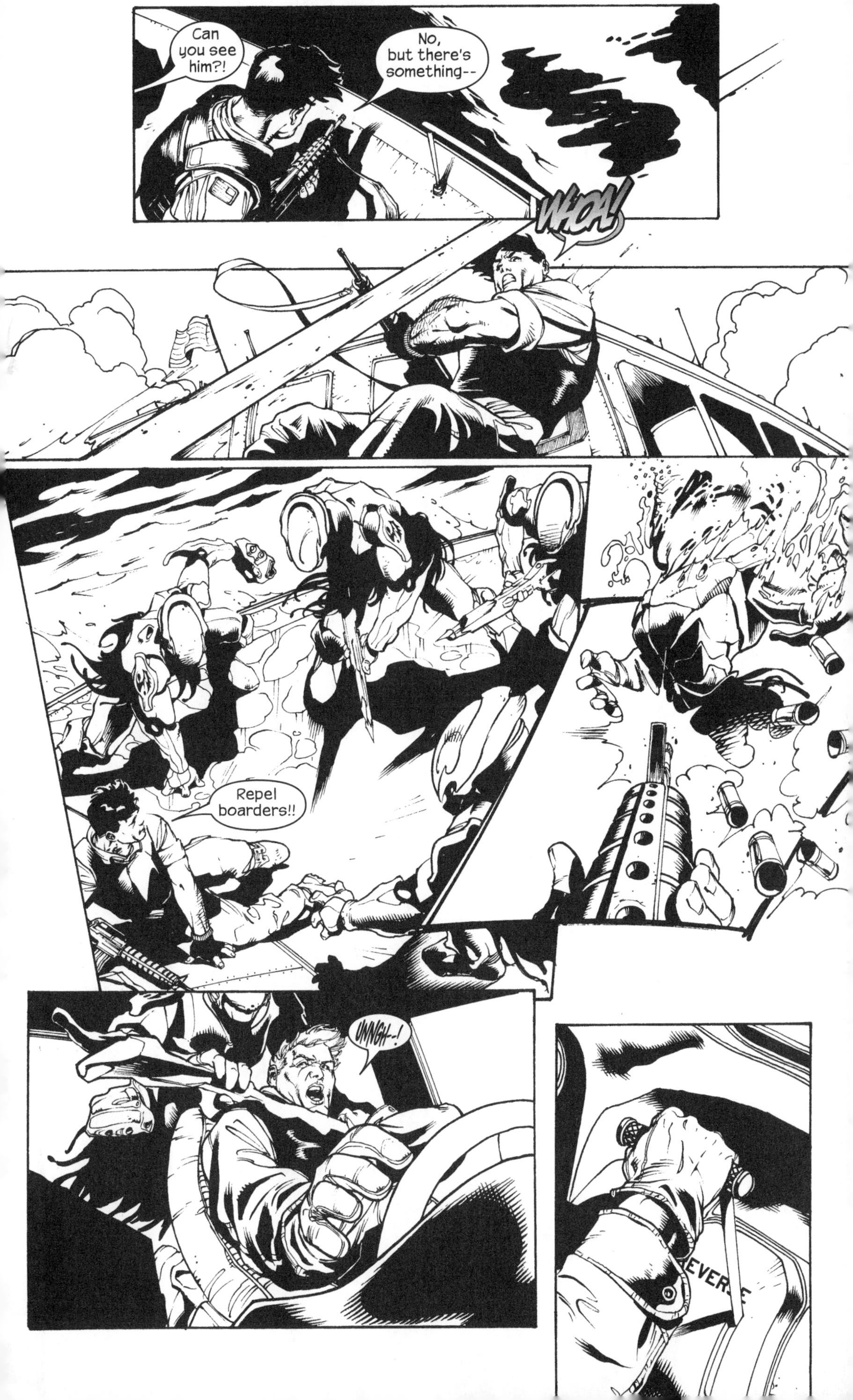

Can you see him?!
No, but there's something--
WHOA!
Repel boarders!!
UNNGH--!
REVERSE

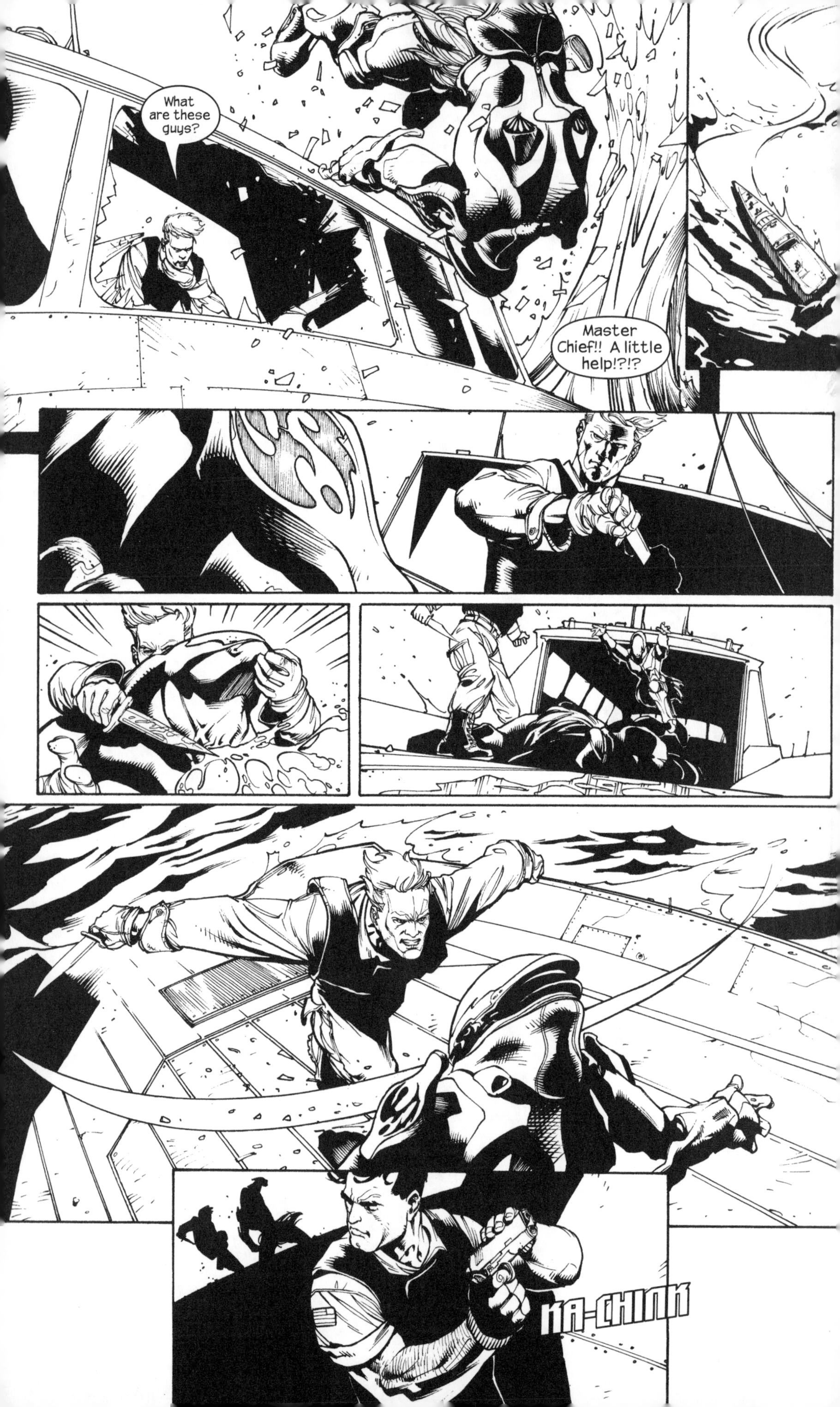

What are these guys?
Master Chief!! A little help!?!?
KA-CHINK

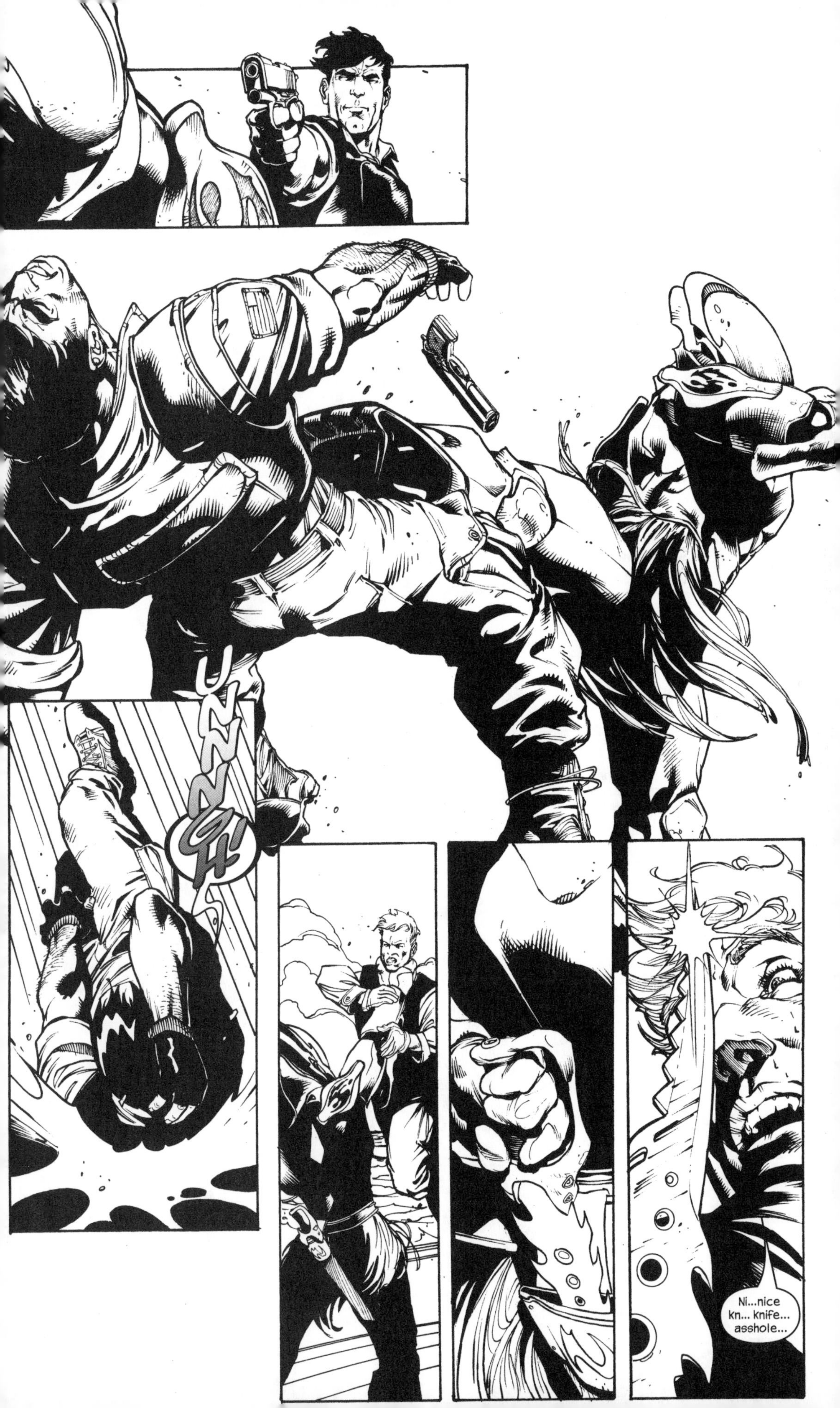
UNNNGH!
Ni...nice
kn... knife...
asshole...

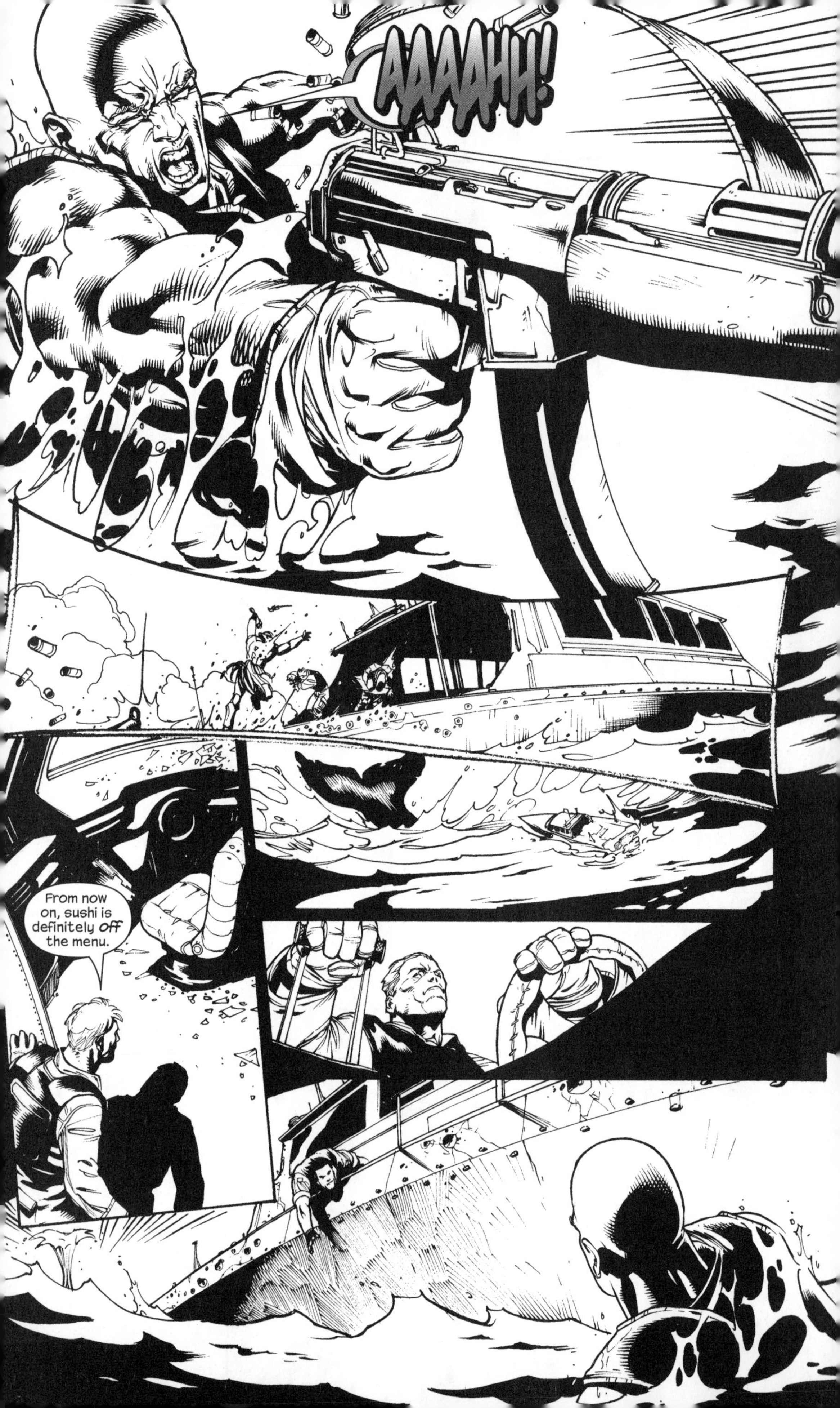
AAAAHH!
From now on, sushi is definitely OFF the menu.

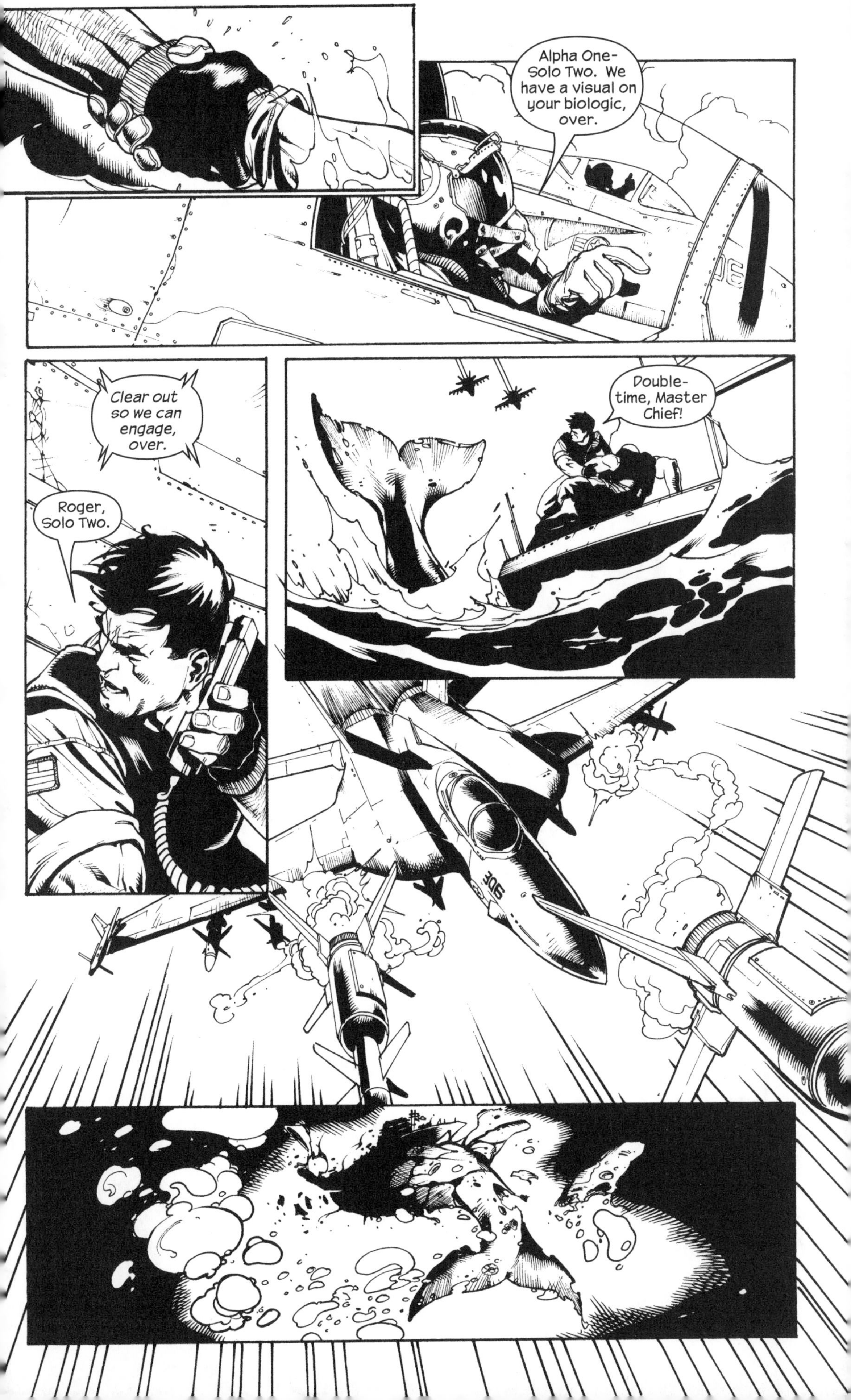
Alpha One-Solo Two. We have a visual on your biologic, over.
Clear out so we can engage, over.
Roger, Solo Two.
Double-time, Master Chief!

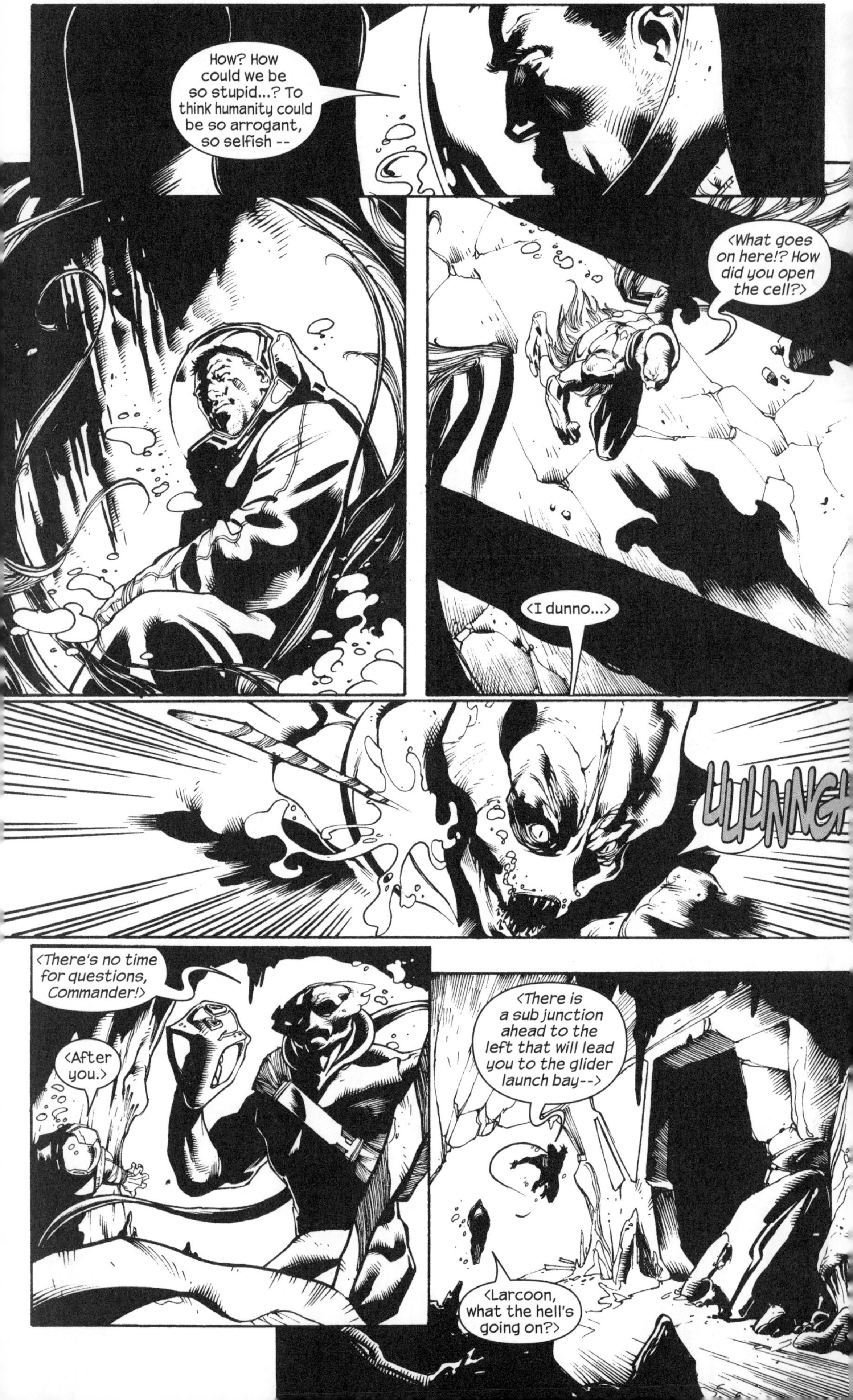
How? How could we be so stupid...? To think humanity could be so arrogant, so selfish --
<What goes on here!? How did you open the cell?>
<I dunno...>
UUUNNGH
<There's no time for questions, Commander!>
<After you.>
<There is a sub junction ahead to the left that will lead you to the glider launch bay-->
<Larcoon, what the hell's going on?>

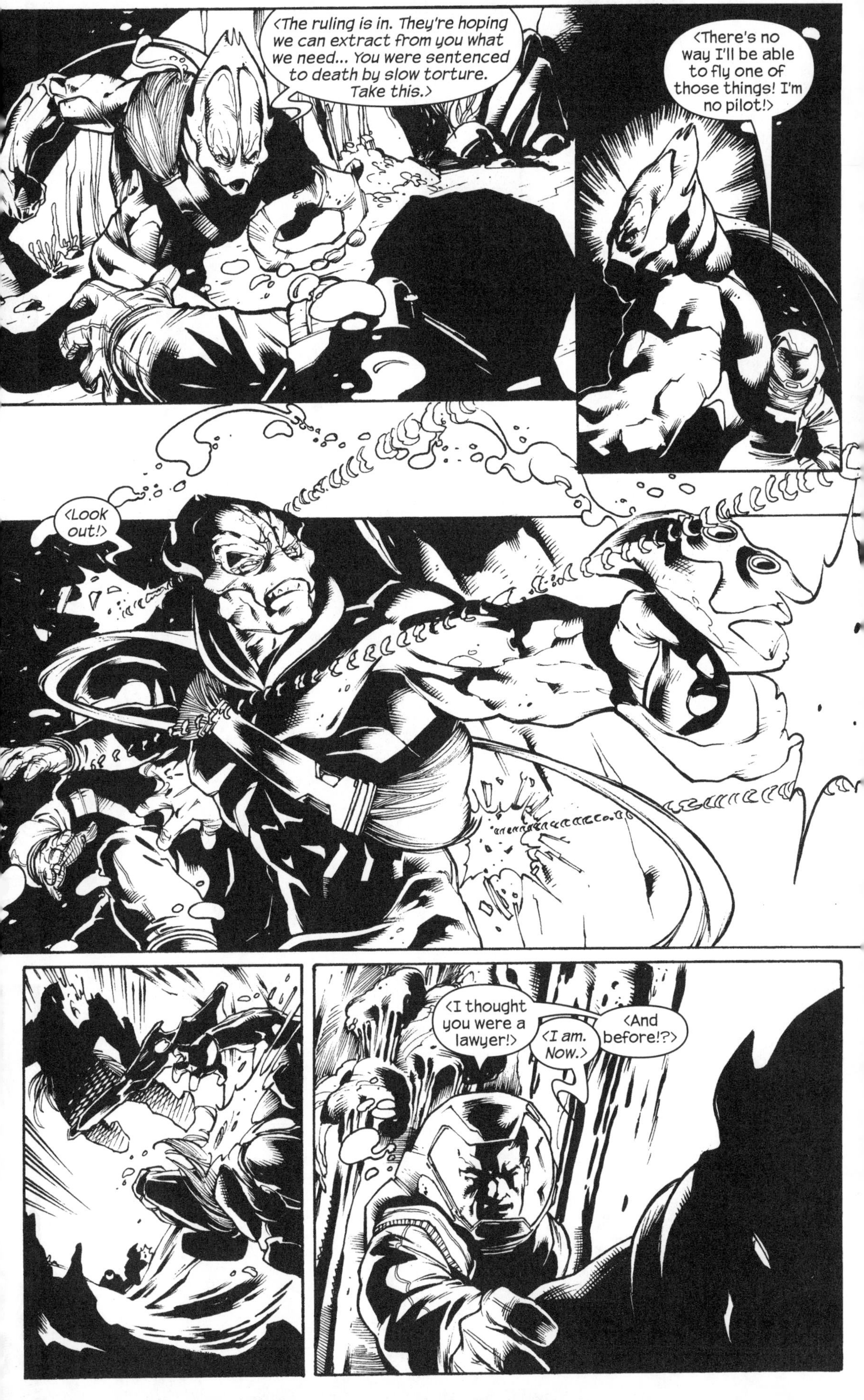
<The ruling is in. They're hoping we can extract from you what we need... You were sentenced to death by slow torture. Take this.>
<There's no way I'll be able to fly one of those things! I'm no pilot!>
<Look out!>
<I thought you were a lawyer!>
<I am. Now.>
<And before!?>

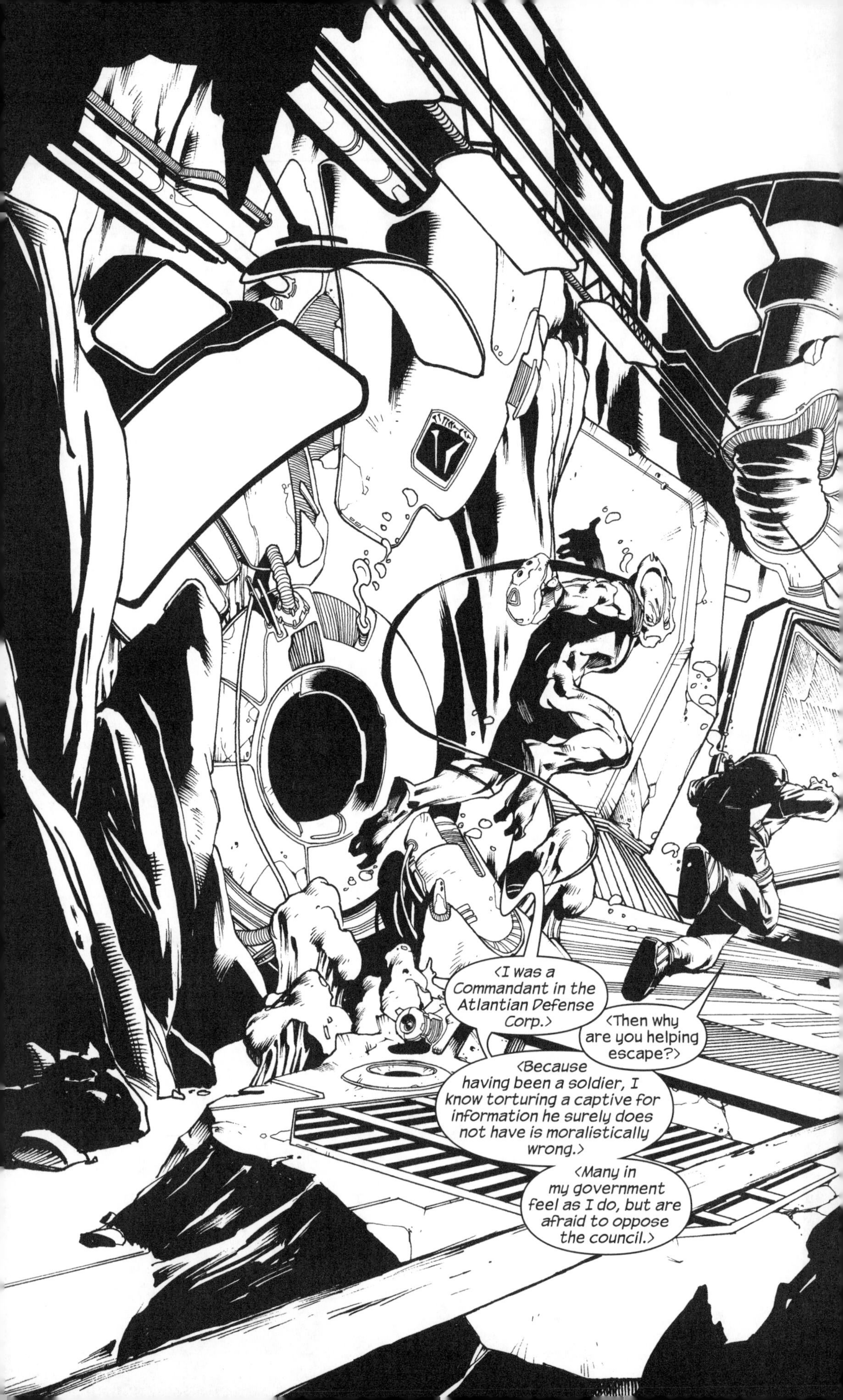

<I was a Commandant in the Atlantian Defense Corp.>
<Then why are you helping escape?>
<Because having been a soldier, I know torturing a captive for information he surely does not have is moralistically wrong.>
<Many in my government feel as I do, but are afraid to oppose the council.>

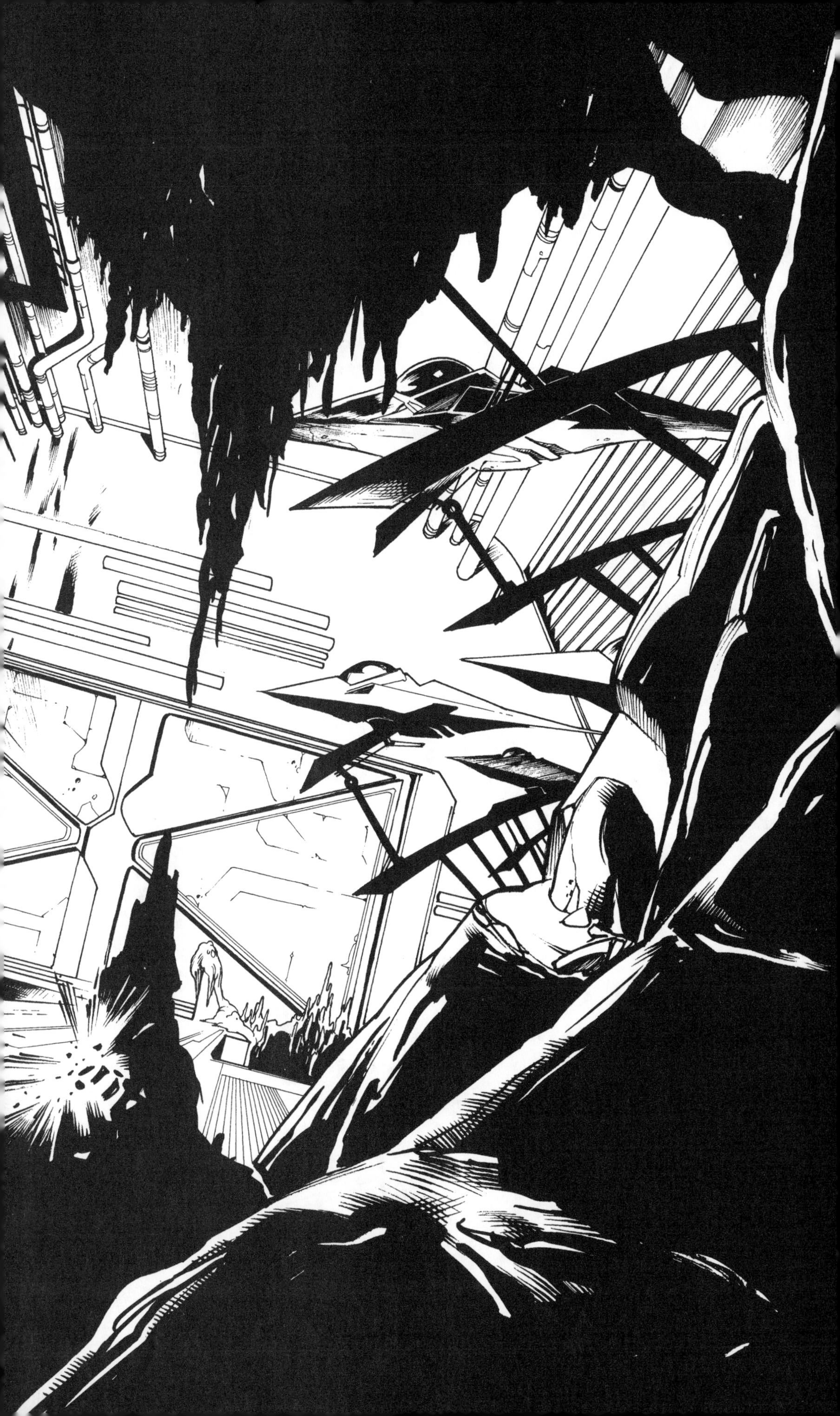

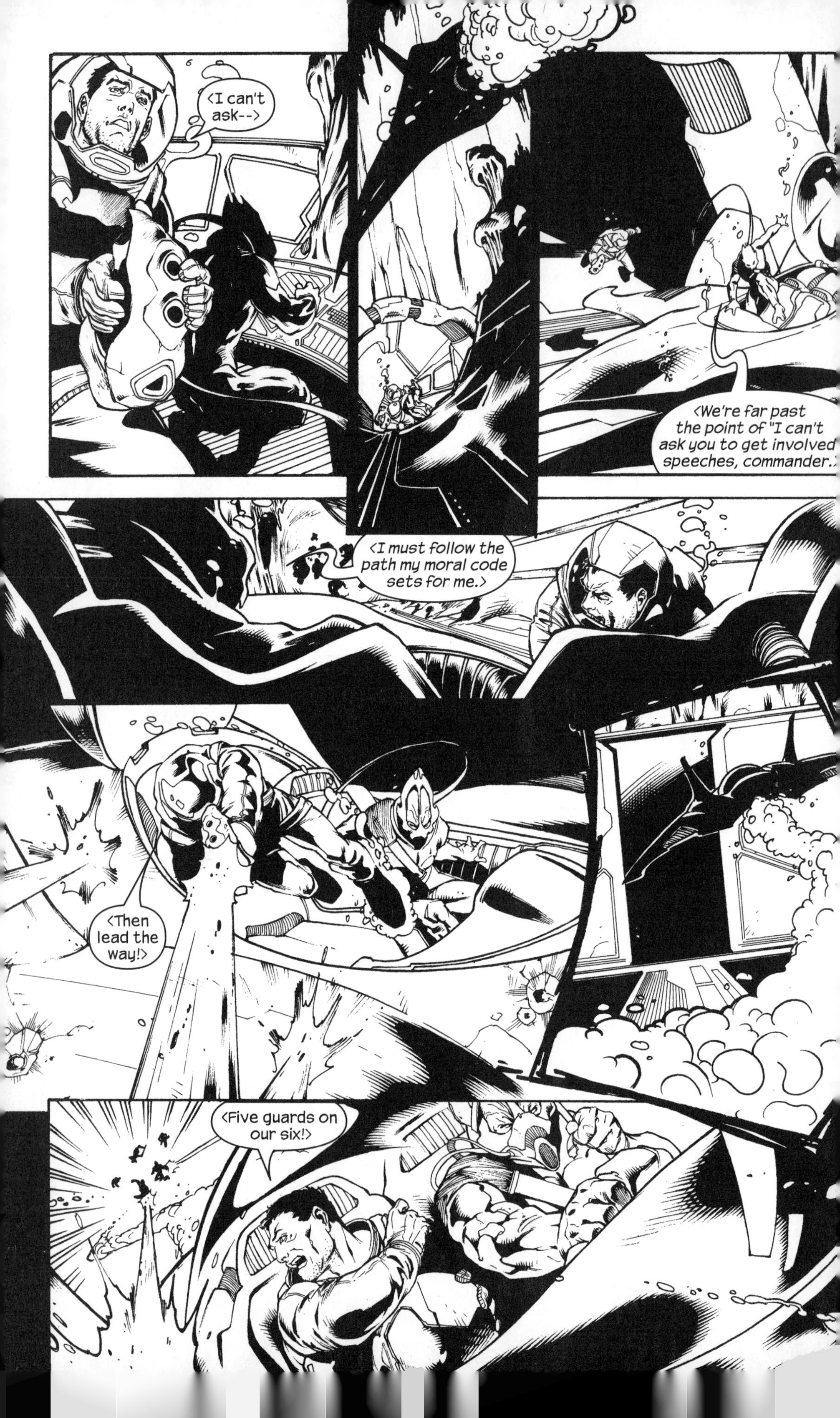

<I can't ask-->
<We're far past the point of "I can't ask you to get involved speeches, commander.>
<I must follow the path my moral code sets for me.>
<Then lead the way!>
<Five guards on our six!>

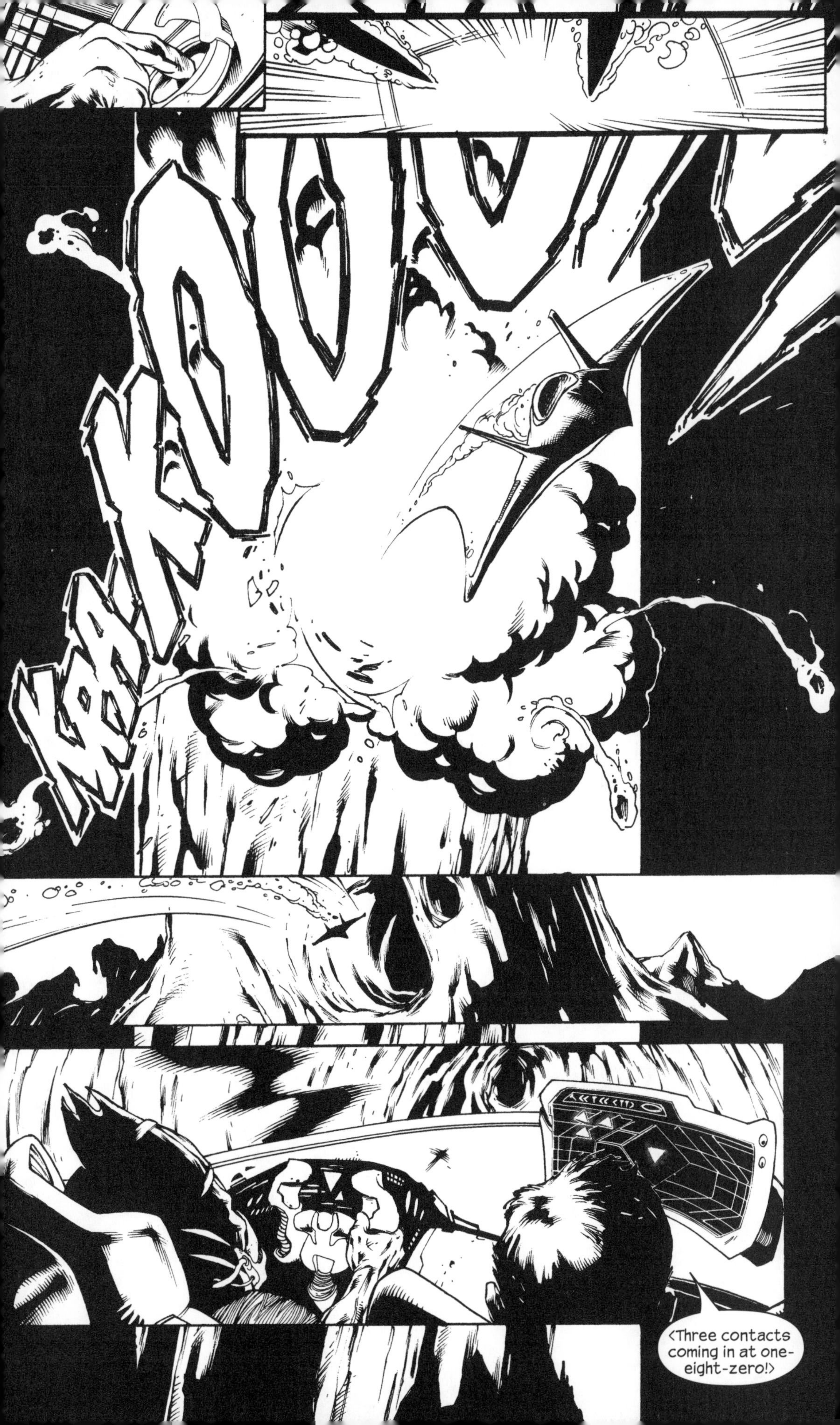

‹Three contacts coming in at one-eight-zero!›

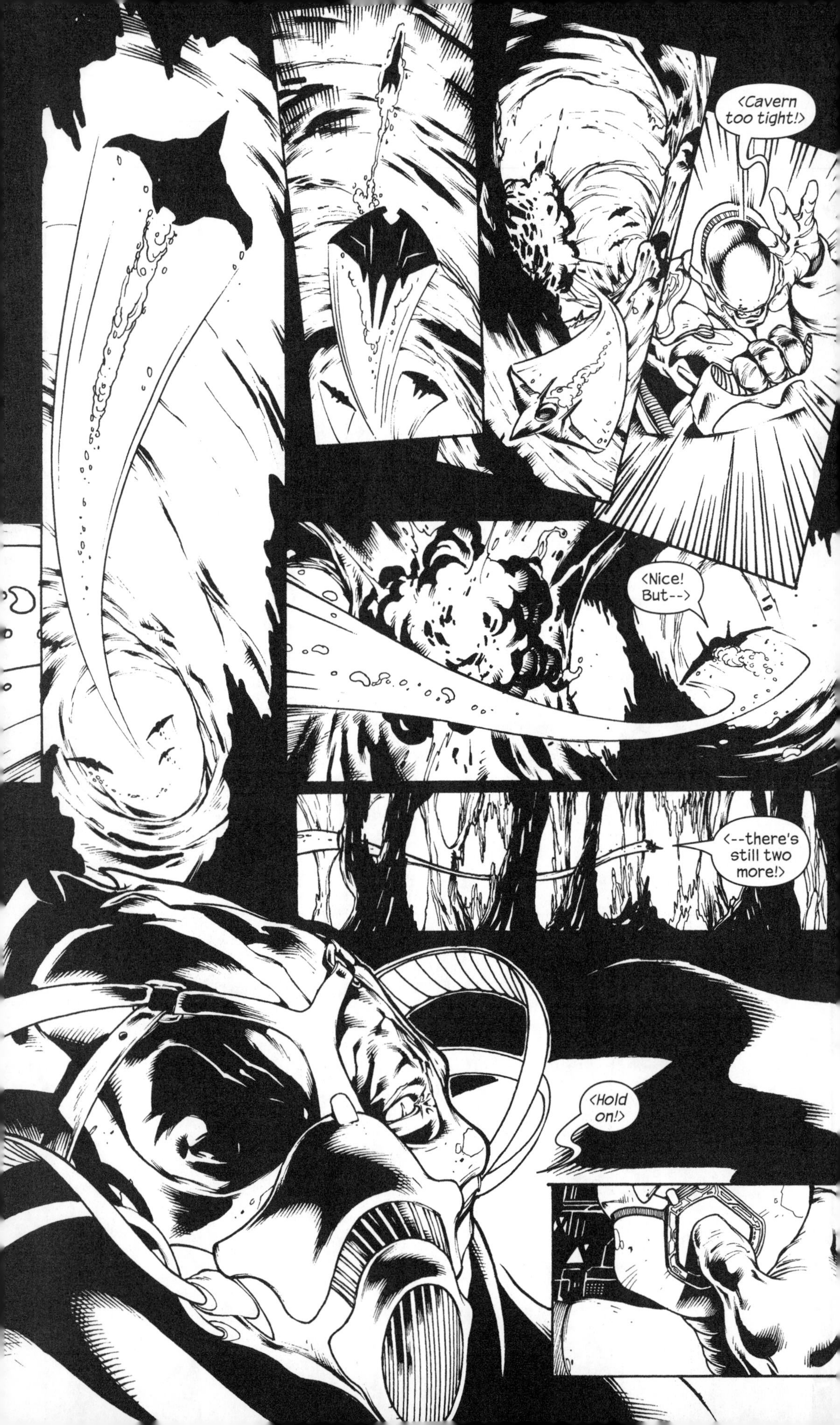

<Cavern too tight!>
<Nice! But-->
<--there's still two more!>
<Hold on!>

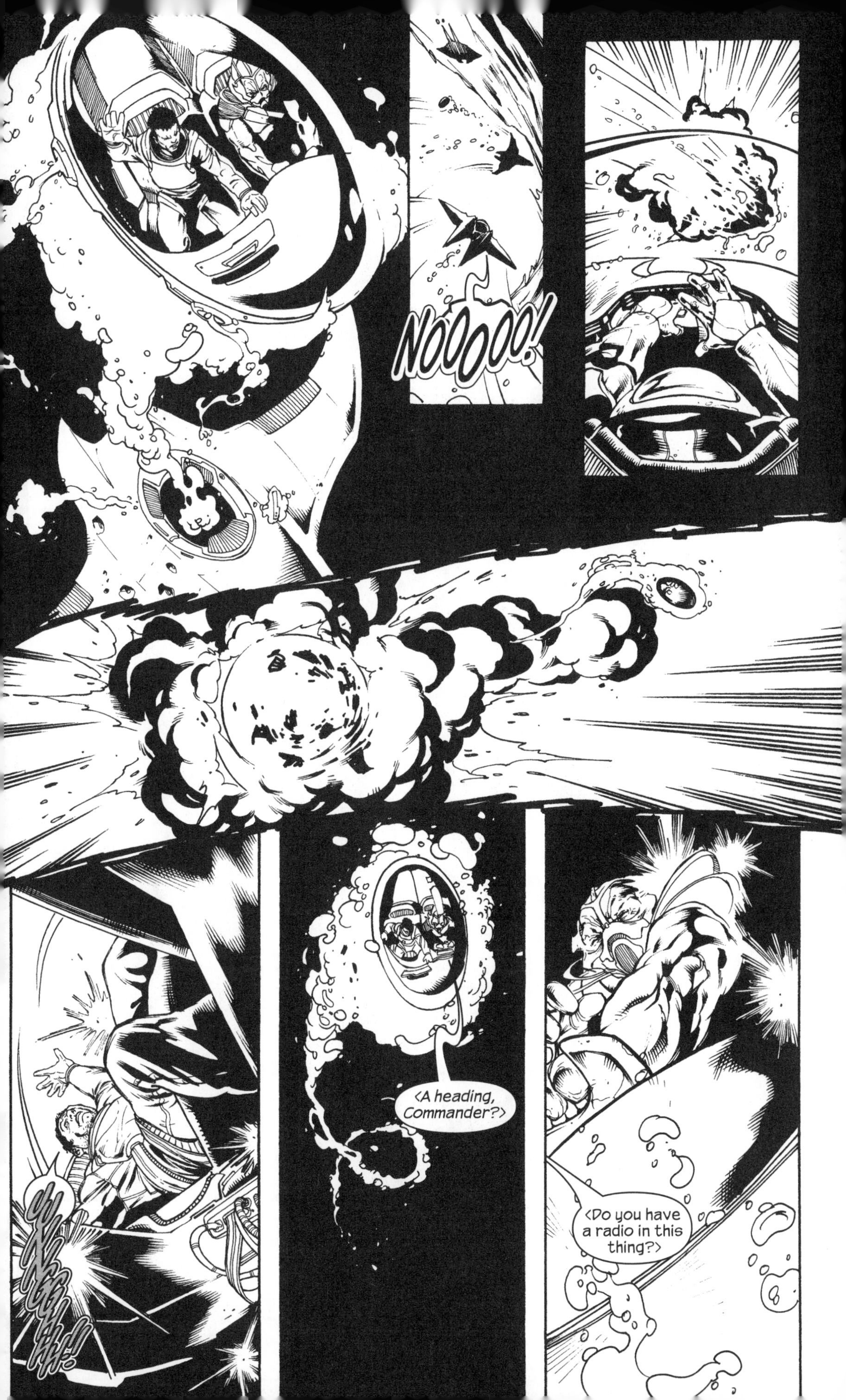
NOOOOO!
<A heading, Commander?>
<Do you have a radio in this thing?>

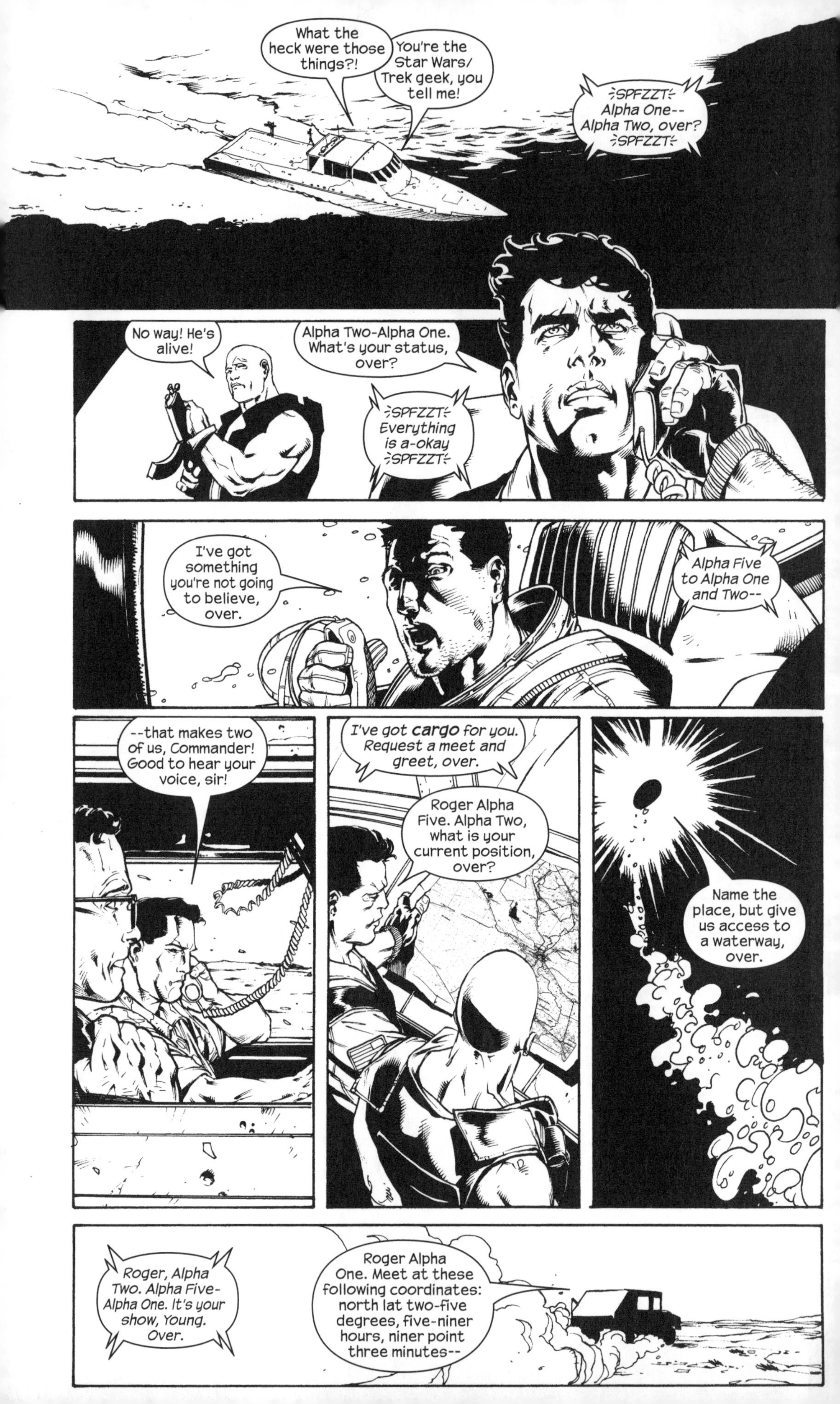

What the heck were those things?!
You're the Star Wars/Trek geek, you tell me!
SPFZZT Alpha One--Alpha Two, over? SPFZZT
No way! He's alive!
Alpha Two-Alpha One. What's your status, over?
SPFZZT Everything is a-okay SPFZZT
I've got something you're not going to believe, over.
Alpha Five to Alpha One and Two--
--that makes two of us, Commander! Good to hear your voice, sir!
I've got cargo for you. Request a meet and greet, over.
Roger Alpha Five. Alpha Two, what is your current position, over?
Name the place, but give us access to a waterway, over.
Roger, Alpha Two. Alpha Five-Alpha One. It's your show, Young. Over.
Roger Alpha One. Meet at these following coordinates: north lat two-five degrees, five-niner hours, niner point three minutes--

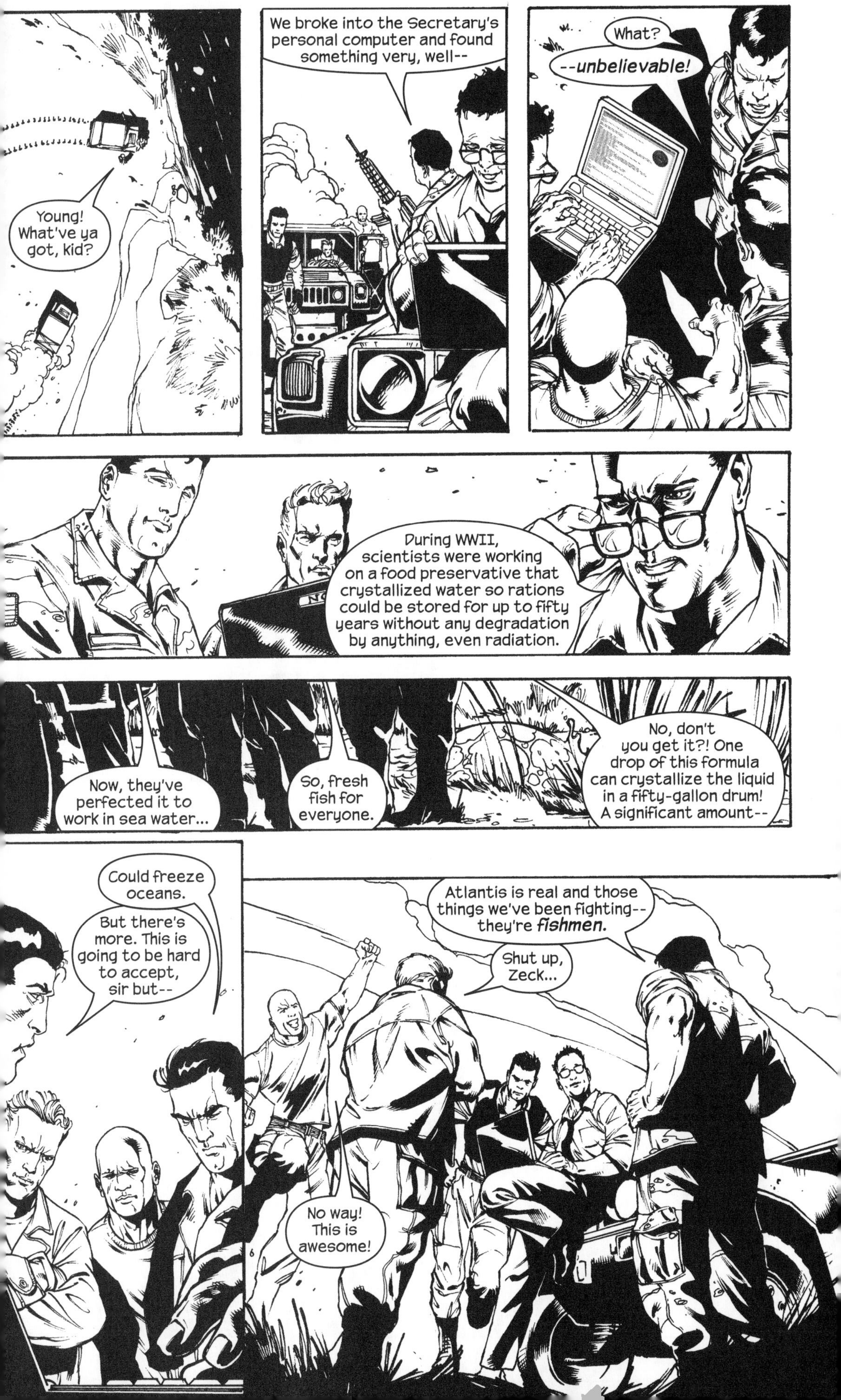

Young! What've ya got, kid?
We broke into the Secretary's personal computer and found something very, well--
What?
--*unbelievable!*
During WWII, scientists were working on a food preservative that crystallized water so rations could be stored for up to fifty years without any degradation by anything, even radiation.
Now, they've perfected it to work in sea water...
So, fresh fish for everyone.
No, don't you get it?! One drop of this formula can crystallize the liquid in a fifty-gallon drum! A significant amount--
Could freeze oceans.
But there's more. This is going to be hard to accept, sir but--
Atlantis is real and those things we've been fighting-- they're *fishmen.*
Shut up, Zeck...
No way! This is awesome!

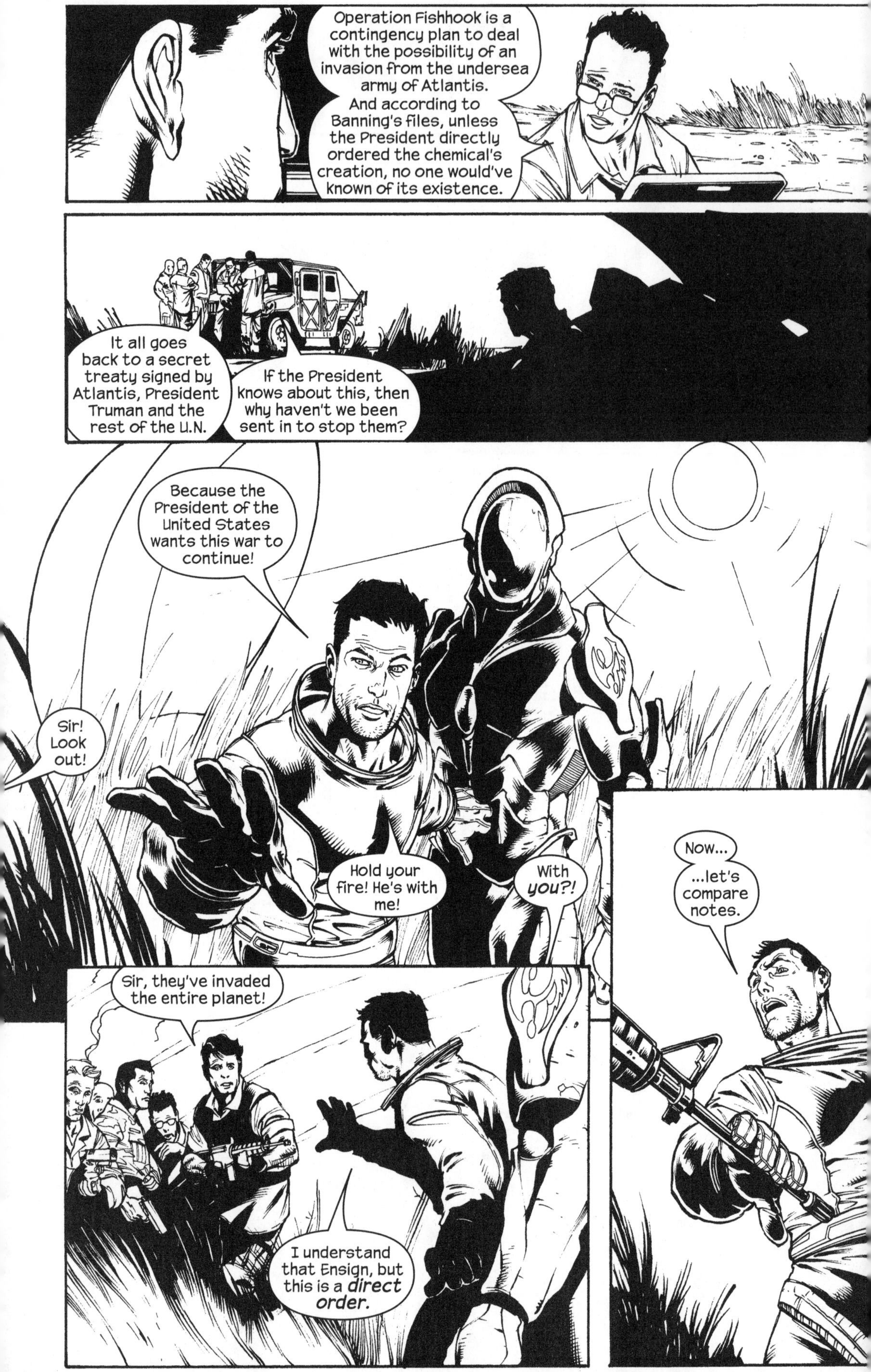
Operation Fishhook is a contingency plan to deal with the possibility of an invasion from the undersea army of Atlantis.
And according to Banning's files, unless the President directly ordered the chemical's creation, no one would've known of its existence.
It all goes back to a secret treaty signed by Atlantis, President Truman and the rest of the U.N.
If the President knows about this, then why haven't we been sent in to stop them?
Because the President of the United States wants this war to continue!
Sir! Look out!
Hold your fire! He's with me!
With *you*?!
Sir, they've invaded the entire planet!
I understand that Ensign, but this is a *direct order.*
Now...
...let's compare notes.

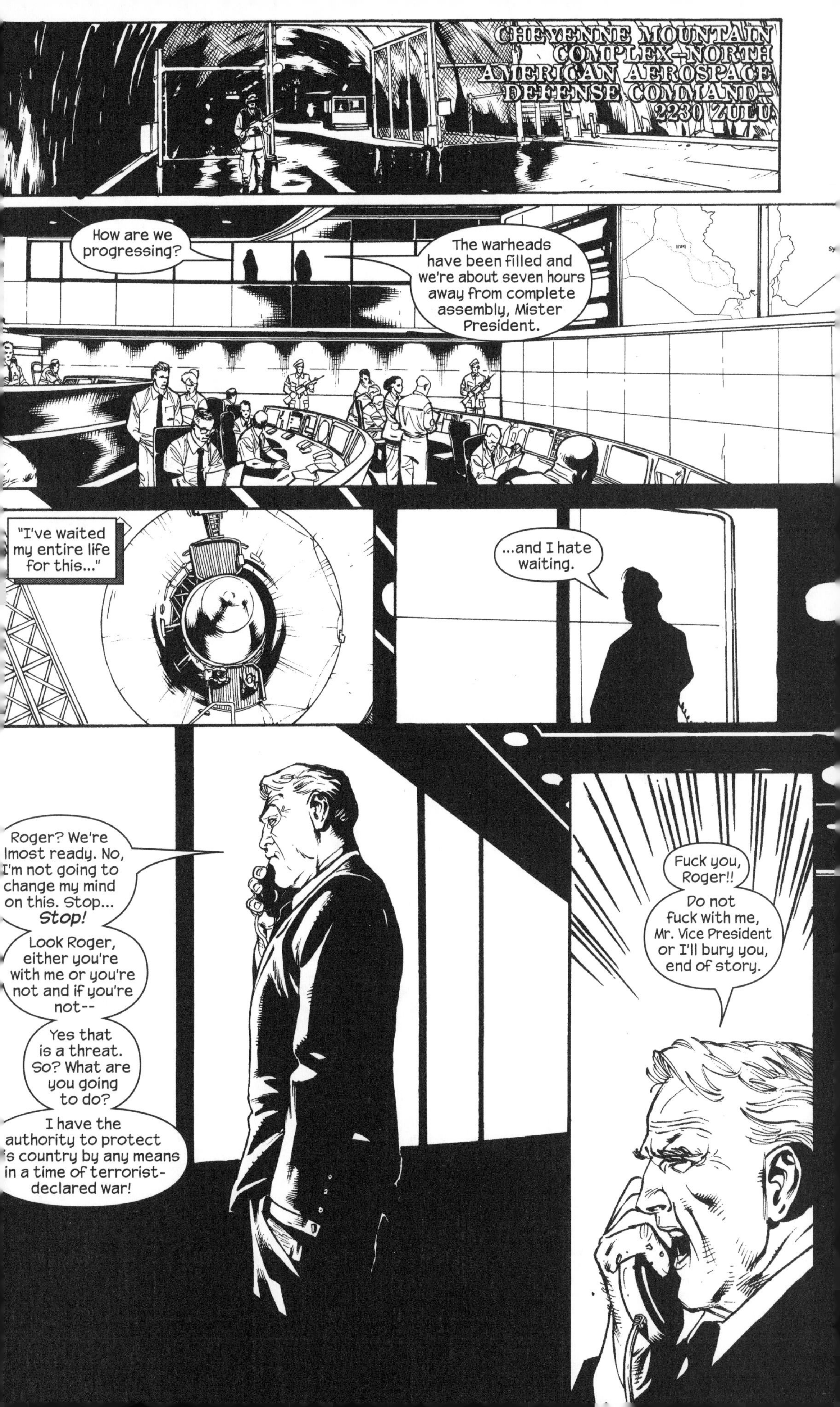
CHEYENNE MOUNTAIN COMPLEX--NORTH AMERICAN AEROSPACE DEFENSE COMMAND--2230 ZULU
How are we progressing?
The warheads have been filled and we're about seven hours away from complete assembly, Mister President.
Iraq
"I've waited my entire life for this..."
...and I hate waiting.
Roger? We're lmost ready. No, I'm not going to change my mind on this. Stop... Stop!
Look Roger, either you're with me or you're not and if you're not--
Yes that is a threat. So? What are you going to do?
I have the authority to protect 's country by any means in a time of terrorist-declared war!
Fuck you, Roger!!
Do not fuck with me, Mr. Vice President or I'll bury you, end of story.

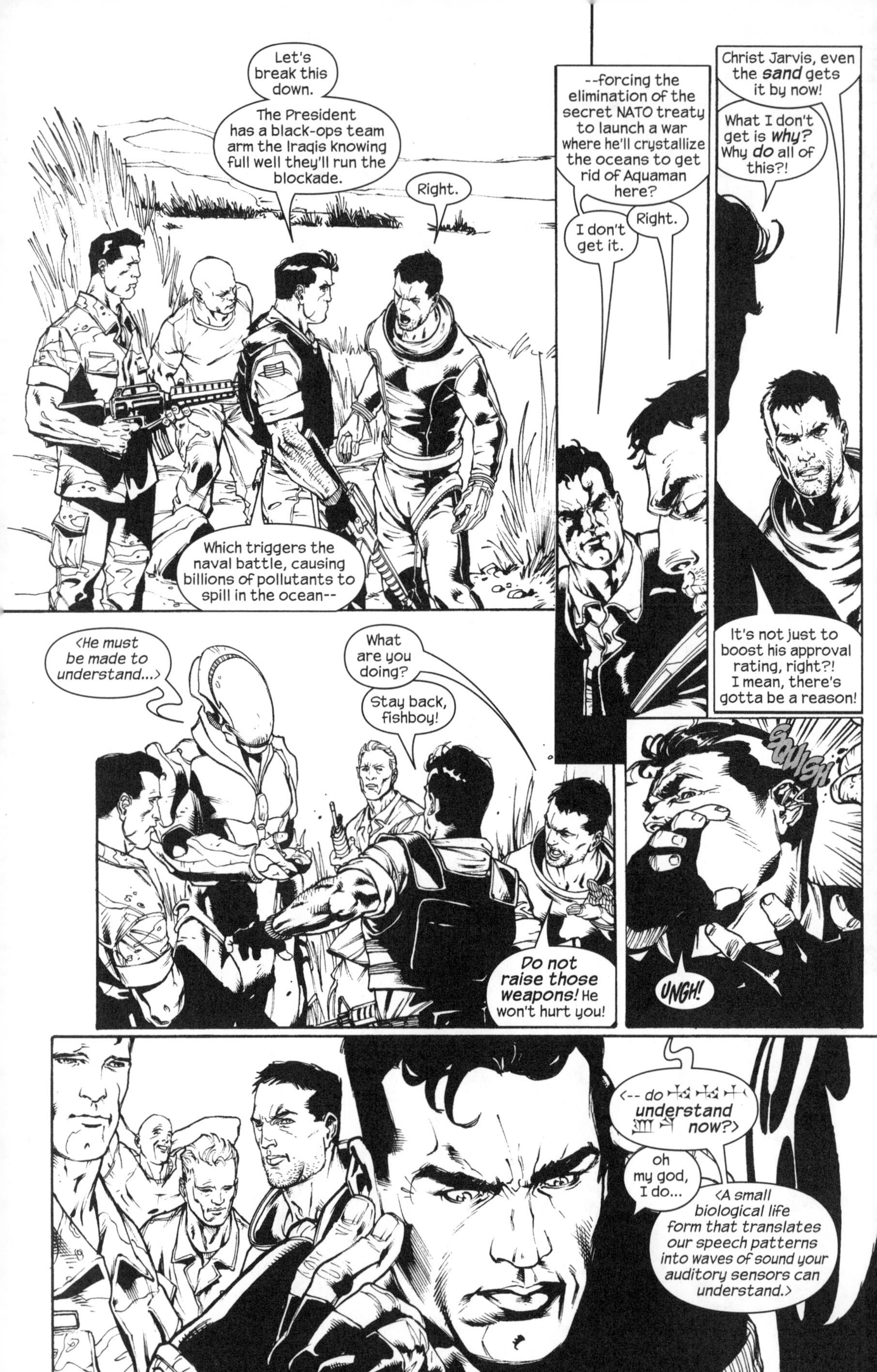
Let's break this down.
The President has a black-ops team arm the Iraqis knowing full well they'll run the blockade.
Right.
Which triggers the naval battle, causing billions of pollutants to spill in the ocean--
--forcing the elimination of the secret NATO treaty to launch a war where he'll crystallize the oceans to get rid of Aquaman here?
I don't get it.
Right.
Christ Jarvis, even the *sand* gets it by now!
What I don't get is *why?* Why *do* all of this?!
It's not just to boost his approval rating, right?! I mean, there's gotta be a reason!
<*He must be made to understand...*>
What are you doing?
Stay back, fishboy!
Do not raise those weapons! He won't hurt you!
SQUISH
UNGH!
<-- do *understand now?*>
oh my god, I do...
<*A small biological life form that translates our speech patterns into waves of sound your auditory sensors can understand.*>

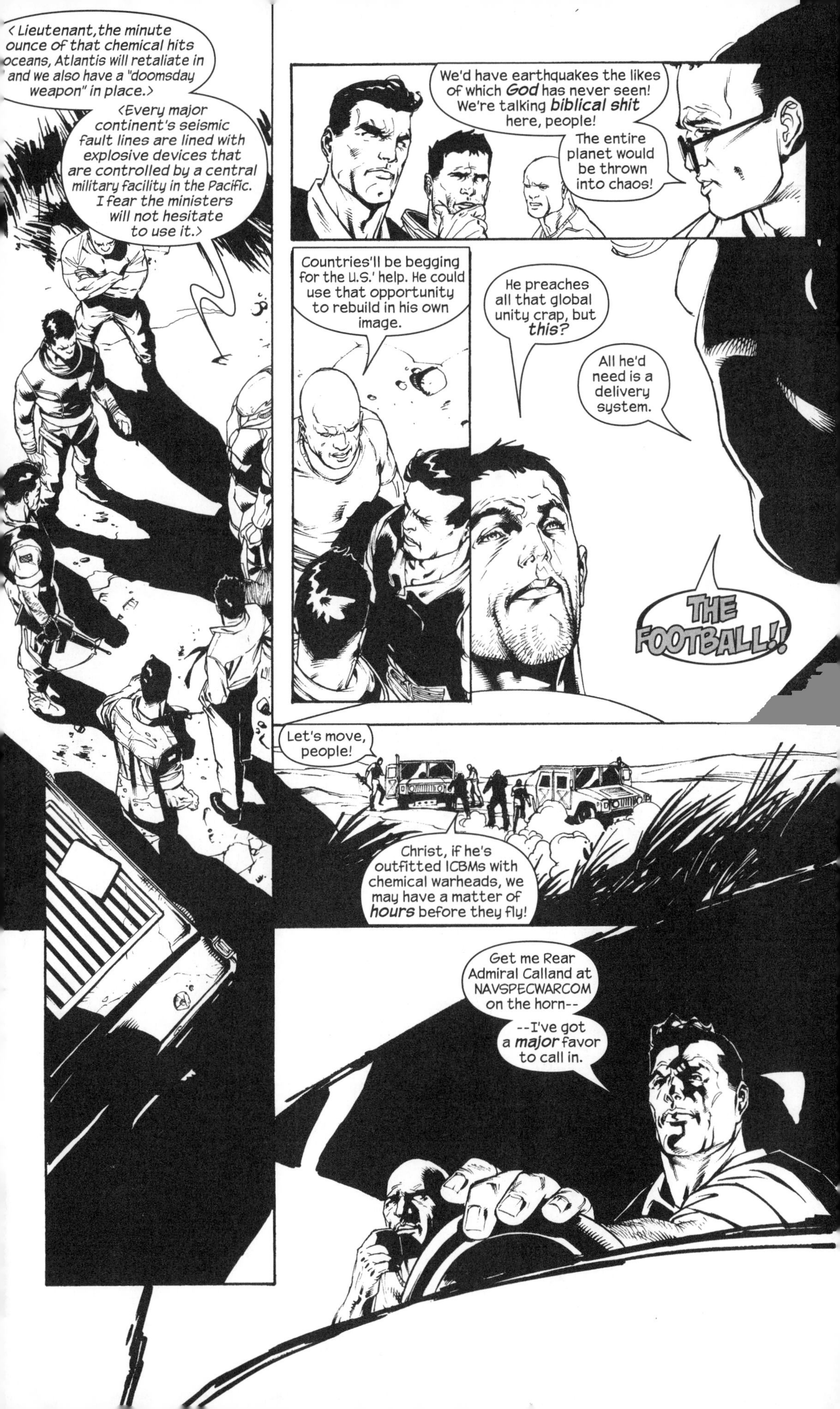
<Lieutenant, the minute ounce of that chemical hits oceans, Atlantis will retaliate in and we also have a "doomsday weapon" in place.>
<Every major continent's seismic fault lines are lined with explosive devices that are controlled by a central military facility in the Pacific. I fear the ministers will not hesitate to use it.>
We'd have earthquakes the likes of which God has never seen! We're talking biblical shit here, people!
The entire planet would be thrown into chaos!
Countries'll be begging for the U.S.' help. He could use that opportunity to rebuild in his own image.
He preaches all that global unity crap, but this?
All he'd need is a delivery system.
THE FOOTBALL!
Let's move, people!
Christ, if he's outfitted ICBMs with chemical warheads, we may have a matter of hours before they fly!
Get me Rear Admiral Calland at NAVSPECWARCOM on the horn--
--I've got a major favor to call in.

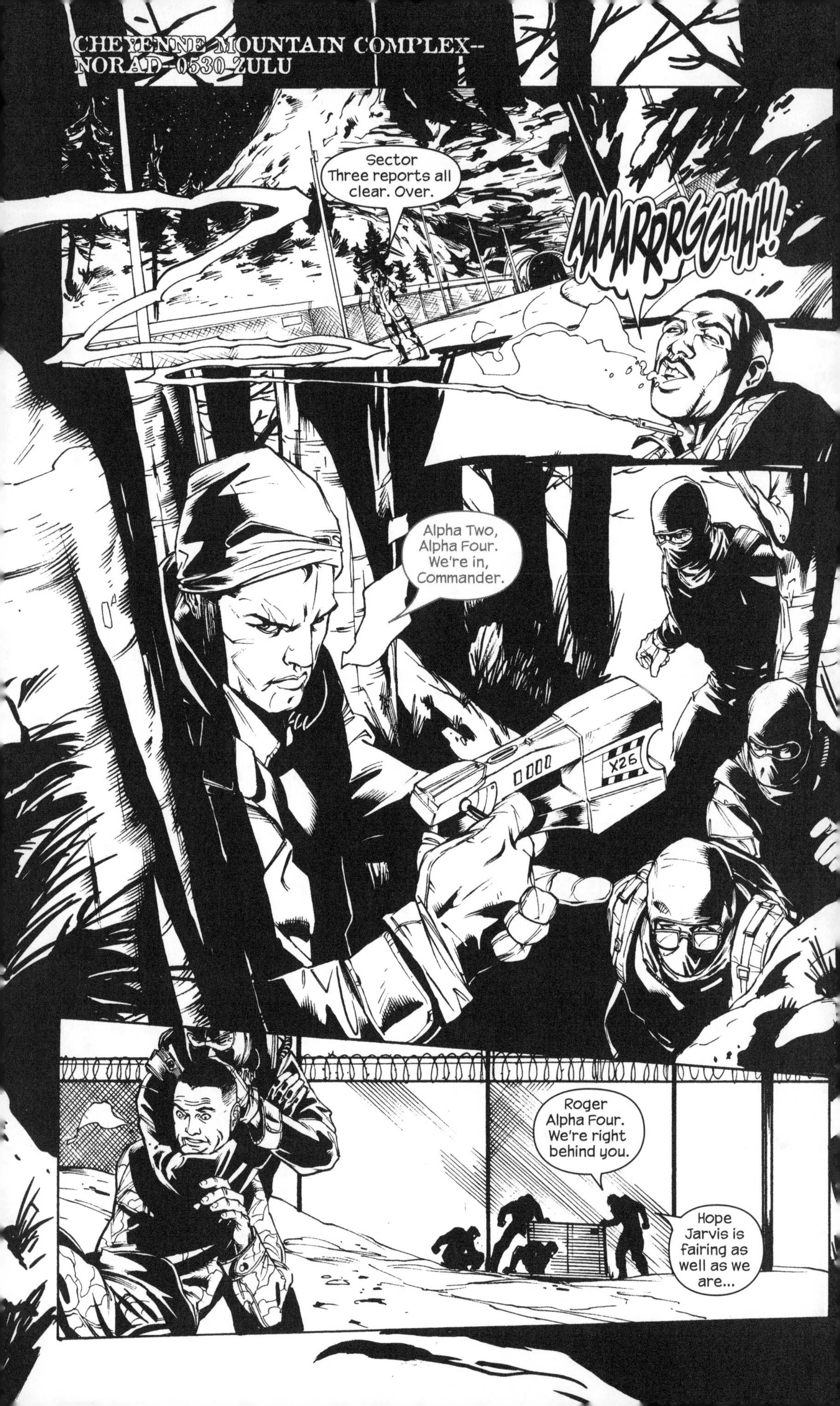
CHEYENNE MOUNTAIN COMPLEX--
NORAD--0530 ZULU
Sector Three reports all clear. Over.
AAAARRRGGHHH!
Alpha Two, Alpha Four. We're in, Commander.
X26
Roger Alpha Four. We're right behind you.
Hope Jarvis is fairing as well as we are...

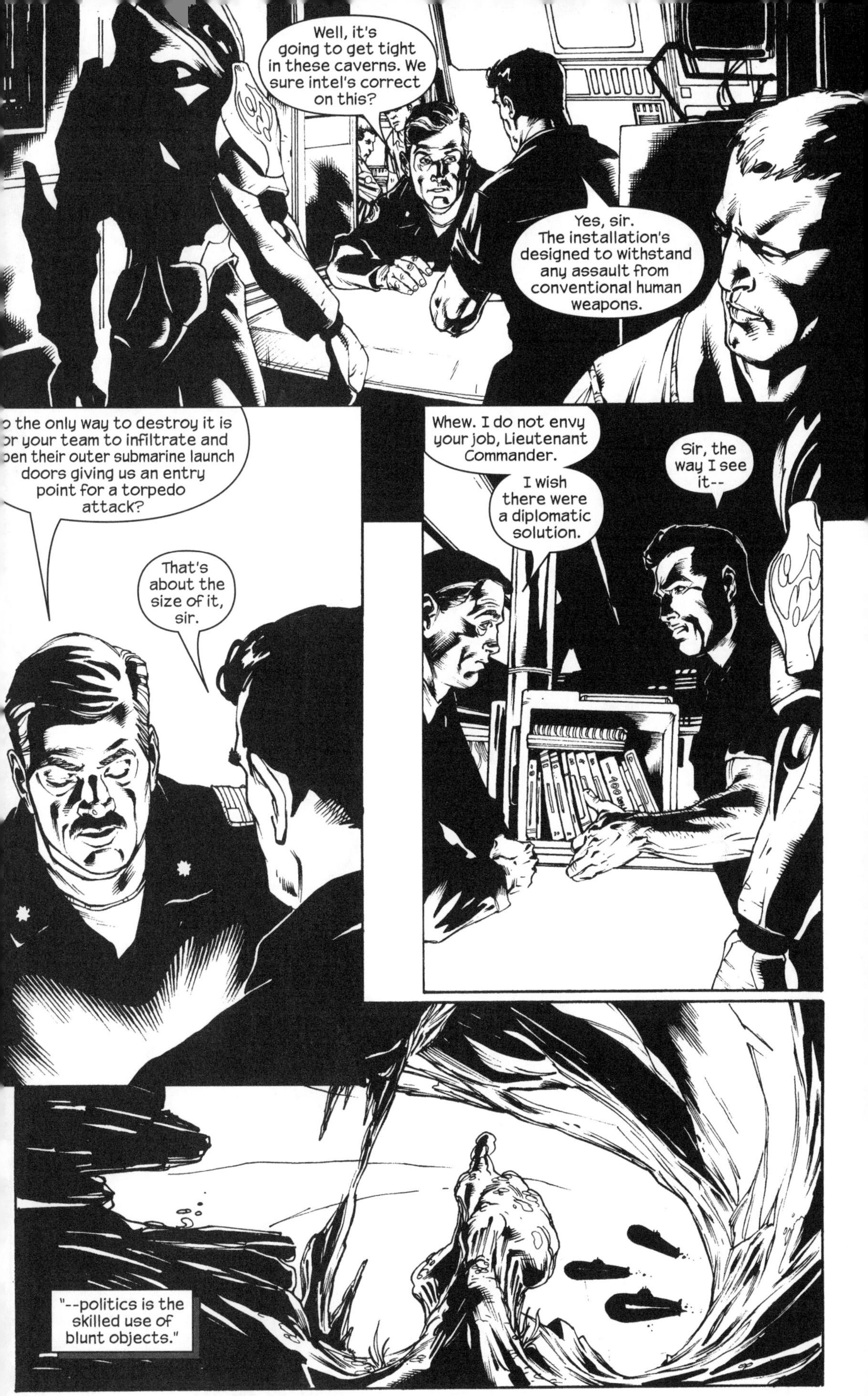
Well, it's going to get tight in these caverns. We sure intel's correct on this?
Yes, sir. The installation's designed to withstand any assault from conventional human weapons.
o the only way to destroy it is or your team to infiltrate and pen their outer submarine launch doors giving us an entry point for a torpedo attack?
That's about the size of it, sir.
Whew. I do not envy your job, Lieutenant Commander.
I wish there were a diplomatic solution.
Sir, the way I see it--
"--politics is the skilled use of blunt objects."

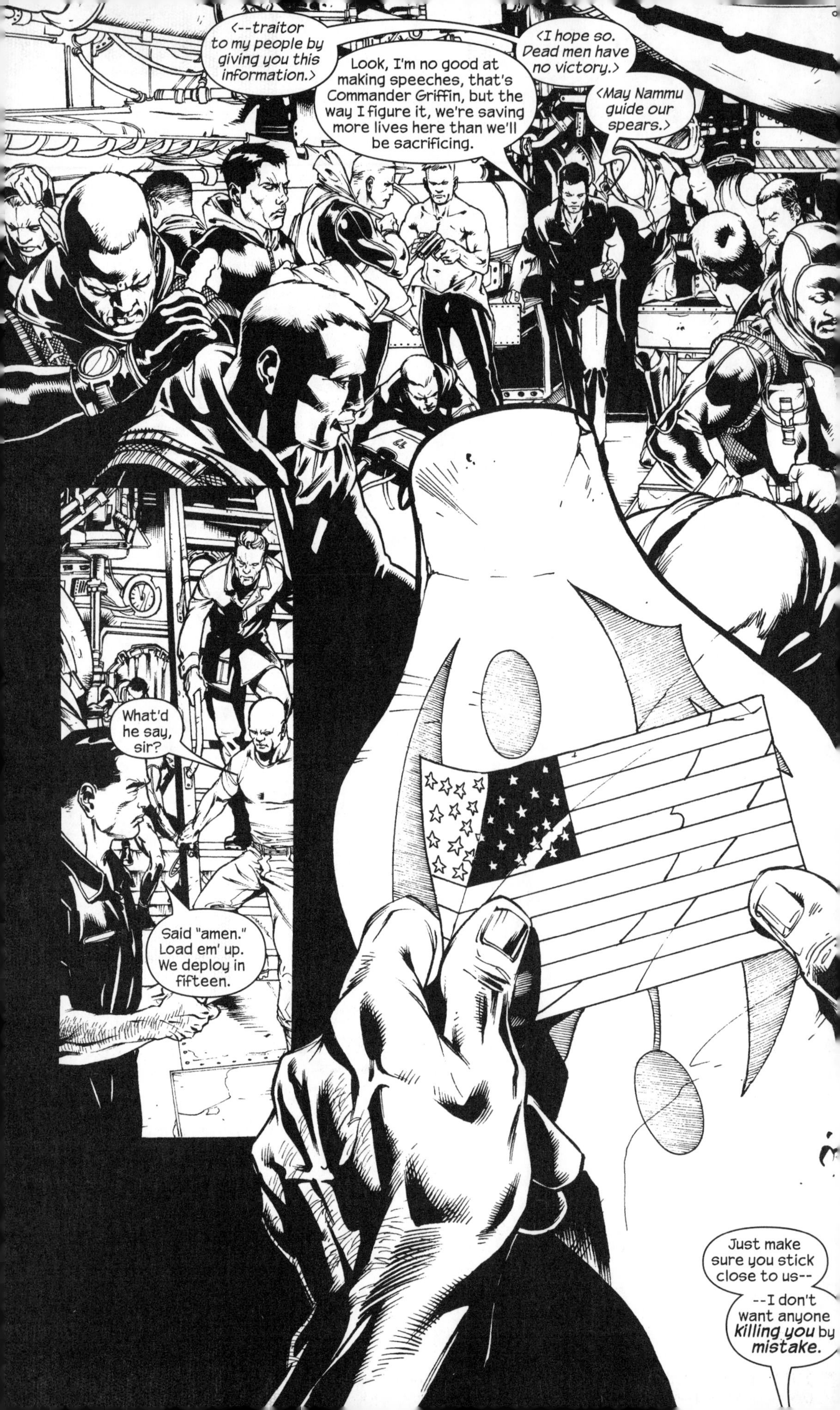

<--traitor to my people by giving you this information.>
Look, I'm no good at making speeches, that's Commander Griffin, but the way I figure it, we're saving more lives here than we'll be sacrificing.
<I hope so. Dead men have no victory.>
<May Nammu guide our spears.>
What'd he say, sir?
Said "amen." Load em' up. We deploy in fifteen.
Just make sure you stick close to us--
--I don't want anyone killing you by mistake.

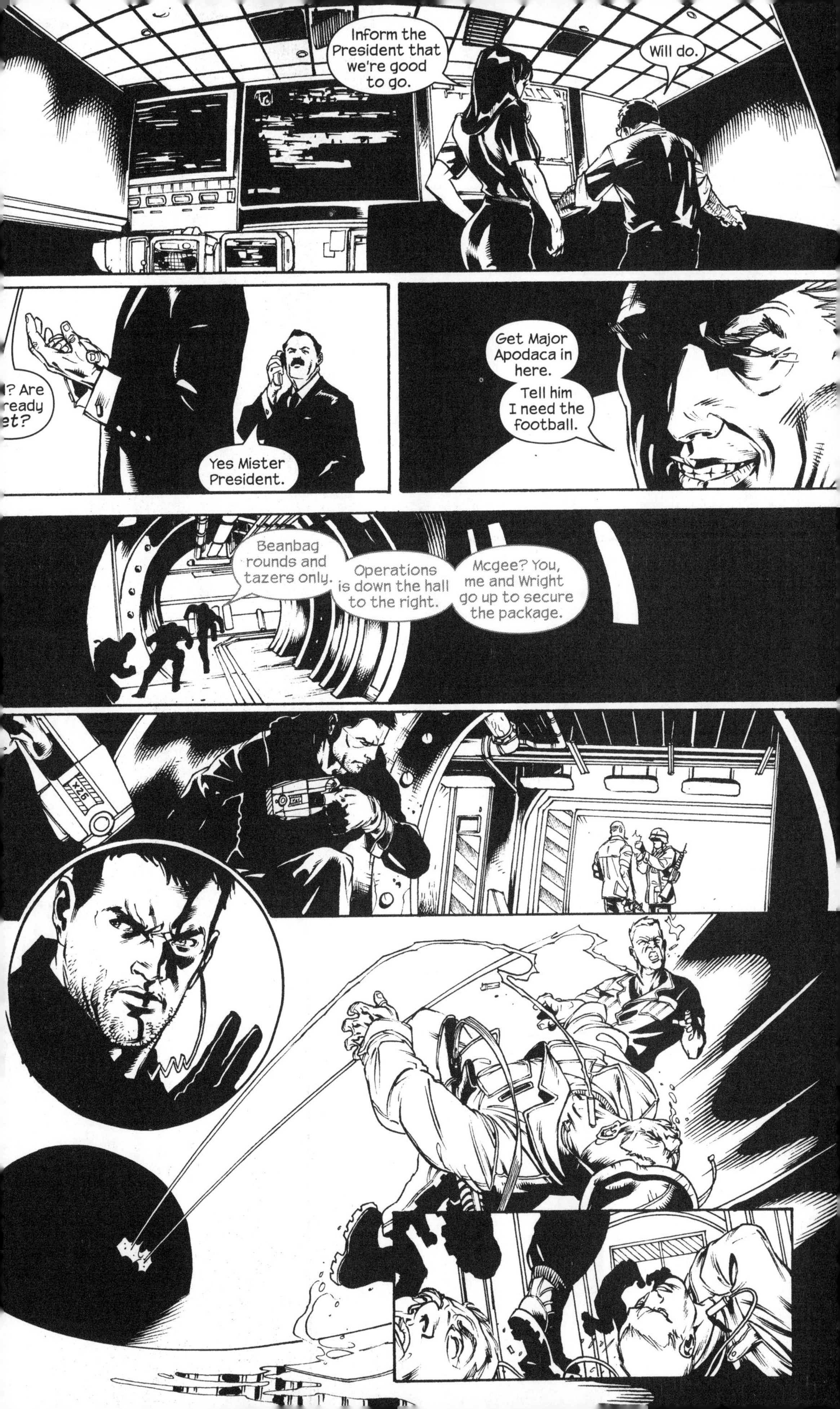
Inform the President that we're good to go.
Will do.
? Are
ready
et?
Yes Mister President.
Get Major Apodaca in here.
Tell him I need the football.
Beanbag rounds and tazers only.
Operations is down the hall to the right.
Mcgee? You, me and Wright go up to secure the package.
X26

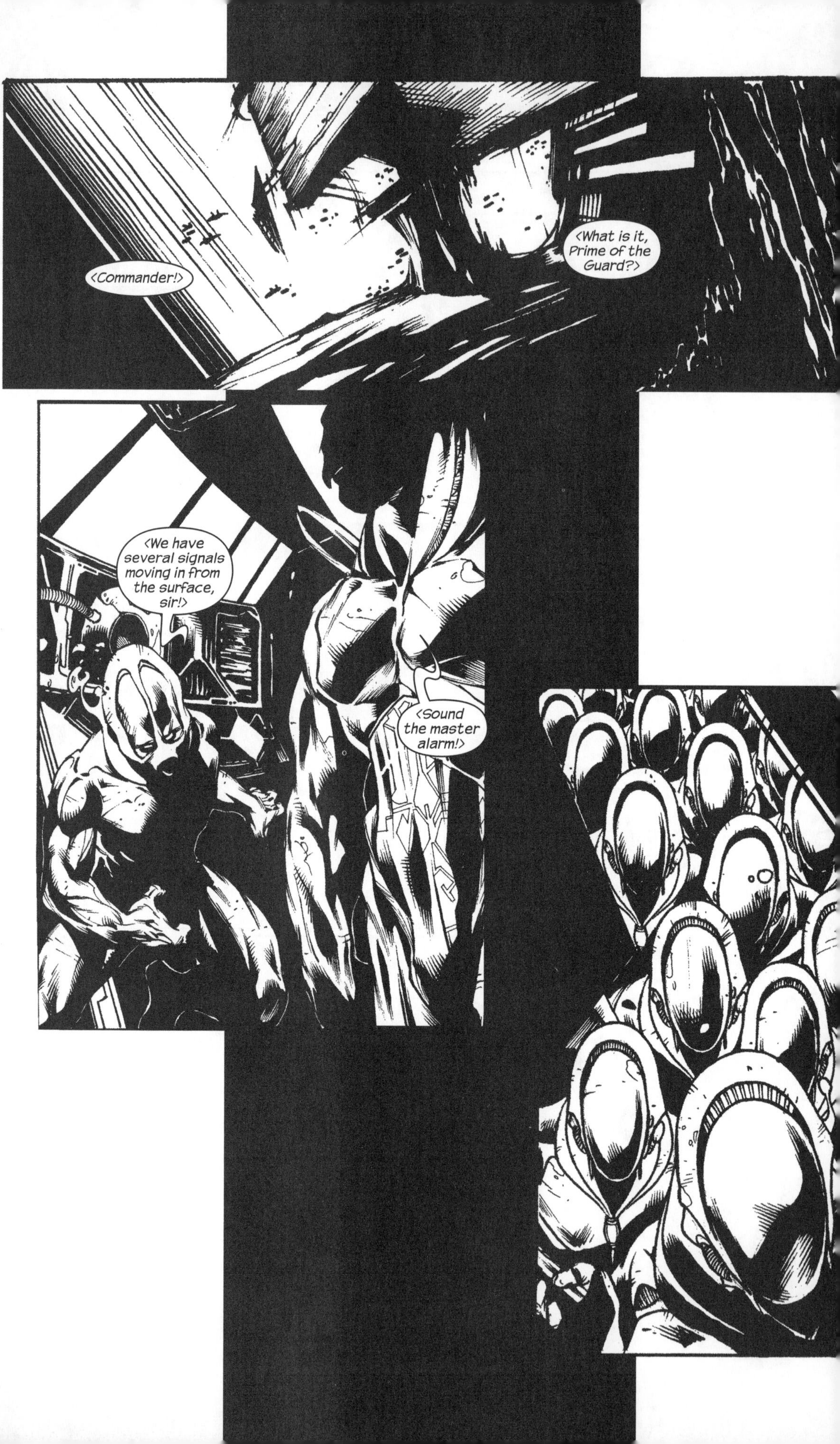

<Commander!>
<What is it, Prime of the Guard?>
<We have several signals moving in from the surface, sir!>
<Sound the master alarm!>

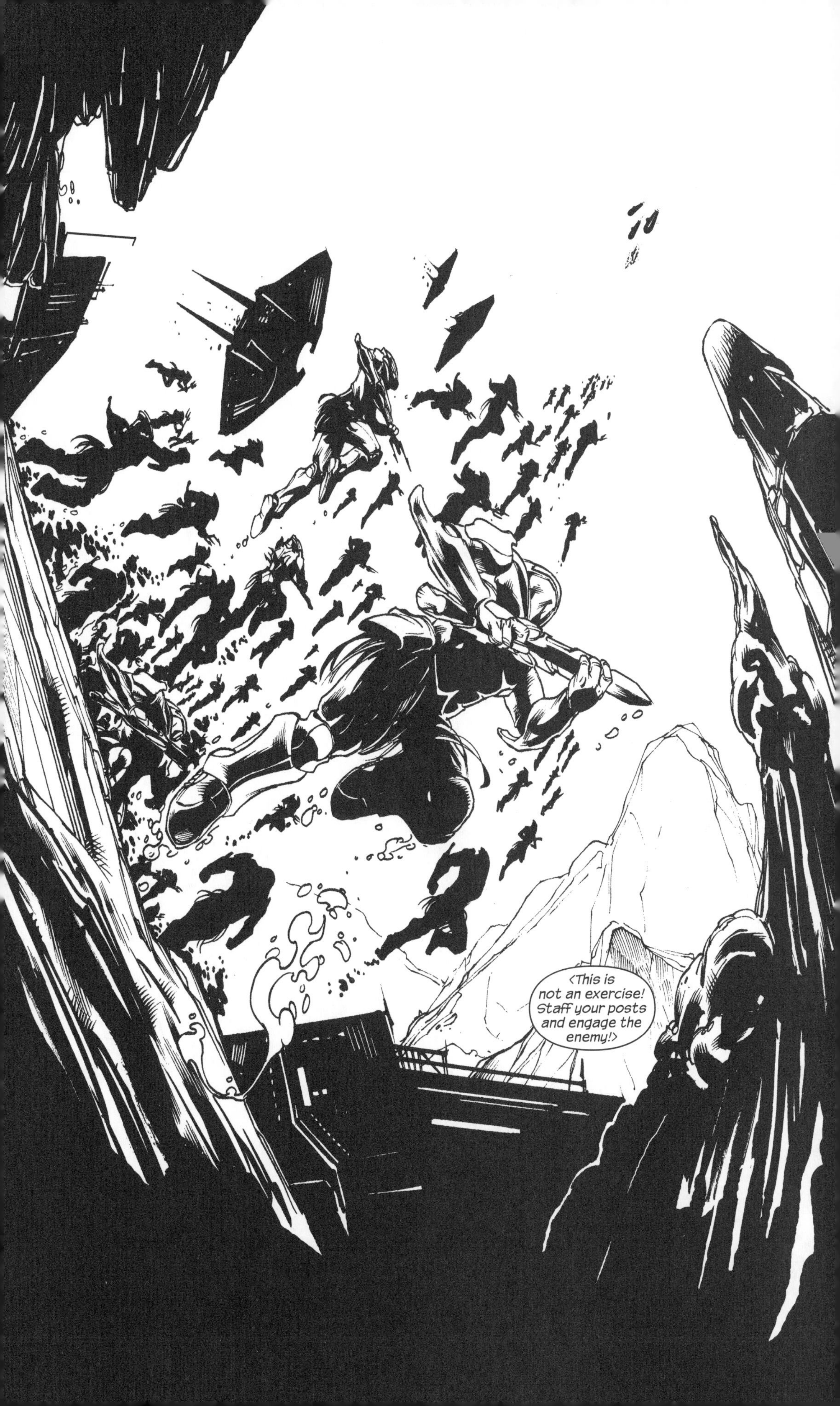
<This is not an exercise! Staff your posts and engage the enemy!>

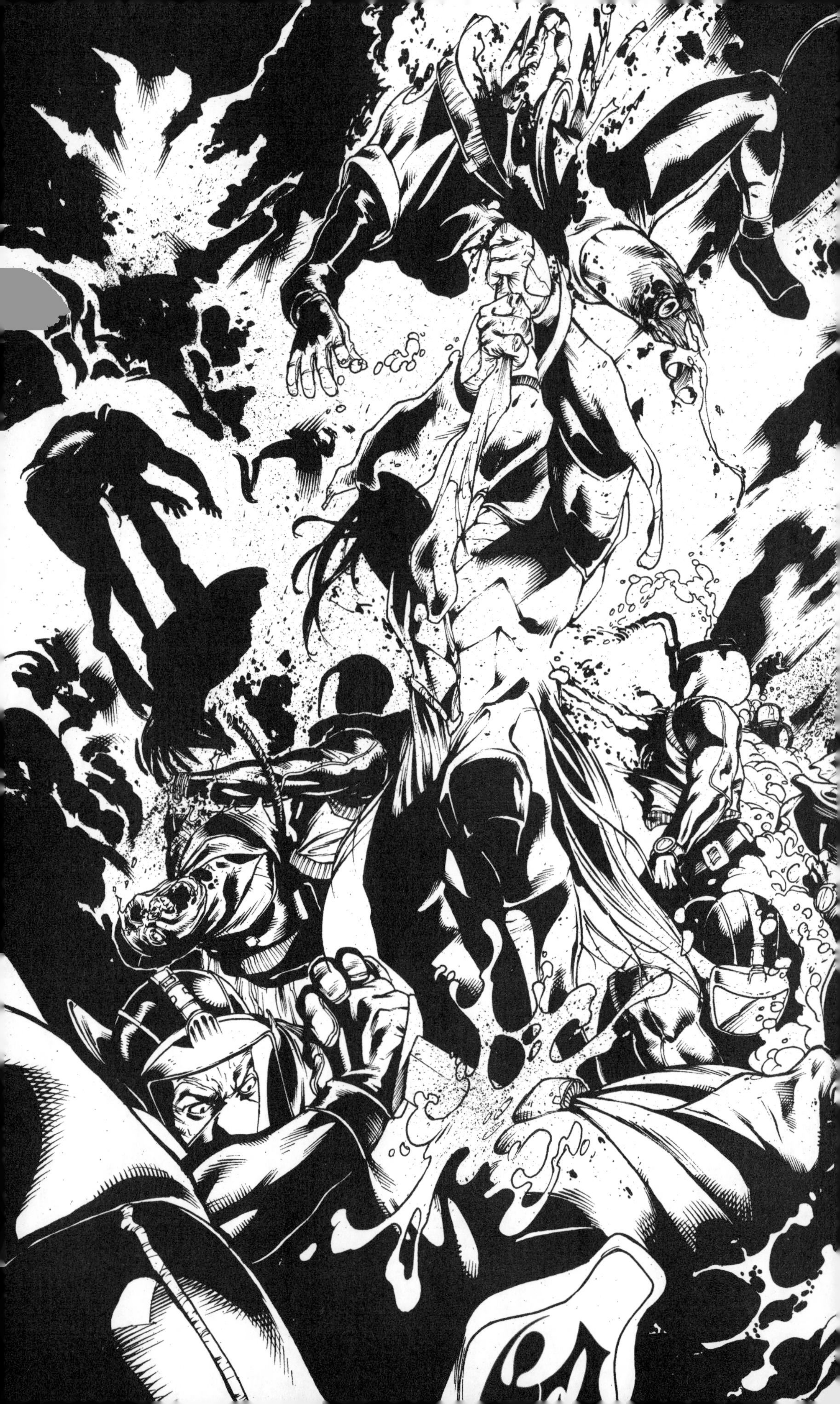

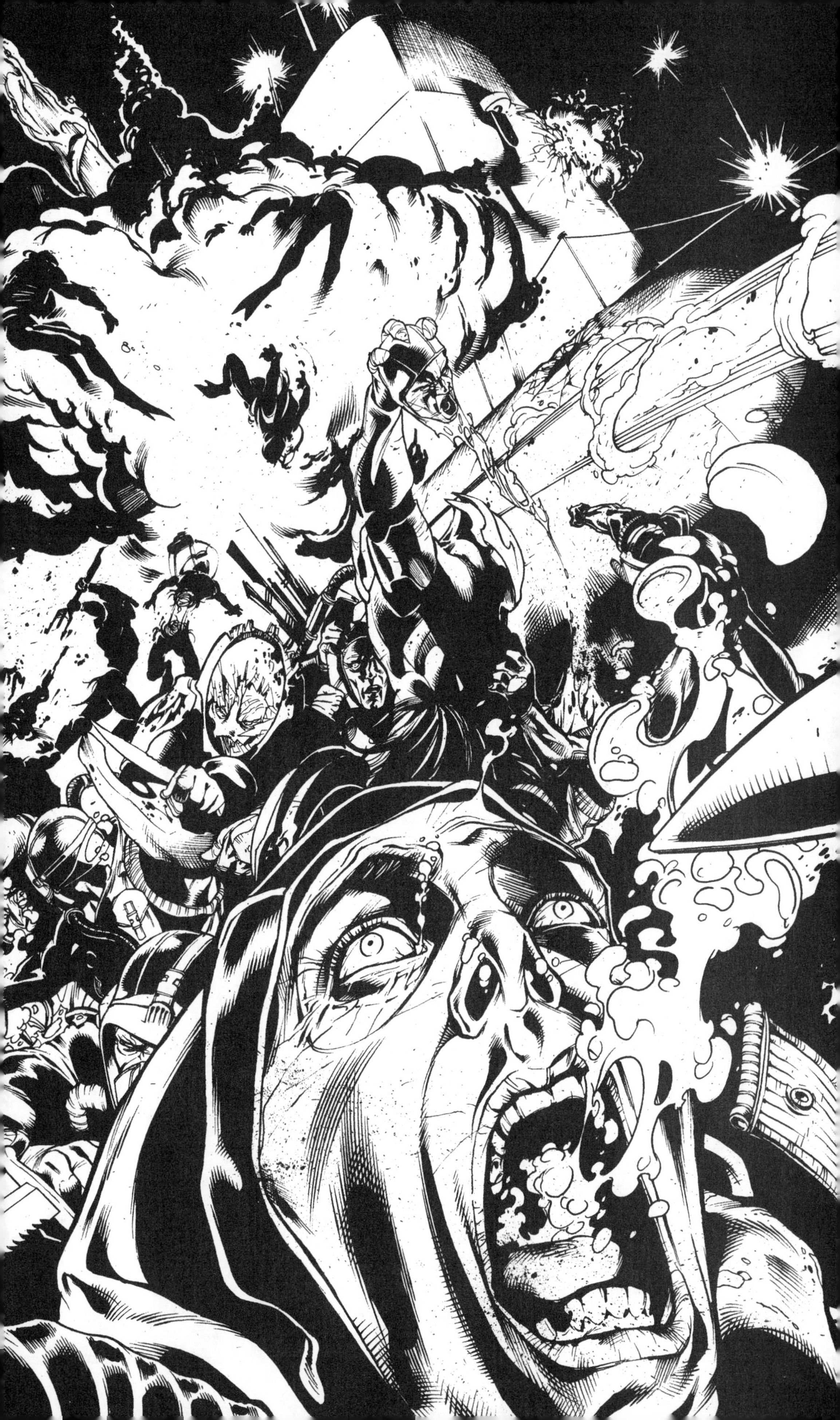

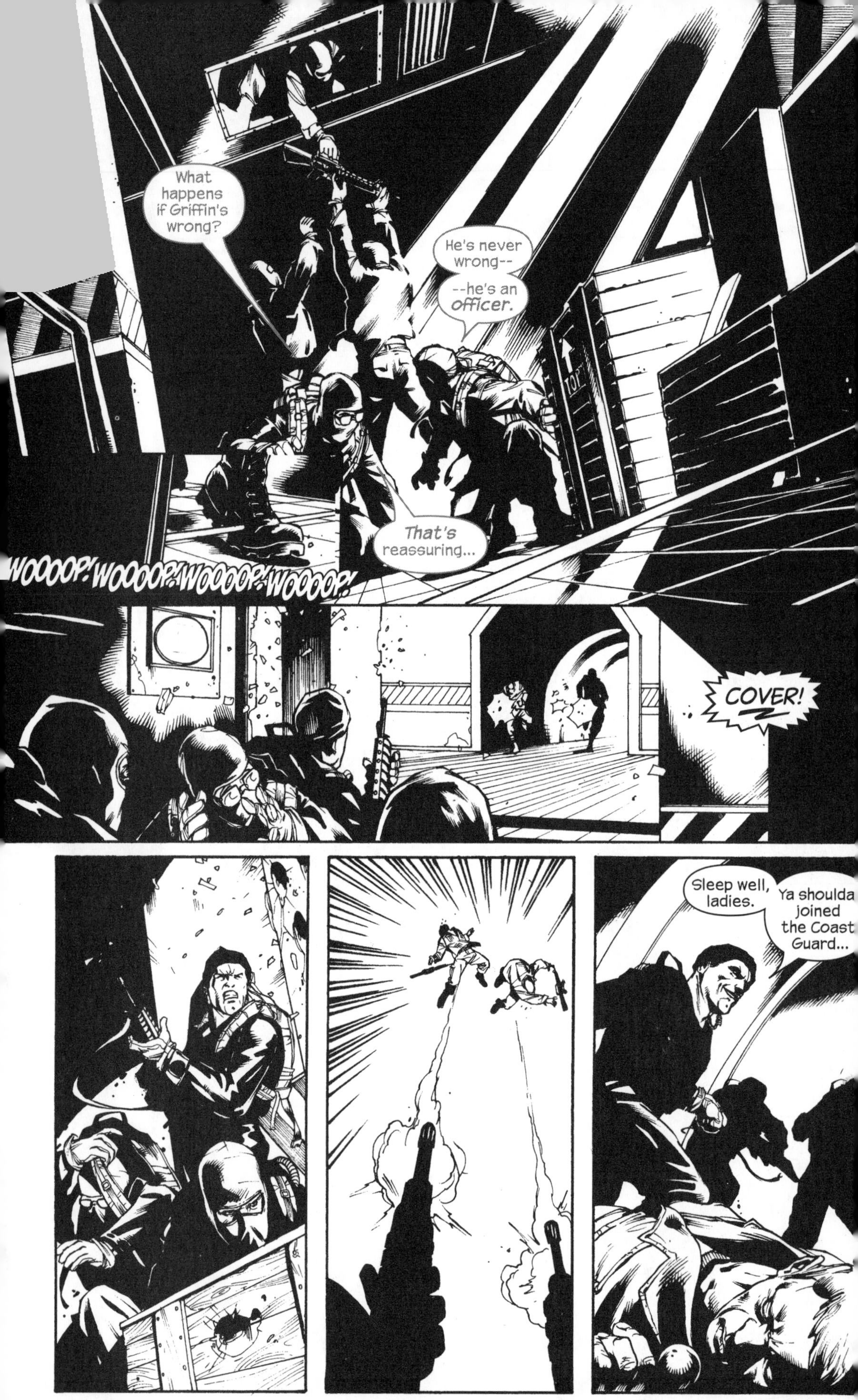
What happens if Griffin's wrong?
He's never wrong--
--he's an *officer.*
That's reassuring...
WOOOOP! WOOOOP! WOOOOP! WOOOOP!
COVER!
Sleep well, ladies.
Ya shoulda joined the Coast Guard...

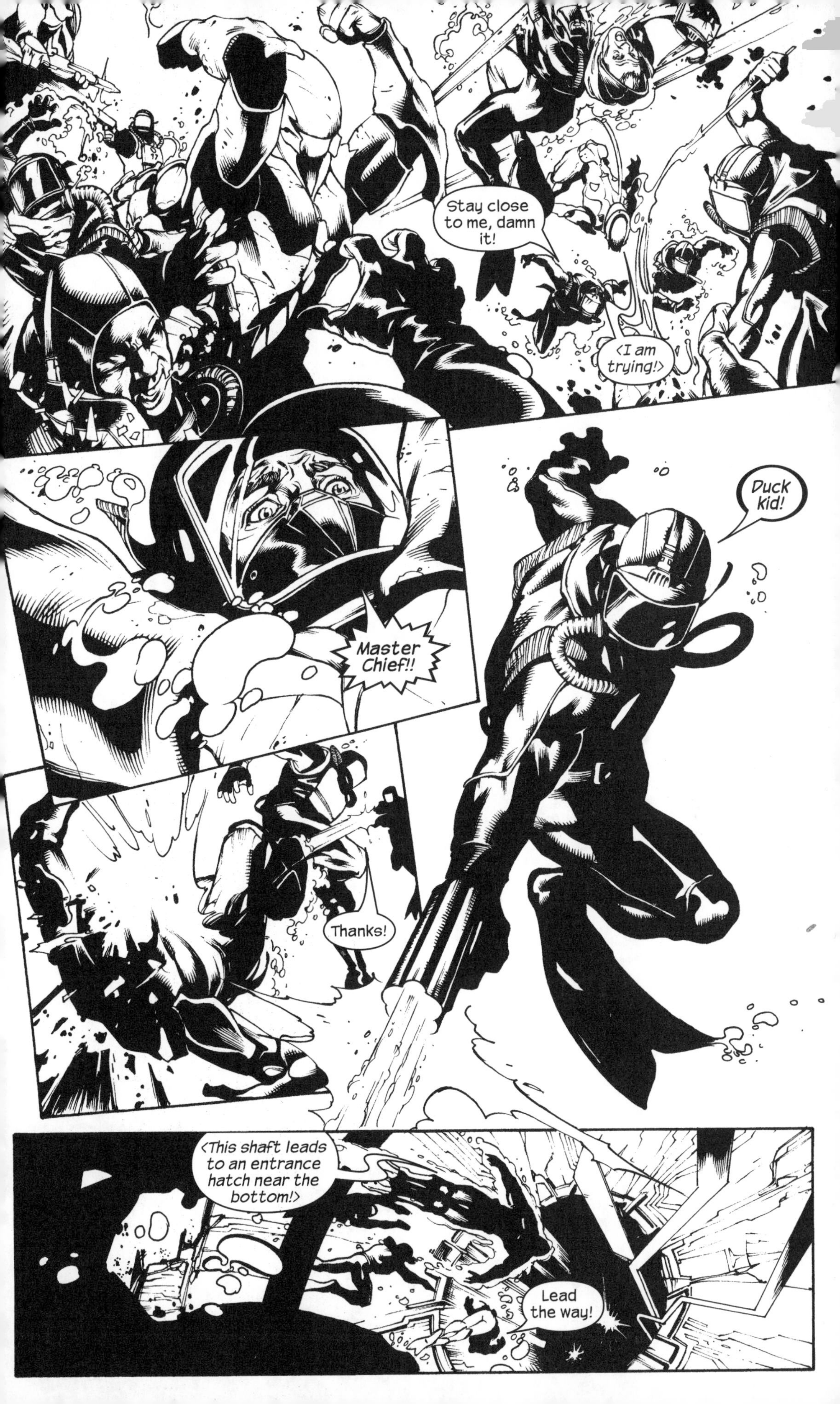
Stay close to me, damn it!
<I am trying!>
Master Chief!!
Duck kid!
Thanks!
<This shaft leads to an entrance hatch near the bottom!>
Lead the way!

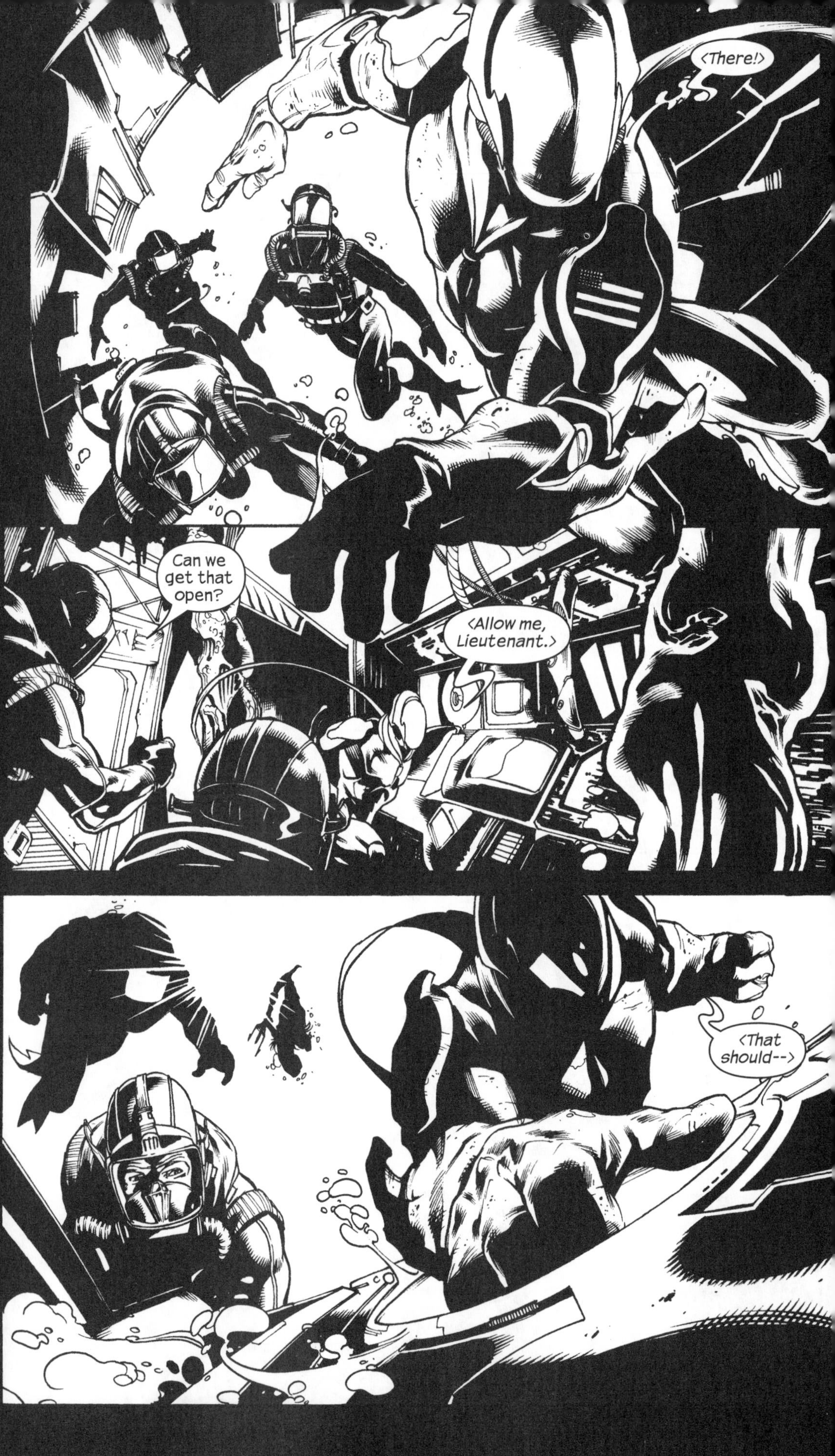

<There!>
Can we get that open?
<Allow me, Lieutenant.>
<That should-->

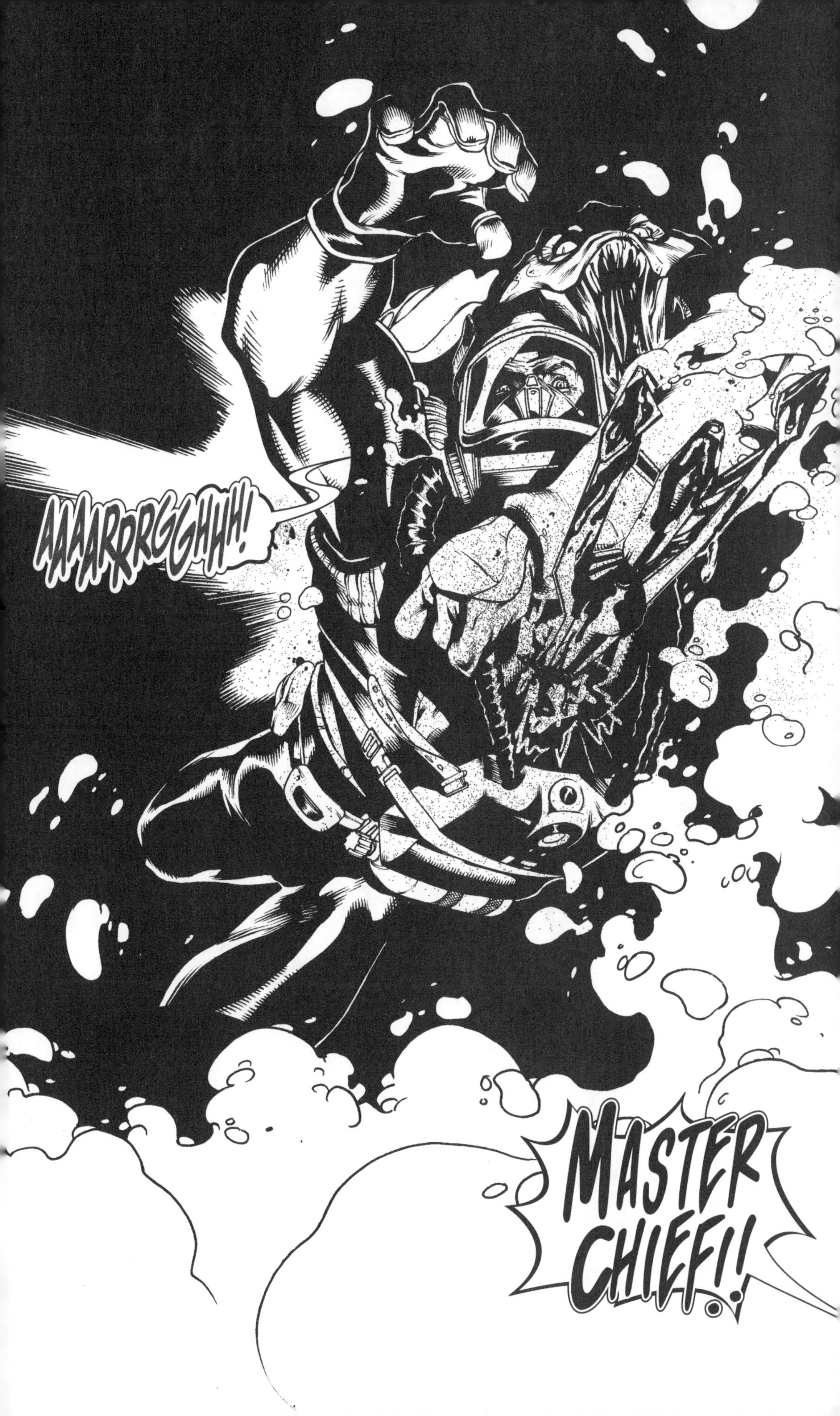
AAAARRRGGHHH!
MASTER CHIEF!!

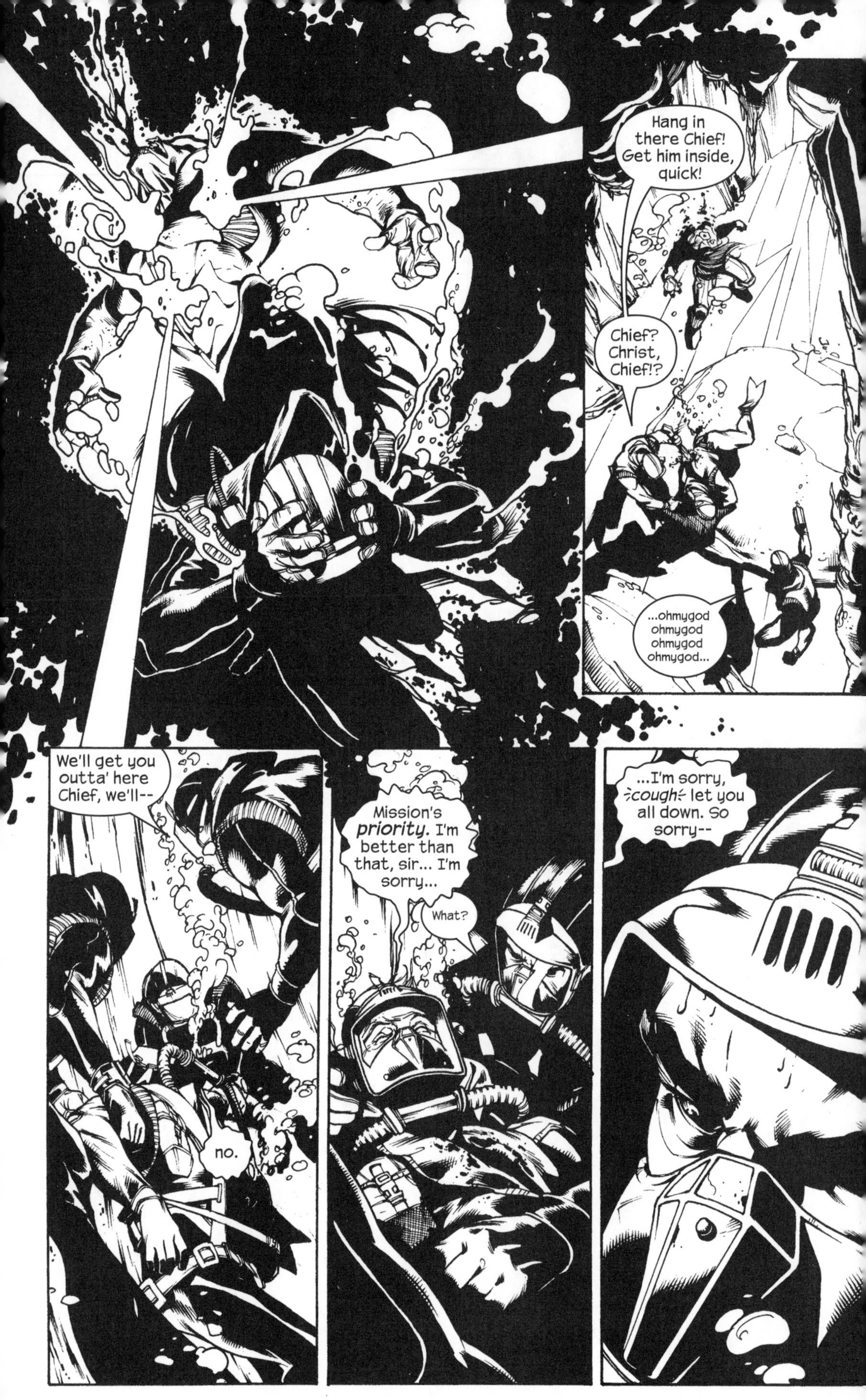
Hang in there Chief! Get him inside, quick!
Chief? Christ, Chief!?
...ohmygod ohmygod ohmygod ohmygod...
We'll get you outta' here Chief, we'll--
no.
Mission's *priority.* I'm better than that, sir... I'm sorry...
What?
...I'm sorry, *cough* let you all down. So sorry--

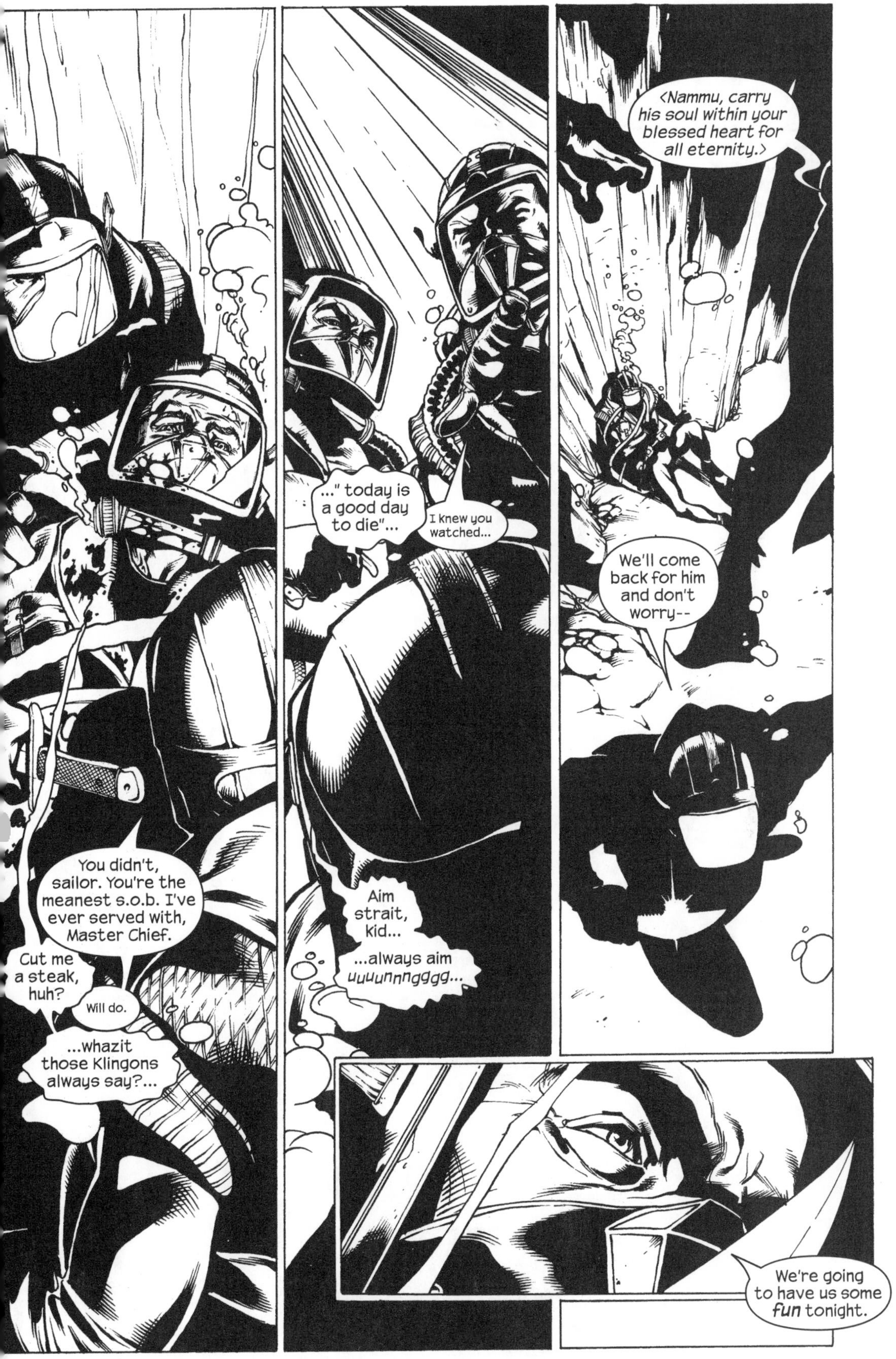
You didn't, sailor. You're the meanest s.o.b. I've ever served with, Master Chief.
Cut me a steak, huh?
Will do.
...whazit those Klingons always say?...
..." today is a good day to die"...
I knew you watched...
Aim strait, kid...
...always aim uuuunnnggg...
<Nammu, carry his soul within your blessed heart for all eternity.>
We'll come back for him and don't worry--
We're going to have us some *fun* tonight.

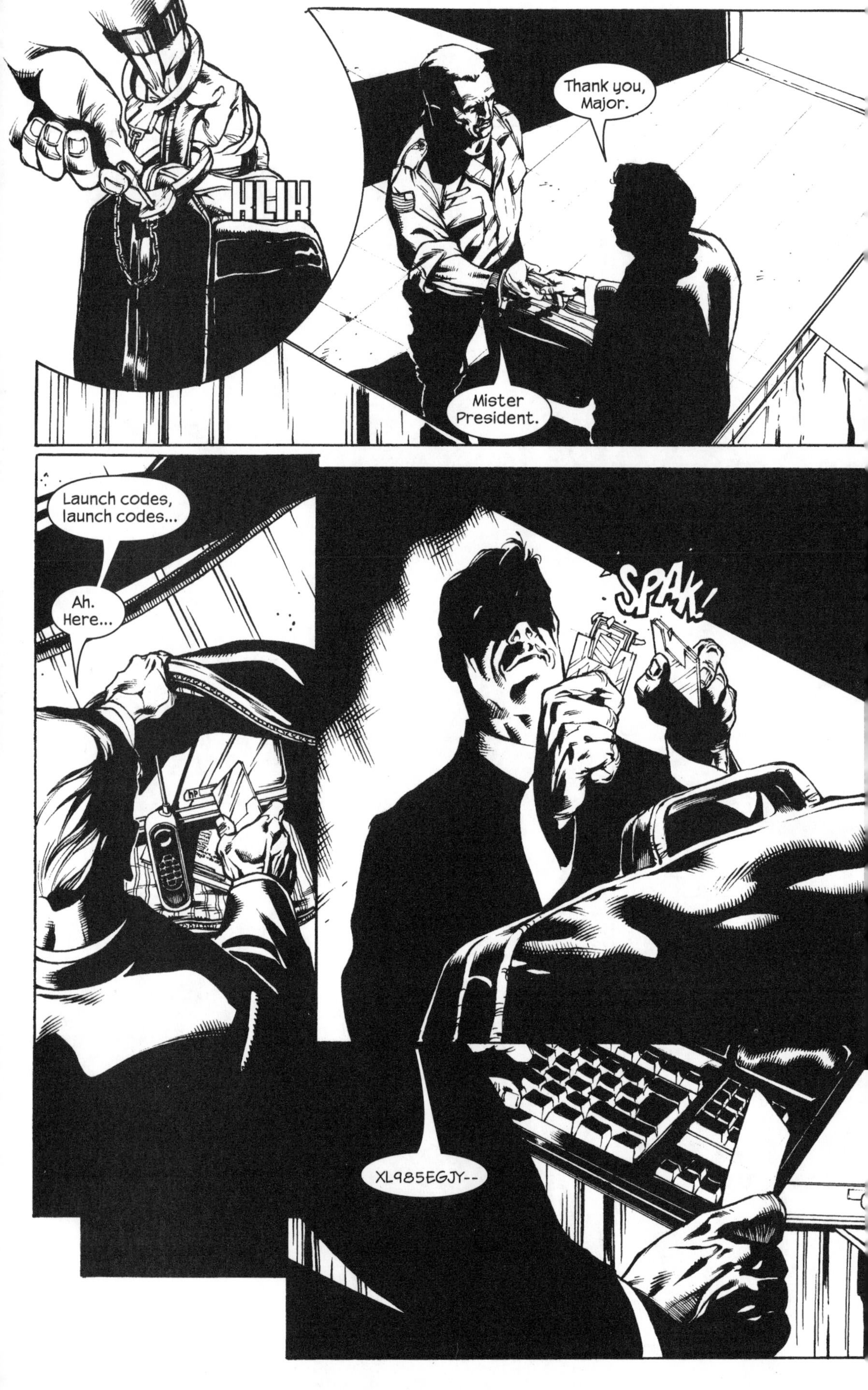
KLIK
Thank you, Major.
Mister President.
Launch codes, launch codes...
Ah. Here...
SPAK!
XL985EGJY--

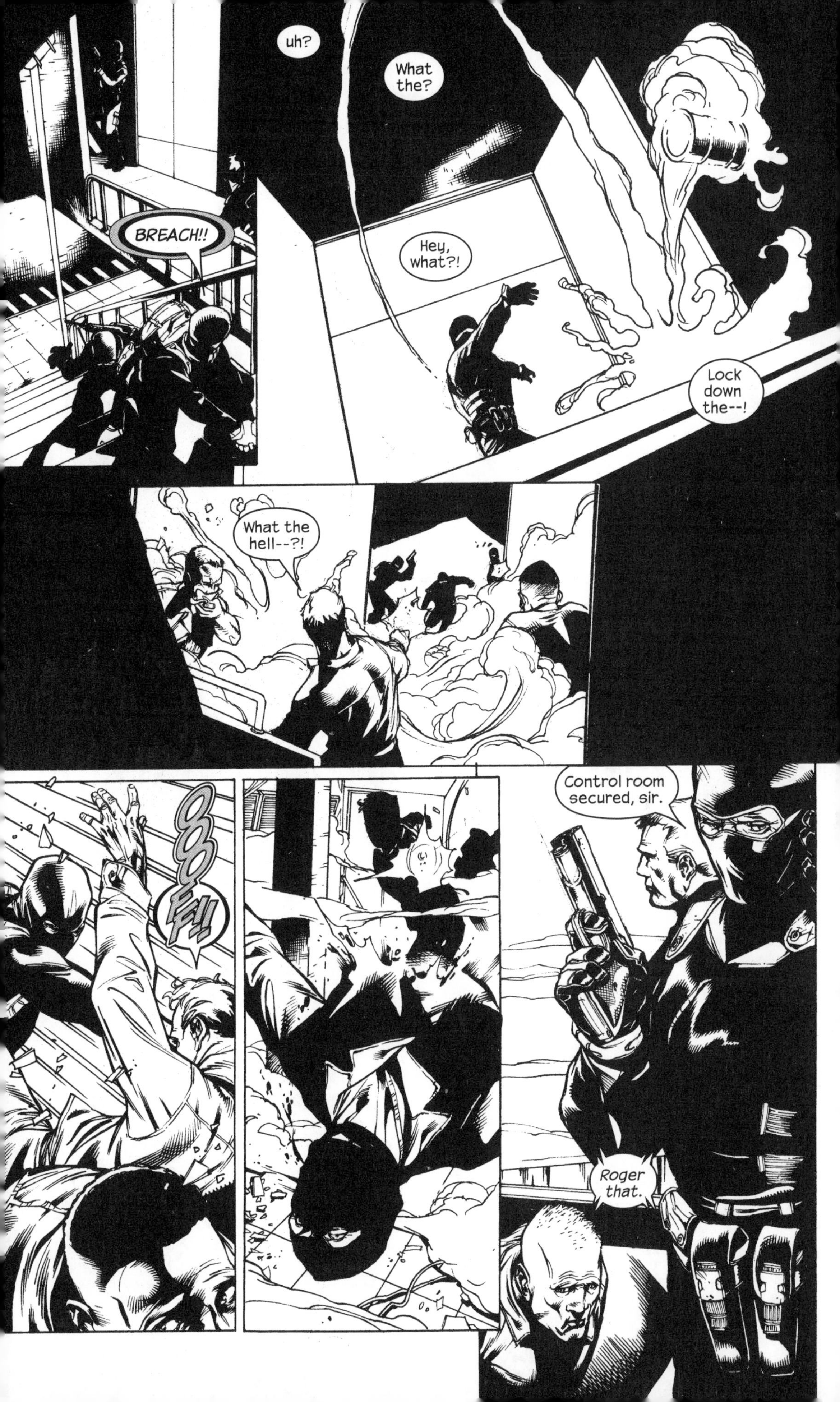
uh?
What the?
BREACH!!
Hey, what?!
Lock down the--!
What the hell--?!
OOOFF!!
Control room secured, sir.
Roger that.

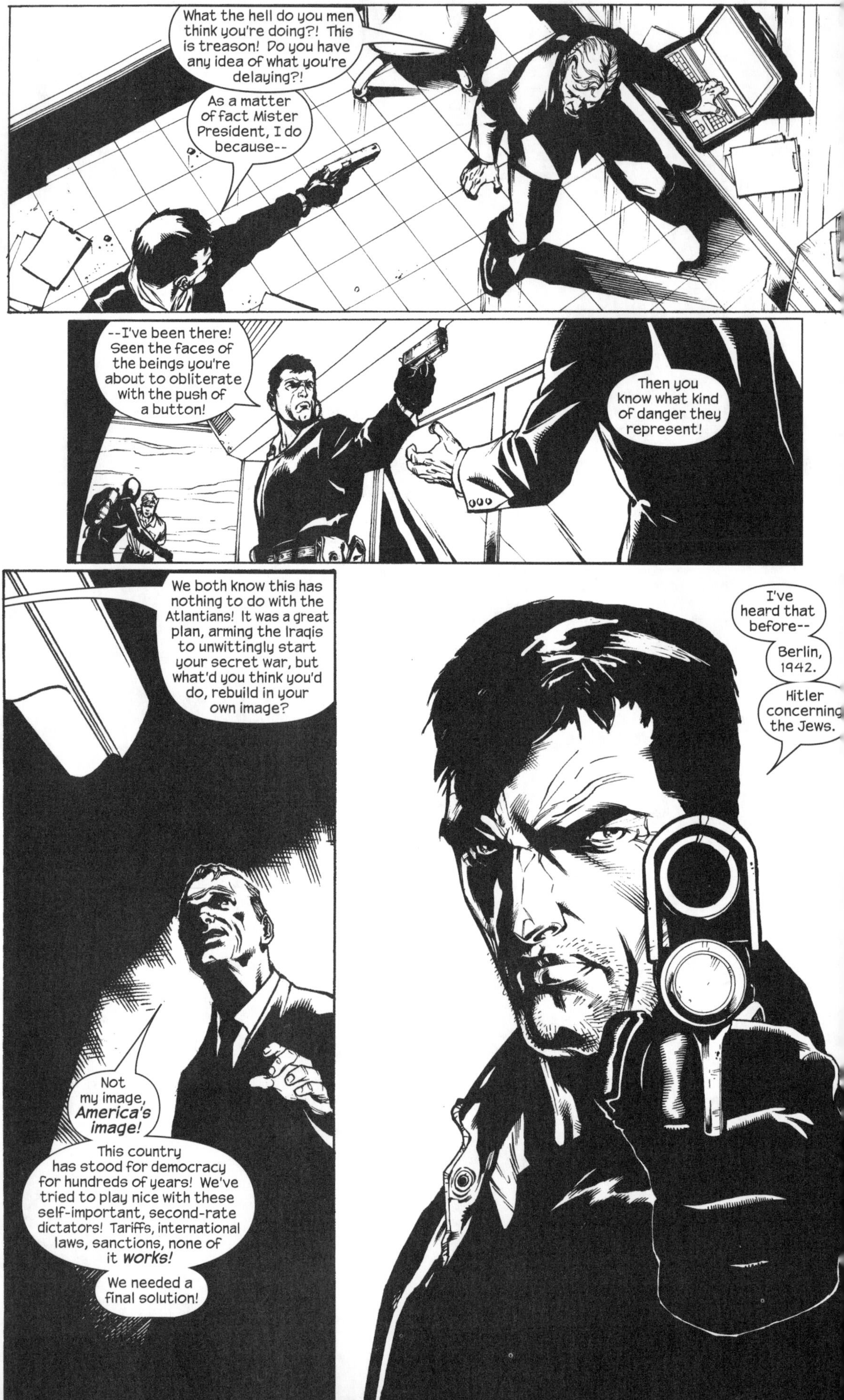

What the hell do you men think you're doing?! This is treason! Do you have any idea of what you're delaying?!
As a matter of fact Mister President, I do because--
--I've been there! Seen the faces of the beings you're about to obliterate with the push of a button!
Then you know what kind of danger they represent!
We both know this has nothing to do with the Atlantians! It was a great plan, arming the Iraqis to unwittingly start your secret war, but what'd you think you'd do, rebuild in your own image?
Not my image, *America's image!*
This country has stood for democracy for hundreds of years! We've tried to play nice with these self-important, second-rate dictators! Tariffs, international laws, sanctions, none of it *works!*
We needed a final solution!
I've heard that before--
Berlin, 1942.
Hitler concerning the Jews.

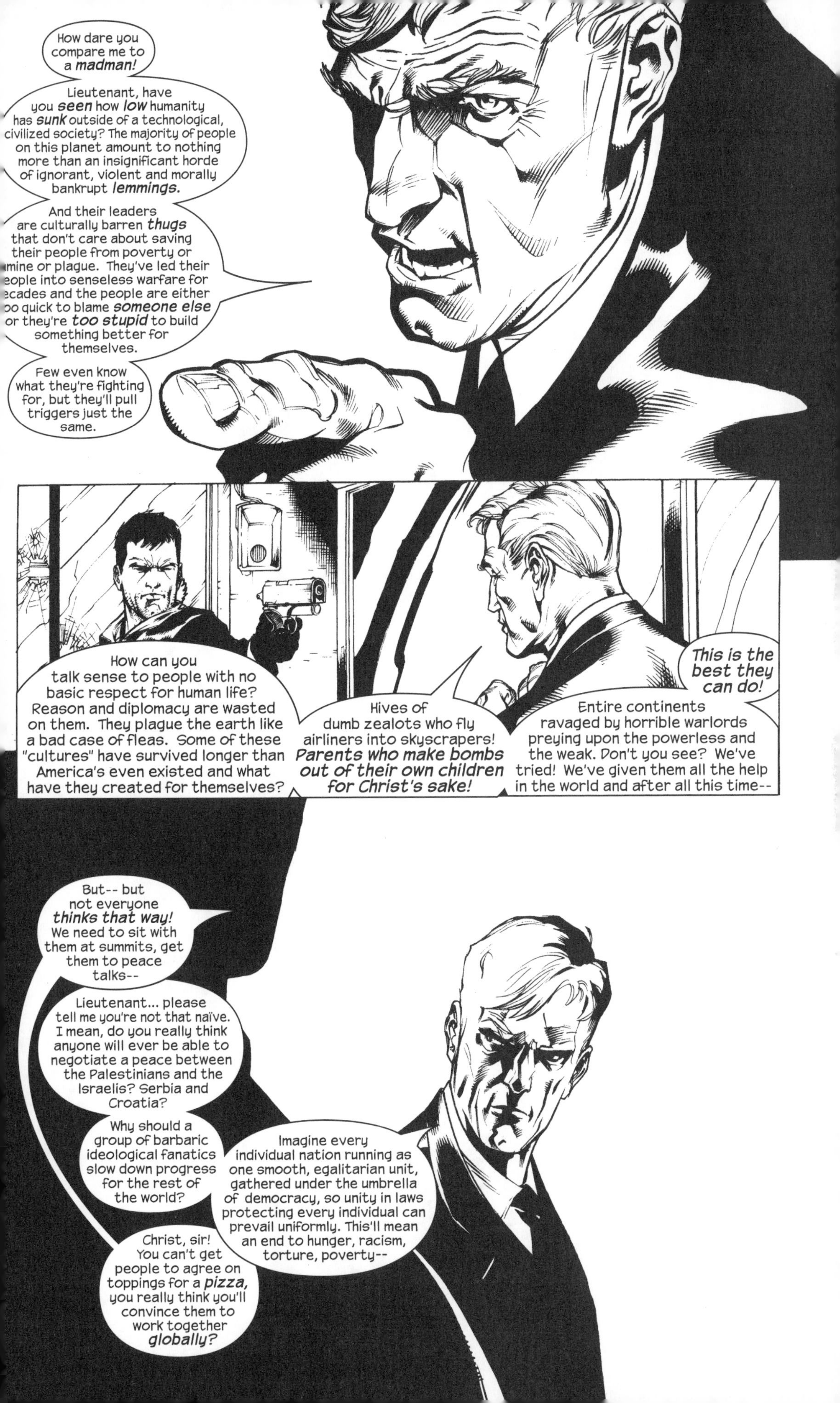

How dare you compare me to a *madman!*
Lieutenant, have you ***seen*** how ***low*** humanity has ***sunk*** outside of a technological, civilized society? The majority of people on this planet amount to nothing more than an insignificant horde of ignorant, violent and morally bankrupt ***lemmings.***
And their leaders are culturally barren ***thugs*** that don't care about saving their people from poverty or mine or plague. They've led their eople into senseless warfare for ecades and the people are either oo quick to blame ***someone else*** or they're ***too stupid*** to build something better for themselves.
Few even know what they're fighting for, but they'll pull triggers just the same.
How can you talk sense to people with no basic respect for human life? Reason and diplomacy are wasted on them. They plague the earth like a bad case of fleas. Some of these "cultures" have survived longer than America's even existed and what have they created for themselves?
Hives of dumb zealots who fly airliners into skyscrapers! ***Parents who make bombs out of their own children for Christ's sake!***
This is the best they can do!
Entire continents ravaged by horrible warlords preying upon the powerless and the weak. Don't you see? We've tried! We've given them all the help in the world and after all this time--
But-- but not everyone ***thinks that way!*** We need to sit with them at summits, get them to peace talks--
Lieutenant... please tell me you're not that naïve. I mean, do you really think anyone will ever be able to negotiate a peace between the Palestinians and the Israelis? Serbia and Croatia?
Why should a group of barbaric ideological fanatics slow down progress for the rest of the world?
Imagine every individual nation running as one smooth, egalitarian unit, gathered under the umbrella of democracy, so unity in laws protecting every individual can prevail uniformly. This'll mean an end to hunger, racism, torture, poverty--
Christ, sir! You can't get people to agree on toppings for a ***pizza,*** you really think you'll convince them to work together ***globally?***

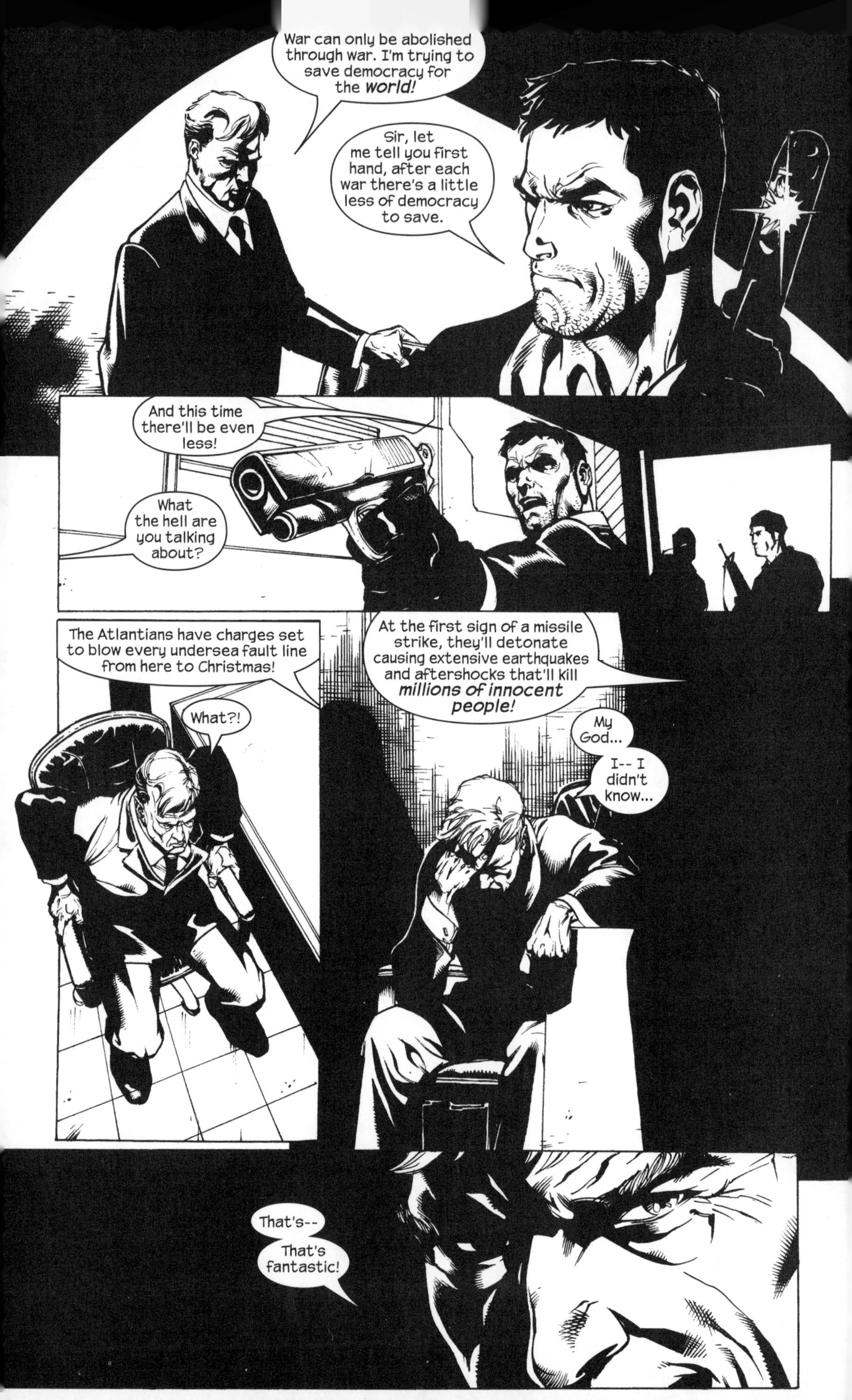
War can only be abolished through war. I'm trying to save democracy for the *world!*
Sir, let me tell you first hand, after each war there's a little less of democracy to save.
And this time there'll be even less!
What the hell are you talking about?
The Atlantians have charges set to blow every undersea fault line from here to Christmas!
What?!
At the first sign of a missile strike, they'll detonate causing extensive earthquakes and aftershocks that'll kill *millions of innocent people!*
My God...
I-- I didn't know...
That's--
That's fantastic!

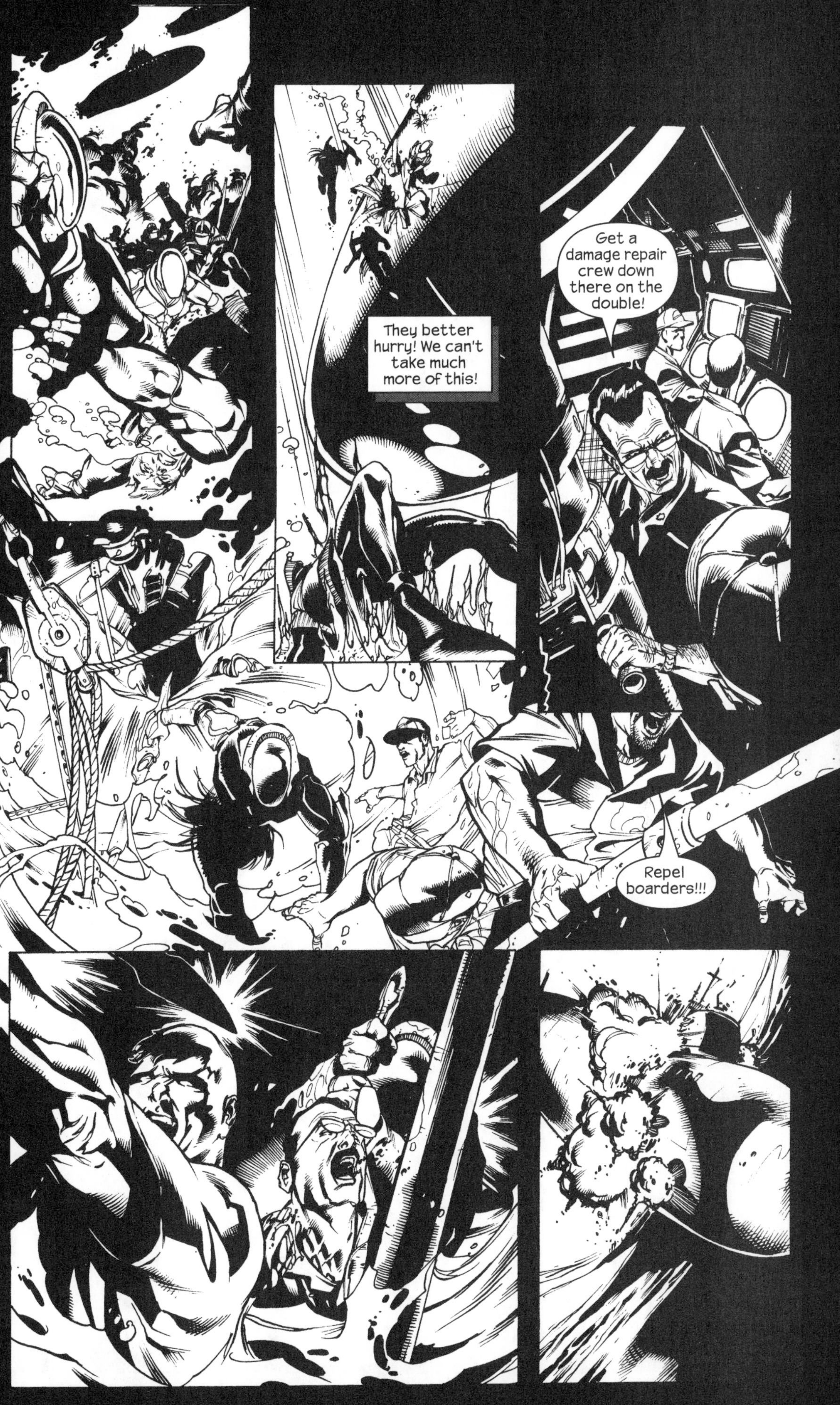
They better hurry! We can't take much more of this!
Get a damage repair crew down there on the double!
Repel boarders!!!

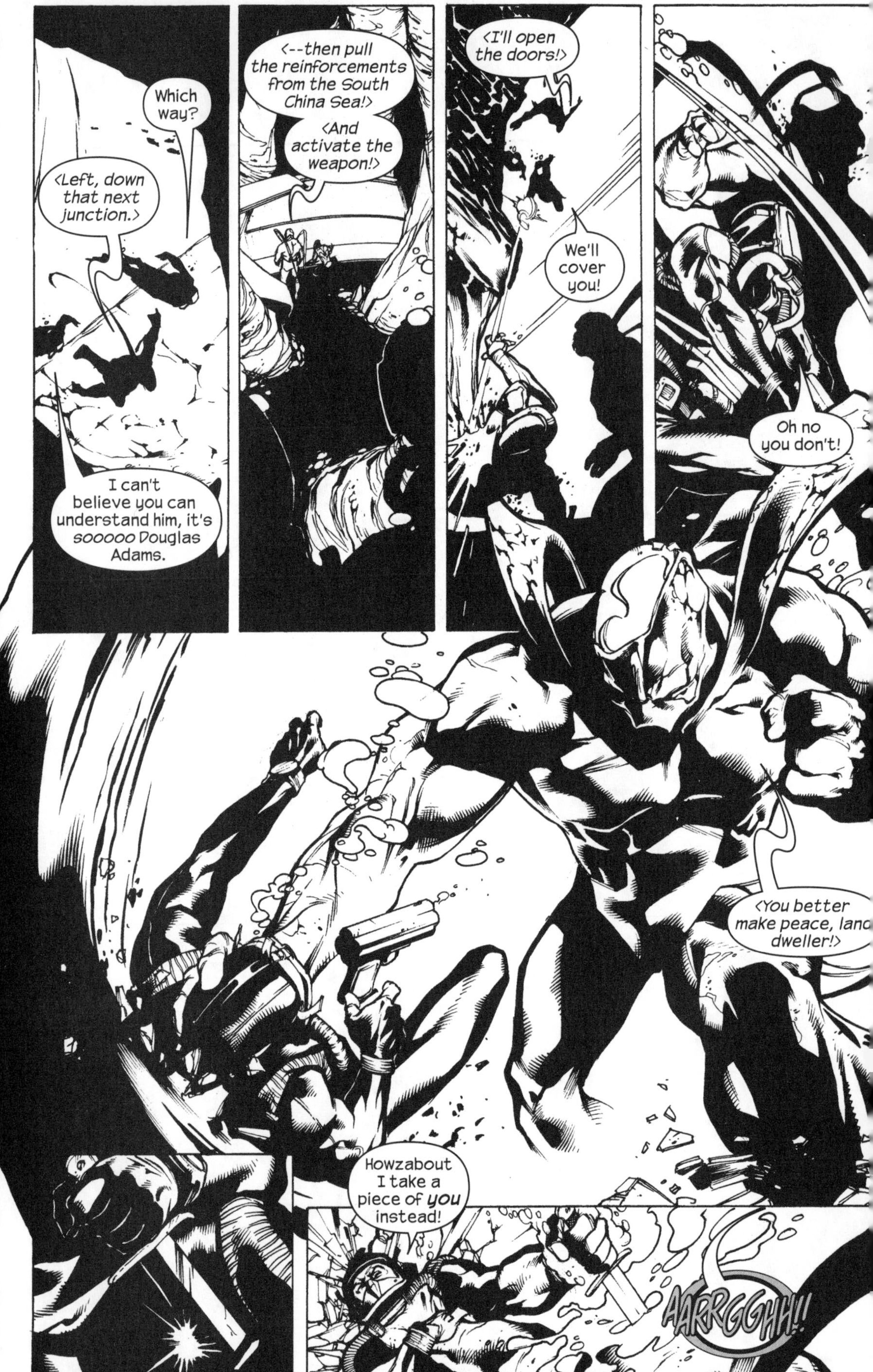

Which way?
<Left, down that next junction.>
I can't believe you can understand him, it's soooooo Douglas Adams.
<--then pull the reinforcements from the South China Sea!>
<And activate the weapon!>
<I'll open the doors!>
We'll cover you!
Oh no you don't!
<You better make peace, land dweller!>
Howzabout I take a piece of you instead!
AARRGGHH!!

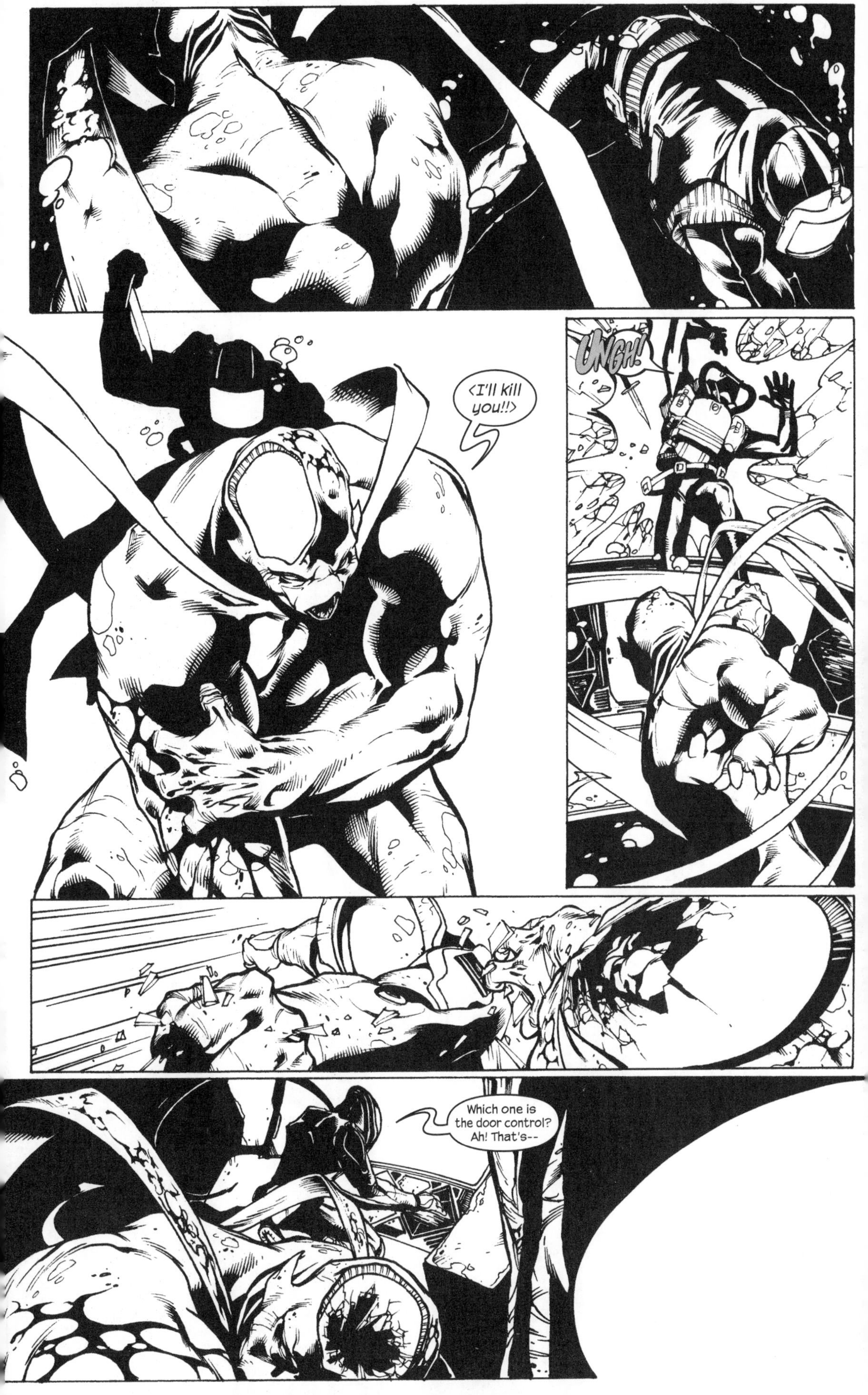
<I'll kill you!!>
UNGH!
Which one is the door control? Ah! That's--

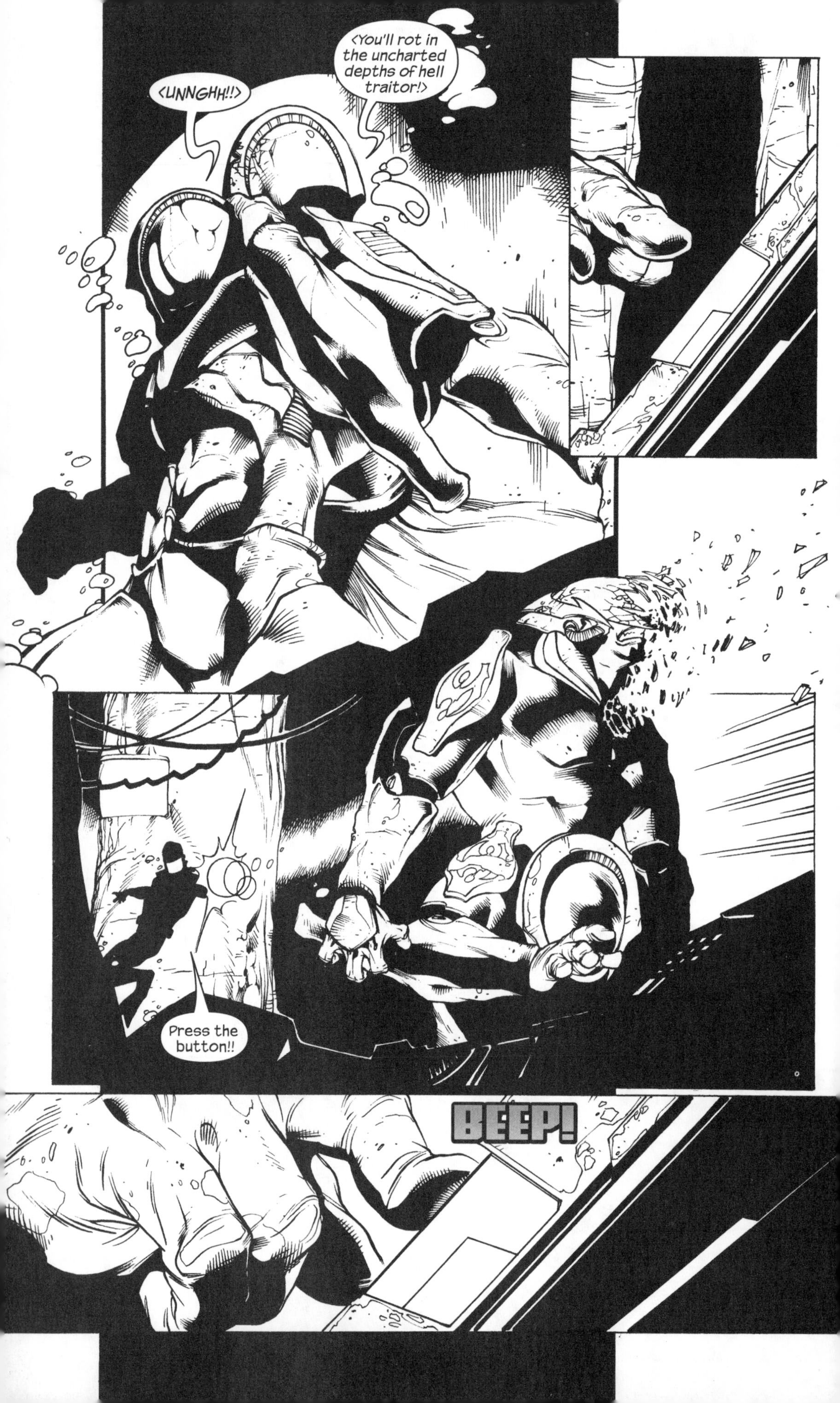
<UNNGHH!!>
<You'll rot in the uncharted depths of hell traitor!>
Press the button!!
BEEP!

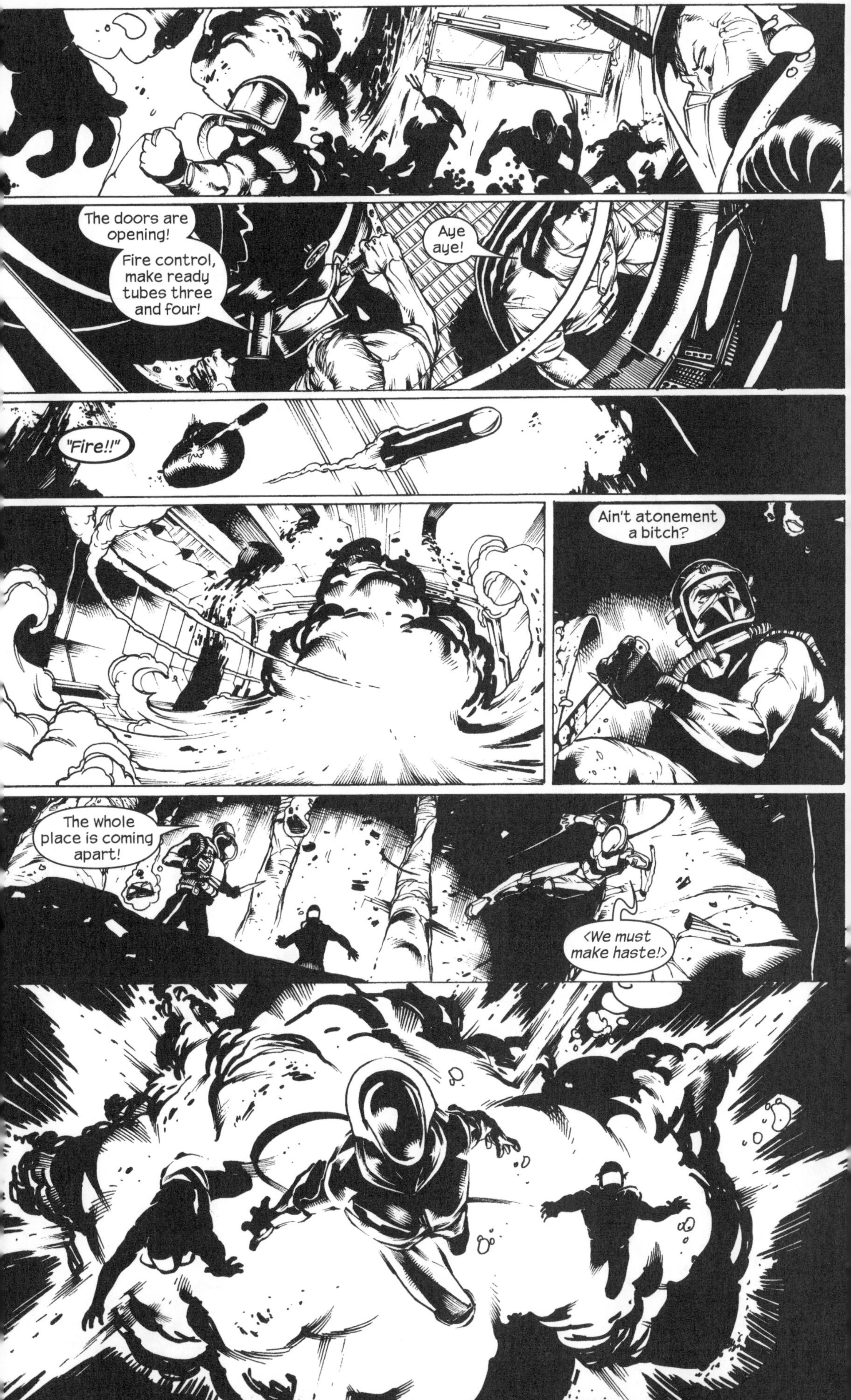
The doors are opening!
Fire control, make ready tubes three and four!
Aye aye!
"Fire!!"
Ain't atonement a bitch?
The whole place is coming apart!
<We must make haste!>

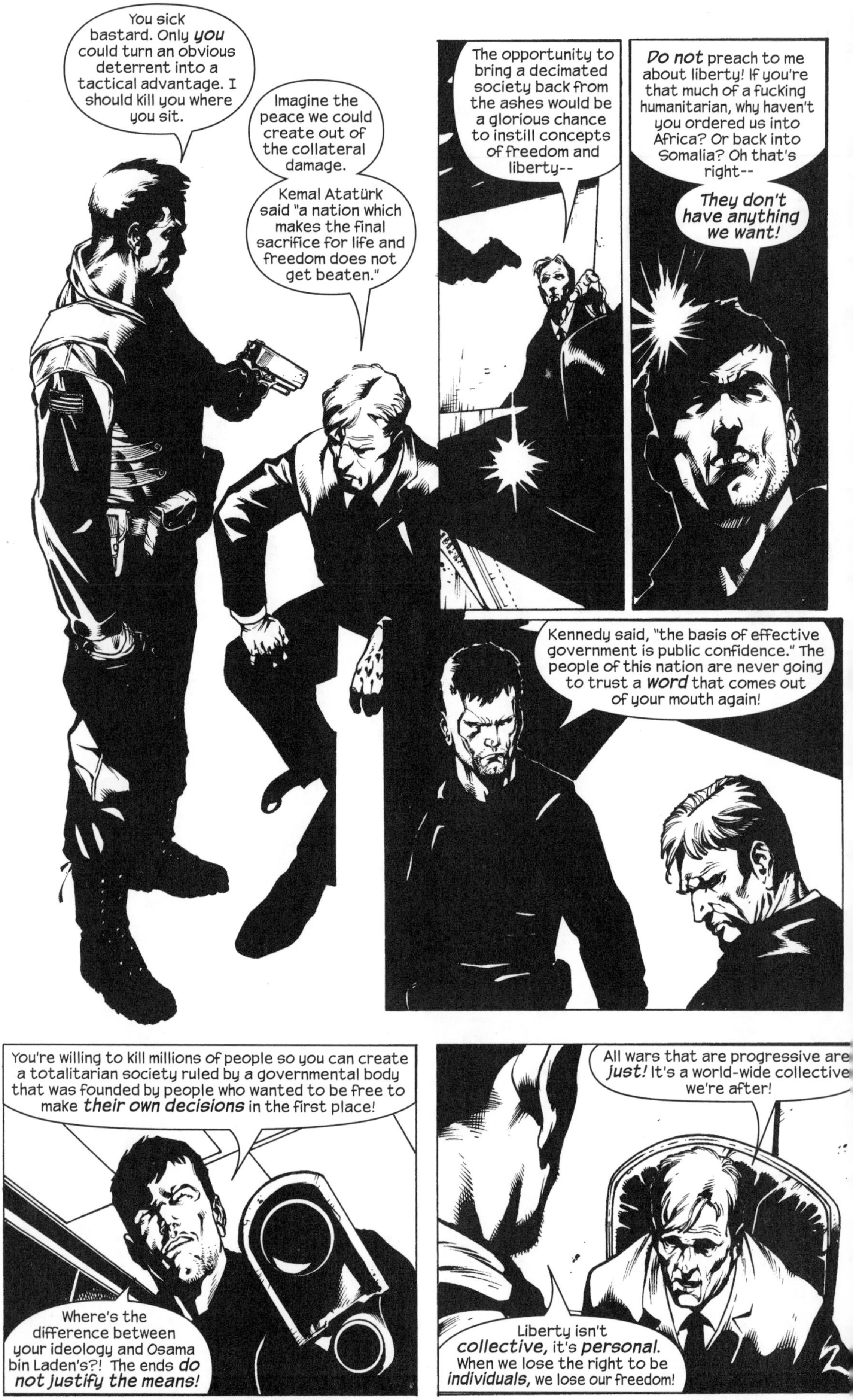
You sick bastard. Only *you* could turn an obvious deterrent into a tactical advantage. I should kill you where you sit.
Imagine the peace we could create out of the collateral damage.
Kemal Atatürk said "a nation which makes the final sacrifice for life and freedom does not get beaten."
The opportunity to bring a decimated society back from the ashes would be a glorious chance to instill concepts of freedom and liberty--
Do not preach to me about liberty! If you're that much of a fucking humanitarian, why haven't you ordered us into Africa? Or back into Somalia? Oh that's right--
They don't have anything we want!
Kennedy said, "the basis of effective government is public confidence." The people of this nation are never going to trust a *word* that comes out of your mouth again!
You're willing to kill millions of people so you can create a totalitarian society ruled by a governmental body that was founded by people who wanted to be free to make *their own decisions* in the first place!
Where's the difference between your ideology and Osama bin Laden's?! The ends *do not justify the means!*
All wars that are progressive are *just!* It's a world-wide collective we're after!
Liberty isn't *collective,* it's *personal.* When we lose the right to be *individuals,* we lose our freedom!

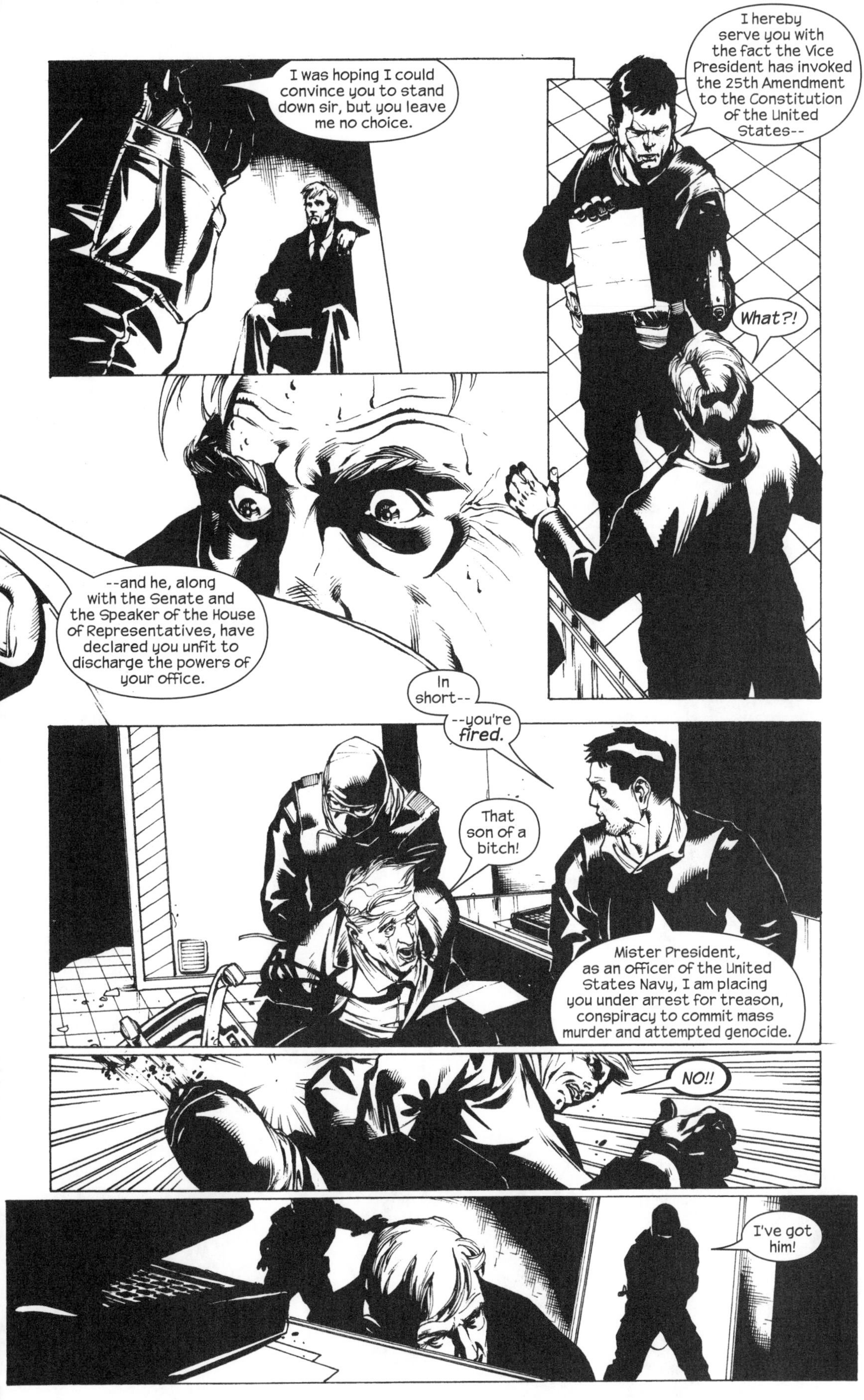

I was hoping I could convince you to stand down sir, but you leave me no choice.
I hereby serve you with the fact the Vice President has invoked the 25th Amendment to the Constitution of the United States--
What?!
--and he, along with the Senate and the Speaker of the House of Representatives, have declared you unfit to discharge the powers of your office.
In short--
--you're fired.
That son of a bitch!
Mister President, as an officer of the United States Navy, I am placing you under arrest for treason, conspiracy to commit mass murder and attempted genocide.
NO!!
I've got him!

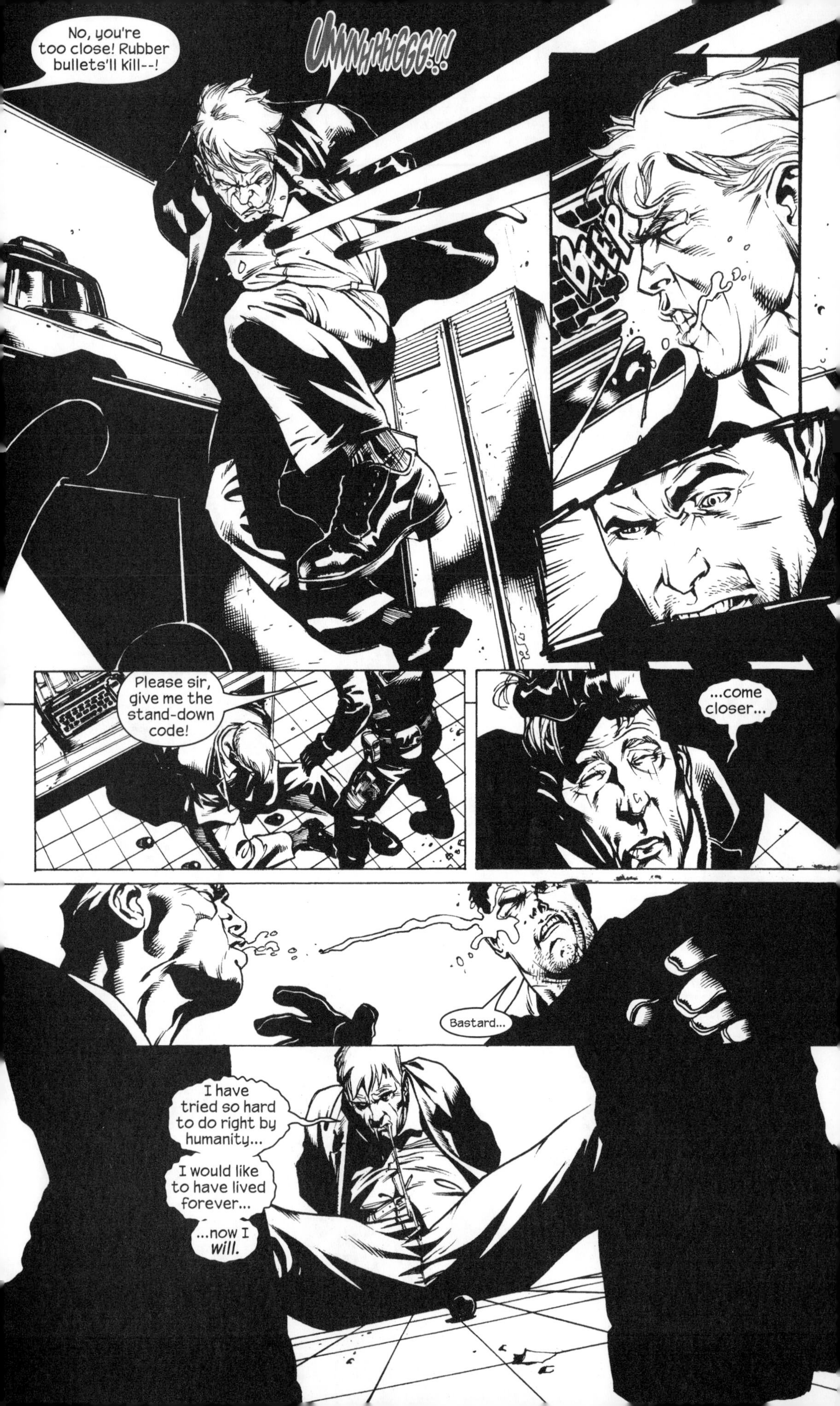
No, you're too close! Rubber bullets'll kill--!
UMNHHHGGG!!!
BEEP
Please sir, give me the stand-down code!
...come closer...
Bastard...
I have tried so hard to do right by humanity...
I would like to have lived forever...
...now I *will.*

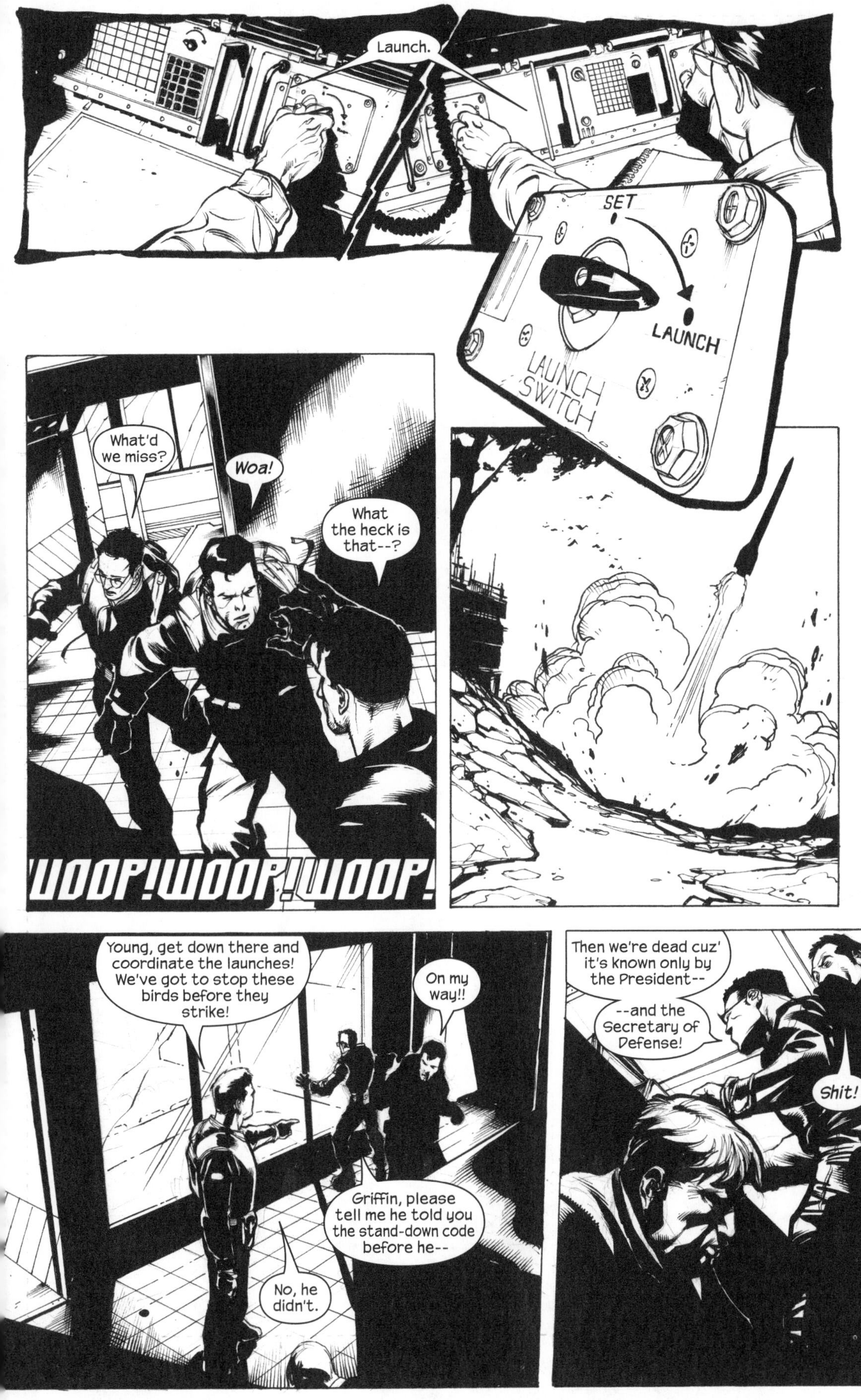
Launch.
SET
LAUNCH
LAUNCH SWITCH
What'd we miss?
Woa!
What the heck is that--?
WOOP! WOOP! WOOP!
Young, get down there and coordinate the launches! We've got to stop these birds before they strike!
On my way!!
Griffin, please tell me he told you the stand-down code before he--
No, he didn't.
Then we're dead cuz' it's known only by the President--
--and the Secretary of Defense!
Shit!

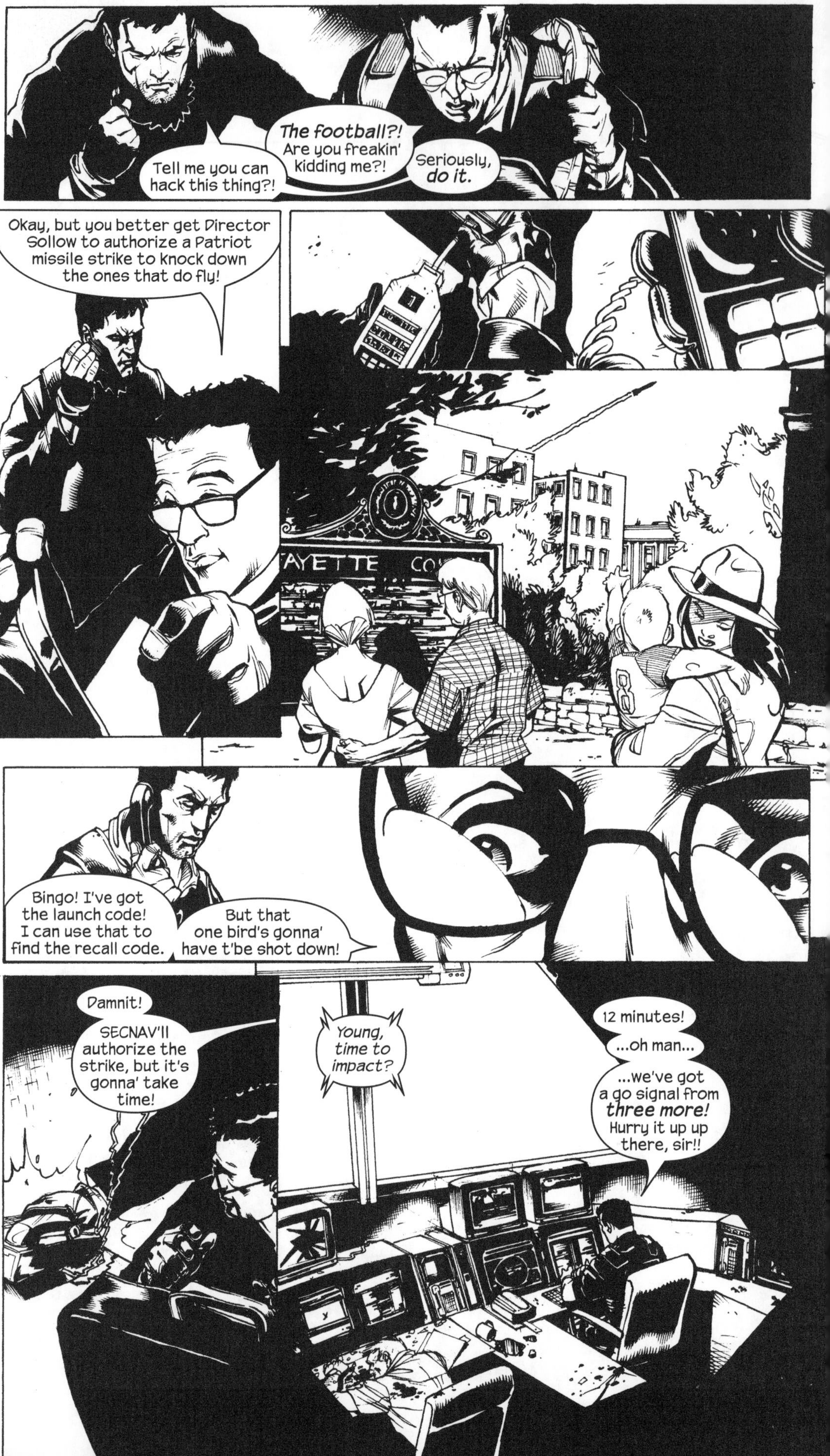

Tell me you can hack this thing?!
The football?! Are you freakin' kidding me?!
Seriously, do it.
Okay, but you better get Director Sollow to authorize a Patriot missile strike to knock down the ones that do fly!
Bingo! I've got the launch code! I can use that to find the recall code.
But that one bird's gonna' have t'be shot down!
Damnit!
SECNAV'll authorize the strike, but it's gonna' take time!
Young, time to impact?
12 minutes!
...oh man...
...we've got a go signal from three more! Hurry it up up there, sir!!

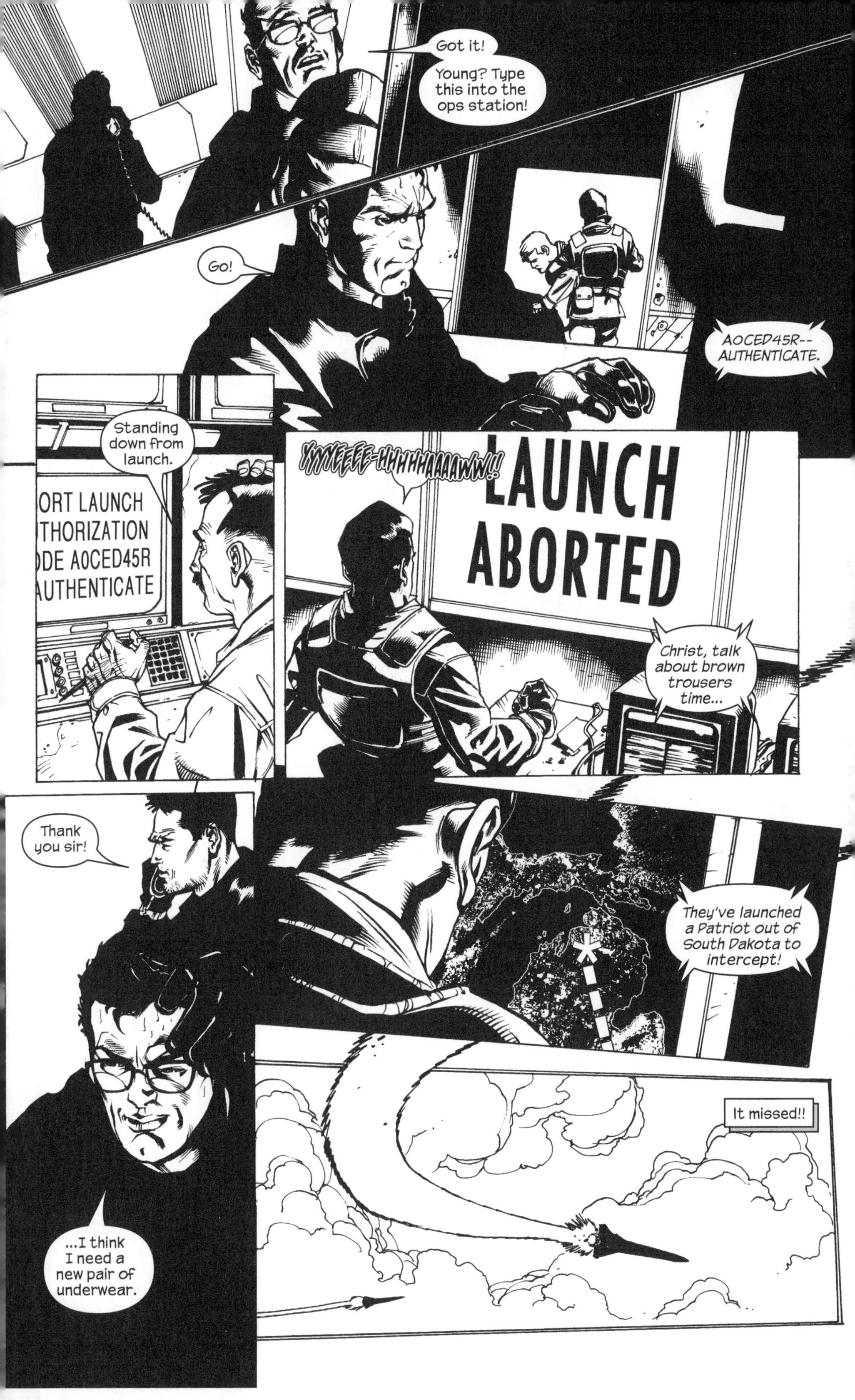
Got it!
Young? Type this into the ops station!
Go!
AOCED45R-- AUTHENTICATE.
Standing down from launch.
ORT LAUNCH
THORIZATION
DE A0CED45R
AUTHENTICATE
YYYYEEEE-HHHHHAAAAWW!!
LAUNCH ABORTED
Christ, talk about brown trousers time...
Thank you sir!
They've launched a Patriot out of South Dakota to intercept!
It missed!!
...I think I need a new pair of underwear.

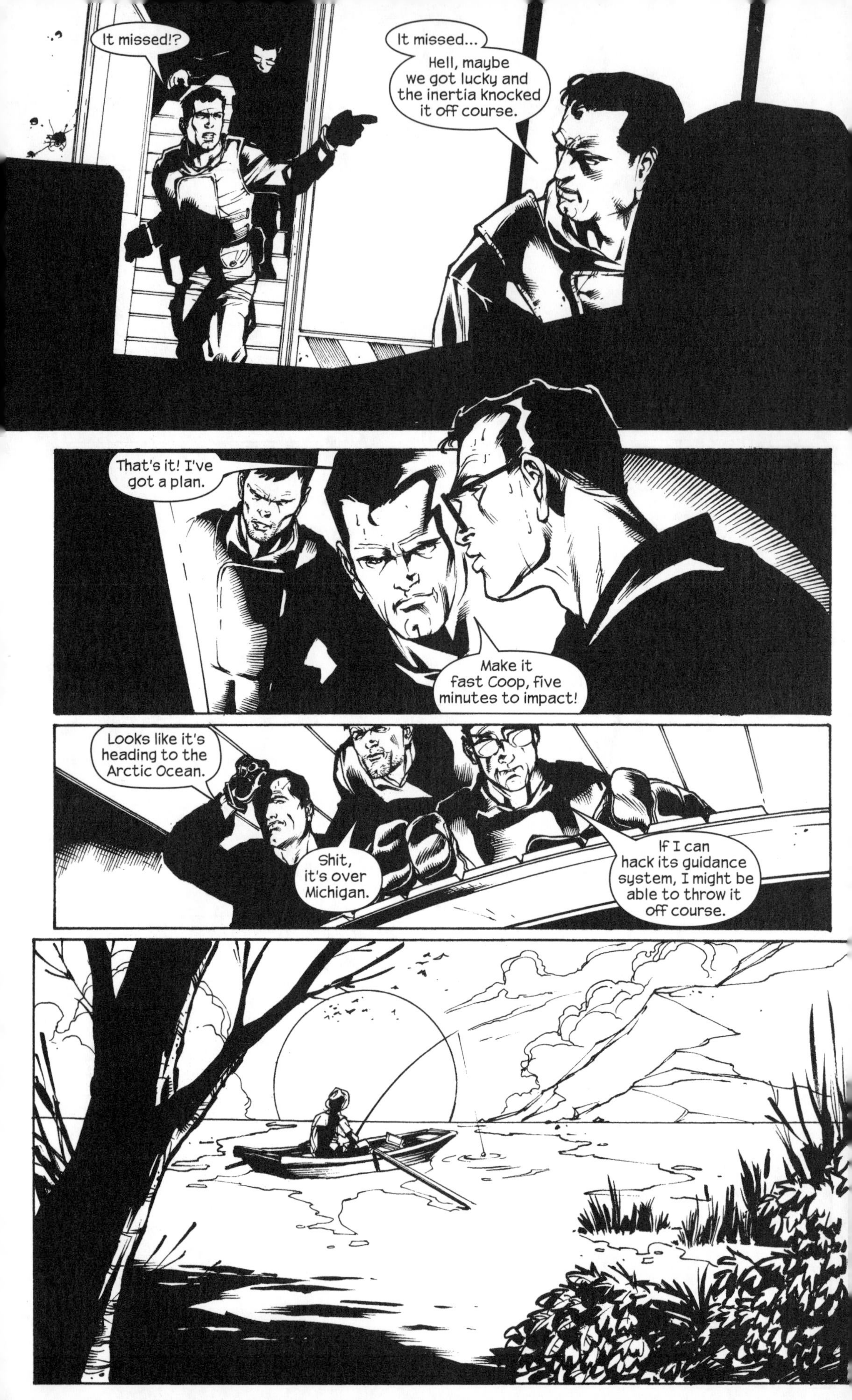
It missed!?
It missed...
Hell, maybe we got lucky and the inertia knocked it off course.
That's it! I've got a plan.
Make it fast Coop, five minutes to impact!
Looks like it's heading to the Arctic Ocean.
Shit, it's over Michigan.
If I can hack its guidance system, I might be able to throw it off course.

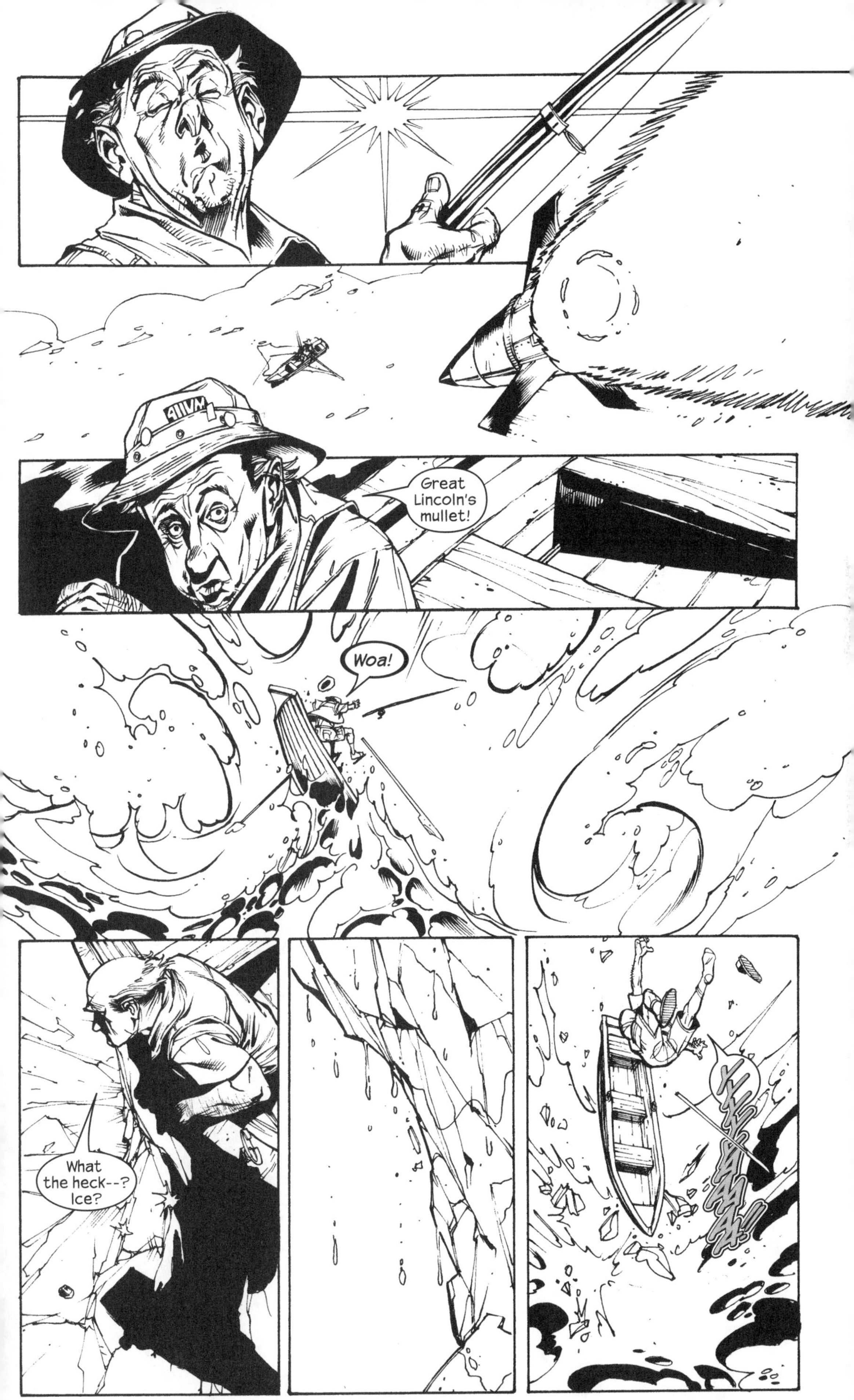
Great Lincoln's mullet!
Woa!
What the heck--? Ice?

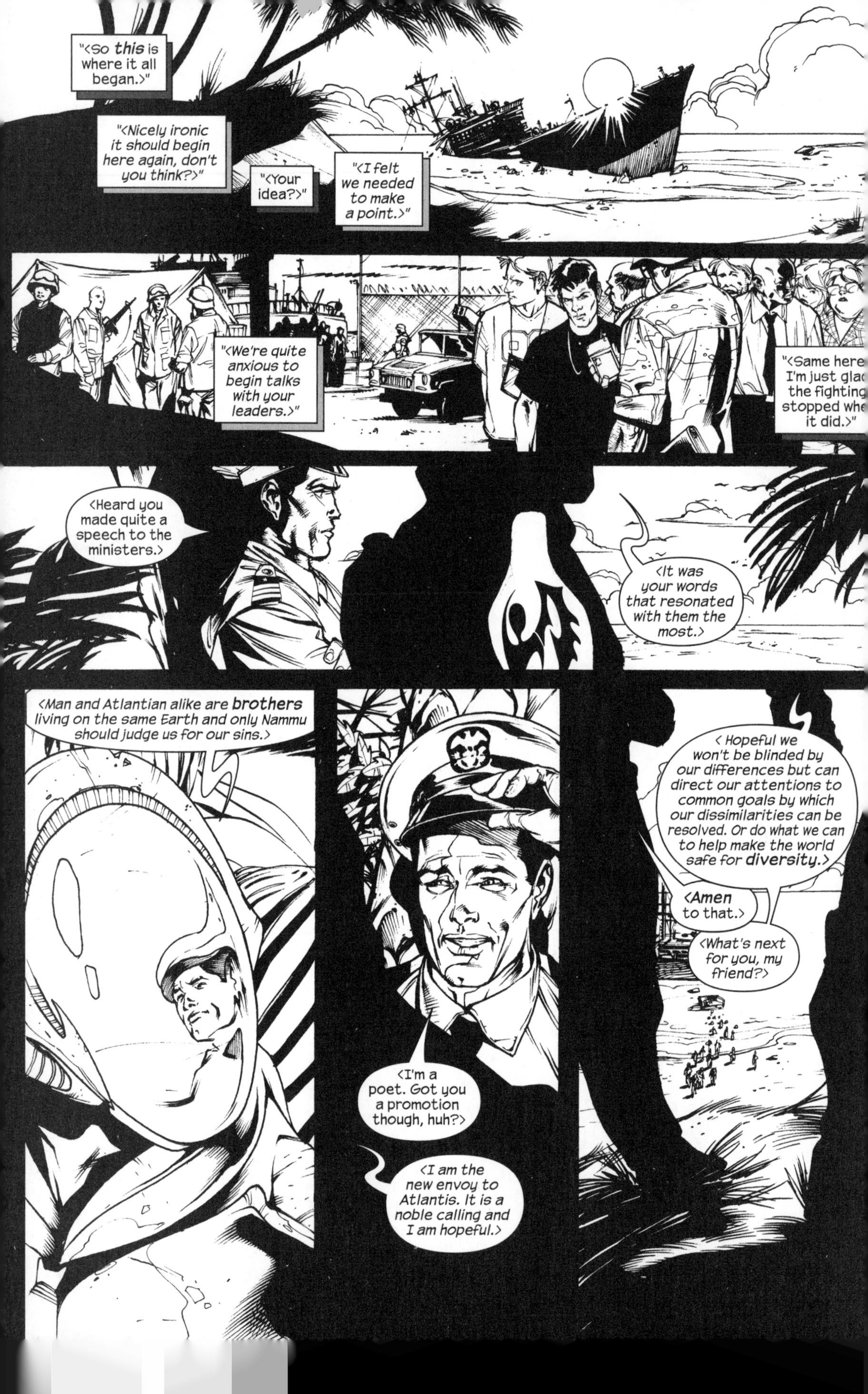

"<So this is where it all began.>"
"<Nicely ironic it should begin here again, don't you think?>"
"<Your idea?>"
"<I felt we needed to make a point.>"
"<We're quite anxious to begin talks with your leaders.>"
"<Same here I'm just glad the fighting stopped whe it did.>"
<Heard you made quite a speech to the ministers.>
<It was your words that resonated with them the most.>
<Man and Atlantian alike are brothers living on the same Earth and only Nammu should judge us for our sins.>
<I'm a poet. Got you a promotion though, huh?>
<I am the new envoy to Atlantis. It is a noble calling and I am hopeful.>
< Hopeful we won't be blinded by our differences but can direct our attentions to common goals by which our dissimilarities can be resolved. Or do what we can to help make the world safe for diversity.>
<Amen to that.>
<What's next for you, my friend?>

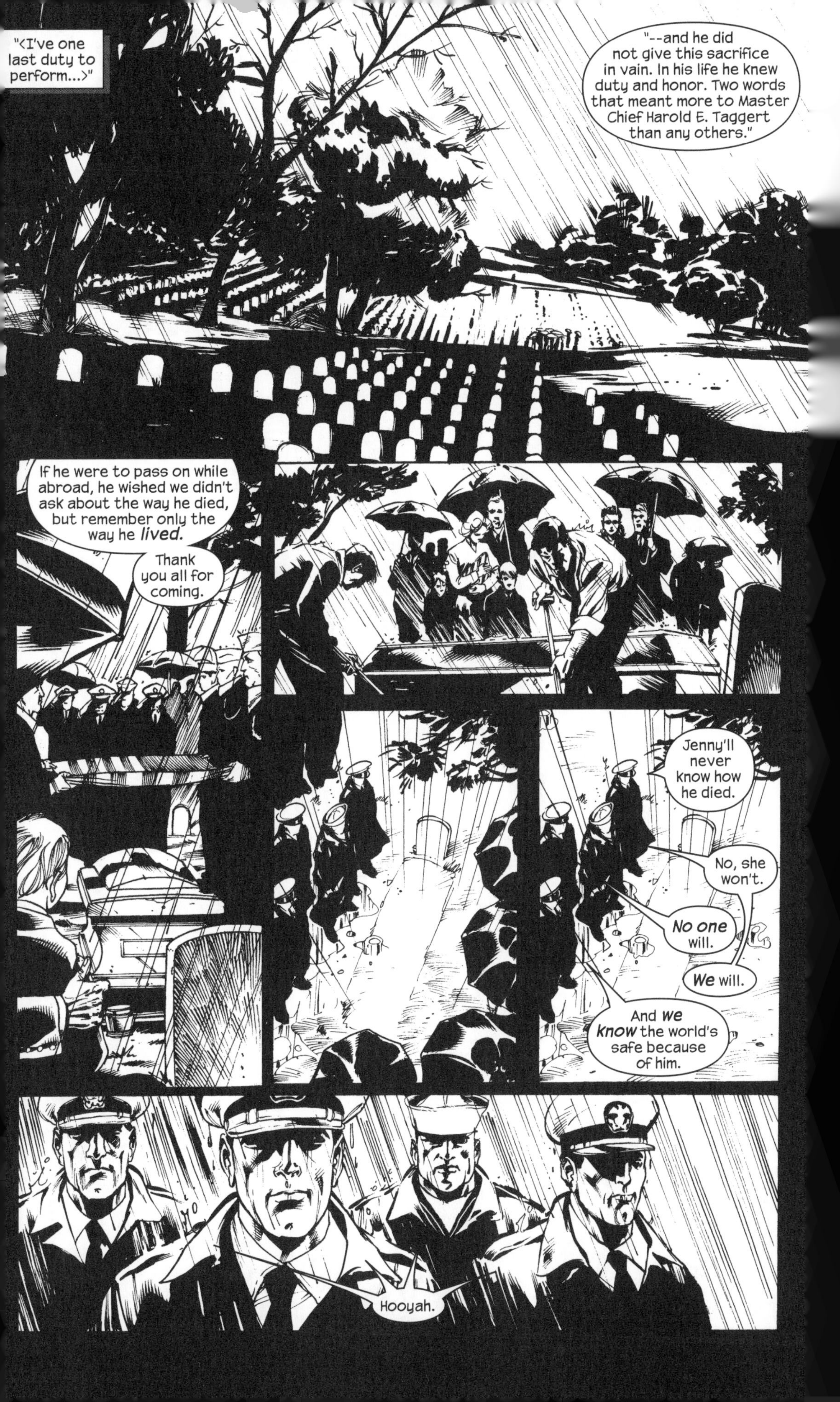
"<I've one last duty to perform...>"
"--and he did not give this sacrifice in vain. In his life he knew duty and honor. Two words that meant more to Master Chief Harold E. Taggert than any others."
If he were to pass on while abroad, he wished we didn't ask about the way he died, but remember only the way he *lived.*
Thank you all for coming.
Jenny'll never know how he died.
No, she won't.
No one will.
We will.
And *we know* the world's safe because of him.
Hooyah.

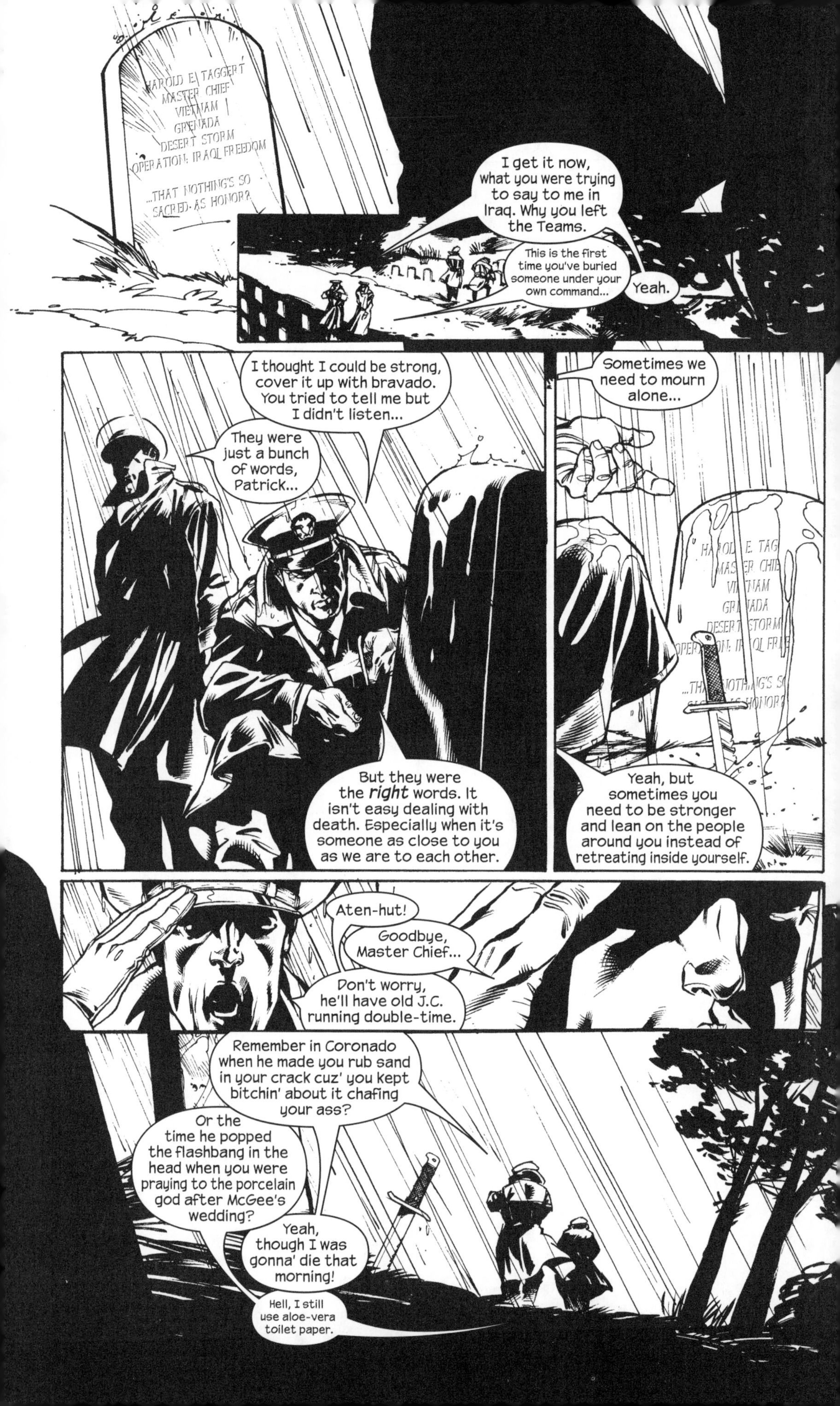
HAROLD E. TAGGERT
MASTER CHIEF
VIETNAM
GRENADA
DESERT STORM
OPERATION: IRAQI FREEDOM
...THAT NOTHING'S SO SACRED AS HONOR?
I get it now, what you were trying to say to me in Iraq. Why you left the Teams.
This is the first time you've buried someone under your own command...
Yeah.
I thought I could be strong, cover it up with bravado. You tried to tell me but I didn't listen...
They were just a bunch of words, Patrick...
But they were the *right* words. It isn't easy dealing with death. Especially when it's someone as close to you as we are to each other.
Sometimes we need to mourn alone...
Yeah, but sometimes you need to be stronger and lean on the people around you instead of retreating inside yourself.
Aten-hut!
Goodbye, Master Chief...
Don't worry, he'll have old J.C. running double-time.
Remember in Coronado when he made you rub sand in your crack cuz' you kept bitchin' about it chafing your ass?
Or the time he popped the flashbang in the head when you were praying to the porcelain god after McGee's wedding?
Yeah, though I was gonna' die that morning!
Hell, I still use aloe-vera toilet paper.

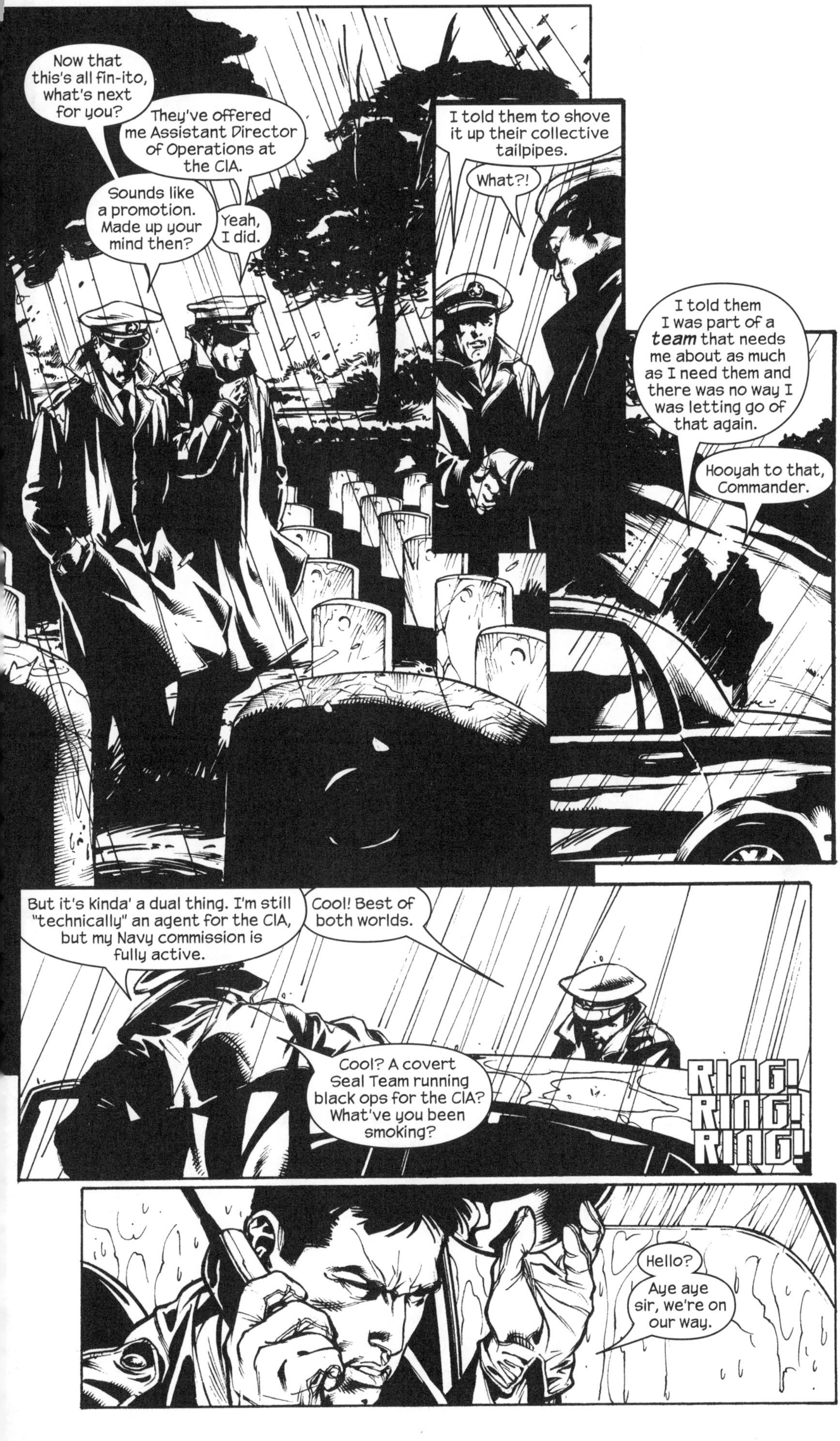
Now that this's all fin-ito, what's next for you?
They've offered me Assistant Director of Operations at the CIA.
Sounds like a promotion. Made up your mind then?
Yeah, I did.
I told them to shove it up their collective tailpipes.
What?!
I told them I was part of a team that needs me about as much as I need them and there was no way I was letting go of that again.
Hooyah to that, Commander.
But it's kinda' a dual thing. I'm still "technically" an agent for the CIA, but my Navy commission is fully active.
Cool! Best of both worlds.
Cool? A covert Seal Team running black ops for the CIA? What've you been smoking?
RING! RING! RING!
Hello?
Aye aye sir, we're on our way.

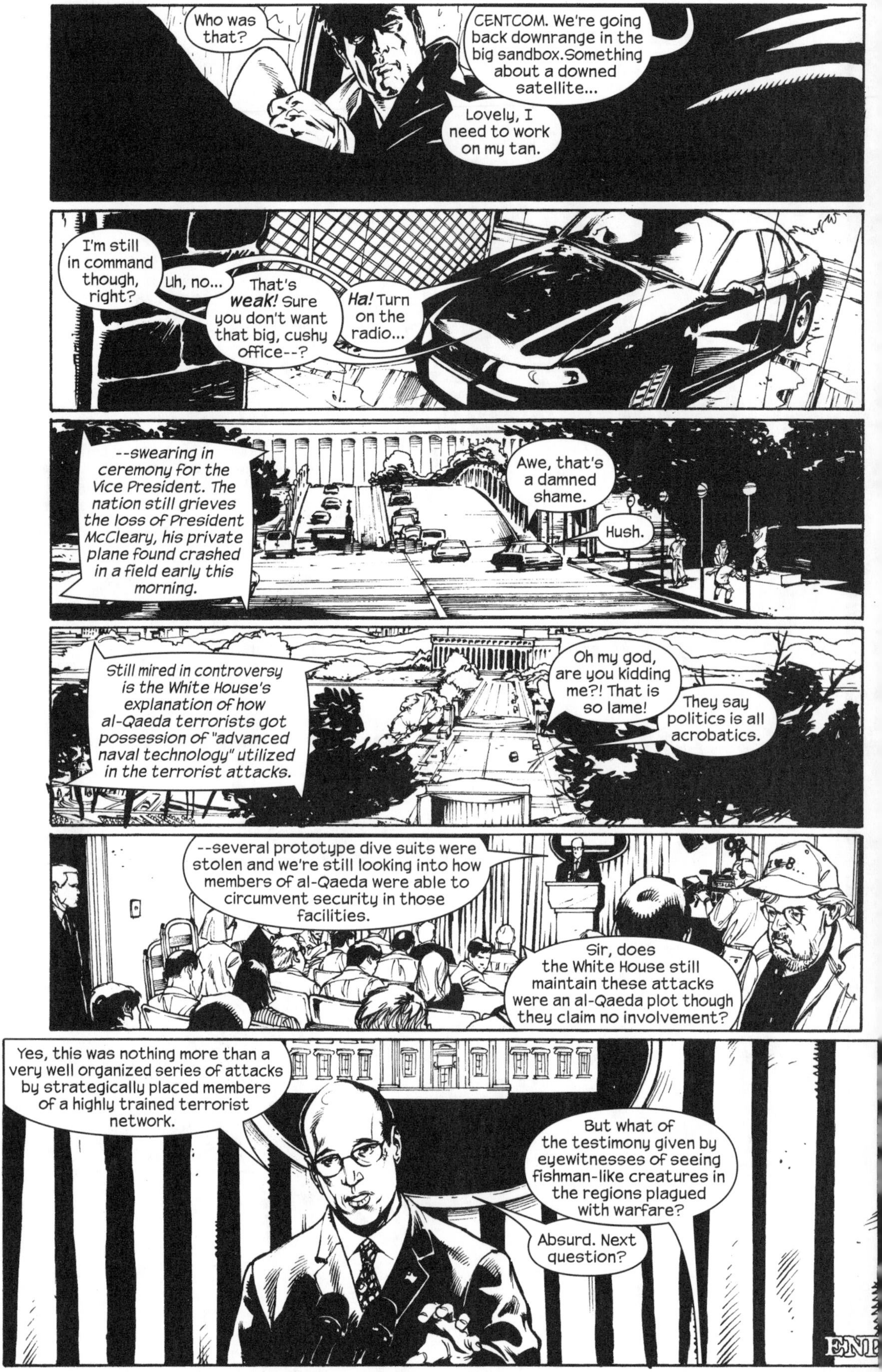
Who was that?
CENTCOM. We're going back downrange in the big sandbox.Something about a downed satellite...
Lovely, I need to work on my tan.
I'm still in command though, right?
Uh, no...
That's *weak!* Sure you don't want that big, cushy office--?
Ha! Turn on the radio...
--swearing in ceremony for the Vice President. The nation still grieves the loss of President McCleary, his private plane found crashed in a field early this morning.
Awe, that's a damned shame.
Hush.
Still mired in controversy is the White House's explanation of how al-Qaeda terrorists got possession of "advanced naval technology" utilized in the terrorist attacks.
Oh my god, are you kidding me?! That is so lame!
They say politics is all acrobatics.
--several prototype dive suits were stolen and we're still looking into how members of al-Qaeda were able to circumvent security in those facilities.
Sir, does the White House still maintain these attacks were an al-Qaeda plot though they claim no involvement?
Yes, this was nothing more than a very well organized series of attacks by strategically placed members of a highly trained terrorist network.
But what of the testimony given by eyewitnesses of seeing fishman-like creatures in the regions plagued with warfare?
Absurd. Next question?
END

DEDICATION

This book is dedicated to Soldiers, Sailors, Airmen and Marines
of the United States Armed Forces.

Without them, this world would most certainly be a more dangerous place.
Those of us who enjoy everything America has to offer
owe them a huge debt of thanks for their willingness
to put themselves in the thick of battle to enable us to live free.

Thank you for your sacrifice.

ACKNOWLEDGEMENTS

A great amount of technical detail and hard work went into
this science fiction book while trying to respect
the real procedures and tactics of the men in the field.
I'd like to thank the people who helped me put this book together:

Captain Michael T. Sherman USN (Ret.) for his technical assistance
Master Chief Journalist Joe Ciokon USN (Ret.) for his invaluable knowledge
Juaqim Dos Santos for his prelim artwork so very long ago
Alex Jaeger for his amazing production designs
Angela Ursillo for her initial character sketches
Doug Wright for having the balls to honestly tell me when the script stunk
and especially
Roberto, the best artist the comics industry is lucky to have found.

And to all the others
who told me their war stories,
all of which helped shape the characters and
keep the world they live in as real as possible when
fish-men from Atlantis invade: thanks
and I hope I got it right.

SOCOM: SEAL TEAM SEVEN

AFTERWORD

Most people think that writing a story about the Navy SEALs would be pretty easy.

Take a few young guys, place them in a hotbed of activity, give them something to shoot at and WHAM! Instant SEAL story.   Well, I'm here to tell you, it ain't so. Writing about SEALs is not an easy thing to do. That is, if you want to get it right.

A majority of them, be they active duty or retired, have been engrained with the inherit trait among all SEALs not to trust anyone who wants to write about them. Forget about the fact that everything they do is completely classified to protect their methods and tactics from our enemies, but look at how they have been so outrageously portrayed by Hollywood. Any time some crappy A-Team-like show needs a mercenary; he always ends up being "an ex-Navy SEAL." And how can we forget about those fantastic SEAL movies with Steven Segal as the SEAL Cook, and the pressure-sickened Team Leader in the Abyss played by Michael Biehn? It's no wonder these men keep their mouths shut. I mean, come on, that'd be like having Carrot Top play John Wayne in his bio-pic. It's because of that a large amount of the stories told are based upon their training at the now infamous BUD/S (Basic Underwater Demolition/SEAL school) and mostly none are told from the perspective of the operator in the field. Truth be told, you'd have to be with them to even get the real stories and to keep up with the Teams, you'd most certainly have to be a SEAL yourself, so sorry Wolf Blitzer, that's why you're not invited to the party.

That being said, I am not a SEAL and would never pretend to be a SEAL. The operators that put their guns into the fight on a daily basis deserve more respect than a USMCR Lance Corporal trying to pass himself off as one of the most elite warriors on the planet. But that hasn't deterred my sense of honor and loyalty to the operators that keep this country safe from harm's way. Remember, the terrorists we're fighting today don't have F-18s or smart bombs. This is an "up-close-and-personal" war that's being fought in the caves of Afghanistan and in the streets of Iraq. And while we, SEALs and Marines, fight side by side on many occasions, our tactics and training are quite different. Sure, we all can be ordered into a domicile to search for illegal weapons, but it's the stuff they do behind the scenes that make them different. Their commitment to training is such a huge part of that. The specialist trains and trains and trains. Their professionalism is a large part of what they do.

I've done my best to get the details right …

Worked with a Naval technical advisor from the first draft of the script all the way up to the final art. Hundreds of man-hours of research on the Navy, the Teams, the tech; everything in here is as accurate as I could make it and still have it be an exciting story. I hope the members of the U.S. Navy agree.

This book is as much for them as it is for anyone and I want them to enjoy it.

Hooyah.

M. Zachary Sherman
Sausalito, California
2005

GLOSSARY OF SEAL AND MILITARY TERMS:

AEC – Atomic Energy Commission. The AEC is a former U.S. government commission created by the Atomic Energy Act of 1946 and charged with the development and control of the U.S. atomic energy program following World War II.

BEAN BAG ROUNDS – Projectiles encased in a durable nylon bag and filled with pellets that can travel at over 250 feet per second. Though they are classified as "non-lethal," when fired at distances under ten feet, there is a high possibility of fatal outcome.

BLACK OPS – Covert operations done in complete secrecy and off the official books.

BUD/S – Basic Underwater Demolition/SEAL training. The most intense military training available to the US military. A 26-week period of instruction conducted at the Naval Amphibious Base located in Coronado, California that all SEAL Team operators must pass in order to qualify as a SEAL.

CENTCOM – United States Central Command is a theatre-level Unified Combatant Command unit of the military established in 1983 under the control of the Department of Defense (DoD). Its forward headquarters are located in Qatar at the Al Udeid airbase.

CHEGET – Name of Russia's nuclear missile launch code suitcase.

CINC – Commander-In-Chief. The President of the United States is designated the CINC of America's armed forces.

CLOSEST POINT OF APPROACH – CPA The range and bearing to the closest point of another vessel's passage, relative to your own ship's location.

COMBAT SEARCH AND RESCUE – An operation to recover downed military personnel at sea or on land.

COMM – Communications.

COMSUBLANT - Commander Submarine Force, U.S. Atlantic Fleet. The principal responsibility of the COMSUBLANT is to operate, maintain, train, and equip submarines in support of Fleet and National tasking in the Atlantic Fleet.

CNO – Chief of Naval Operations. The CNO is the senior military officer of the department of the Navy. A member of the Joint Chiefs of Staff, the CNO is the principal advisor to the President of the United States and the Secretary of the Navy on the conduct of war. Usually a four-star Admiral, he is answerable to the Secretary of the Navy for the utilization, command, and operating efficiency of the operating forces of the Naval Service. This includes all Naval assets, including surface forces.

CORONADO – Often called Coronado Island, it is a spit of land that makes up the southern most part of San Diego harbor. It is the main Naval hub in Southern California and houses NAS North Island, Naval Amphibious Base, as well as the Commander Naval Air Force, US Pacific Fleet (COMNAVAIRPAC). Coronado is also the base for all West-Coast SEAL Teams.

CORPSMAN - Naval equivalent to an army medic, corpsman serve in both Marine and Navy units.

DATUM - A point or location where a submarine has been detected or has made its own detection possible.

FLASHBANG – A stun grenade that renders individuals powerless with a flash of blinding-white light (1 million candles) and a deafening bang (180 decibels).

THE FOOTBALL - The Football is a specially outfitted briefcase used by the President of the United States to authorize the use of nuclear weapons. It has been suggested that the nickname Football was derived from an attack plan codenamed Drop-Kick and its exact contents are classified. The bag itself is a metallic, possibly bullet-proof, modified Zero-Haliburton briefcase which is carried inside of a leather "jacket". The entire package weights approximately 40 pounds (18 kg). It is carried by a military officer who accompanies the President everywhere he goes.

HACK – Synchronize the time on a series of watches down to the second.

IBS – Inflatable boat, small.

ICBM – Intercontinental Ballistic Missile.

INTEL – Military Intelligence, intelligence data.

IRON MIKE – An auto-pilot used by comercial vessels.

JOOD – Junior Officer of the Deck; second to the OOD; normally a young line officer in training.

MARINE ONE - Marine One is the call sign of any United States Marine Corps aircraft carrying the President of the United States. It usually denotes one of 19 helicopters operated by the HMX-1 "Nighthawks" squadron, either a H-3 Sea King or UH-60 Black Hawk.

NAS North Island – Naval Air Station North Island is part of the largest aerospace-industrial complex in the Navy. It's 57,000 acres and is credited as the "Birthplace of Naval Aviation." It hosts over 30 commands including the headquarters for Naval Special Weapons Command. Its airfield houses over 230 aircraft, is the home port to three major aircraft carriers and is home to over 35,000 active duty, reserve and civilian personnel.

NATO – North Atlantic Treaty Organization. It is an international organization for defense collaboration established in 1949, in support of the North Atlantic Treaty signed in Washington, D.C., on April 4, 1949.

NSC – National Security Council. The National Security Council is the President's principal forum for considering national security and foreign policy matters with his senior national security advisors and cabinet officials. It is chaired by the Vice President, the Secretary of State, the Secretary of the Treasury, the Secretary of Defense, and the Assistant to the President for National Security Affairs. The Chairman of the Joint Chiefs of Staff is the statutory military advisor to the Council, and the Director of Central Intelligence is the intelligence advisor.

NAVSPECWARCOM – Naval Special Weapons Command

OOD – The Officer of the Deck. The OOD is the officer that runs the day-to-day operations of the ship while at sea, at the Captain's discretion.

RUBBER BULLETS – Rubber, or PVC, bullets have been deployed heavily as a non-lethal alternative to live fire. They have been widely deployed by the British and the US Military. A major constrain on the use of these projectiles is due to the fact that when fired in close proximity to the subject, serious or fatal injuries can occur.

SAMS – Surface-to-air-missiles.

SATRECON – Satellite reconnaissance

SEA HAWK – SH-60 Sea Hawk helicopter. It is the Naval variant of the MH-60 Black Hawk helicopter. In it's ASW (anti-submarine warfare) role, it carries a 2000 pound avionics package and sonar operator to hunt enemy submarines.

SECNAV – The Secretary of the Navy. The Secretary of the Navy is responsible for, and has the authority under Title 10 of the United States Code, to conduct all the affairs of the Department of the Navy, including: recruiting, organizing, supplying, equipping, training, mobilizing, and demobilizing the United States Navy and the United States Marine Corps and their reserve components.

SITREP – Situation report.

SKIPPER – Slang for the Captain of a ship or air squadron.

SOSUS – The Sound Surveillance System is a deep-water, long-rage detection network consisting of high-gain fixed arrays of acoustic sensors installed in the deep ocean under operational command of the Navy's CUS (Commander Undersea Surveillance). It is a long life, passive acoustic surveillance system that can be configured for multiple mission objectives. It can provide long-term barrier and field acoustic surveillance, long-range acoustic surveillance coverage of the open ocean and acoustic surveillance in areas with high ambient noise. The ears on the ocean floor, it's primary use is the detection of submarines.

TRIDENT D5 – A submarine-launched ballistic missile. It is a three-staged device with a range of over 4,000 nautical miles (7,360 km) and is fueled by a solid propellant. Standing at over 44 feet tall, it is armed with up to twelve thermonuclear MIRV (Multiple Independency Targetable re-entry Vehicle) warheads. Its primary function is as a deterrence in the arms race.

UN - The United Nations is the international organization established in 1945 as a "global association of governments facilitating cooperation in international law, international security, economic development, and social equity." It was founded by 51 states and as of 2005 it consists of 191 member states, including virtually all internationally recognized nations, with the exception of Vatican City (the Holy See), which has declined membership. From its headquarters in New York City, the member countries of the UN and its specialized agencies give guidance and make decisions on substantive and administrative issues in regular meetings held throughout each year.

XO – Executive Officer. The second in command to the Captain on a ship.

ZULU – In reference to the time at the prime meridian, which is zero degrees on a globe and runs directly through the Royal Greenwich Observatory in Greenwich, England. When the concepts for "time zones" (of which there are 25 world-wide) were created, the starting point for the calculation of these time zones was designated from zero outwards both east and west from the starting point. The military, as well as civilian aviation, adapted the use of the term Zulu, which is also the designator for the letter "Z" in the military alphabet. Zulu time is also referred to as "Greenwich Mean Time."

SOCOM: SEAL TEAM SEVEN

CHARACTERS, DESIGNS AND LAYOUTS

ake a glimpse behind the scenes of SOCOM: Seal Team Seven with these amazing illustrations by Roberto de la Torre and Alex Jaeger.

CHARACTERS:

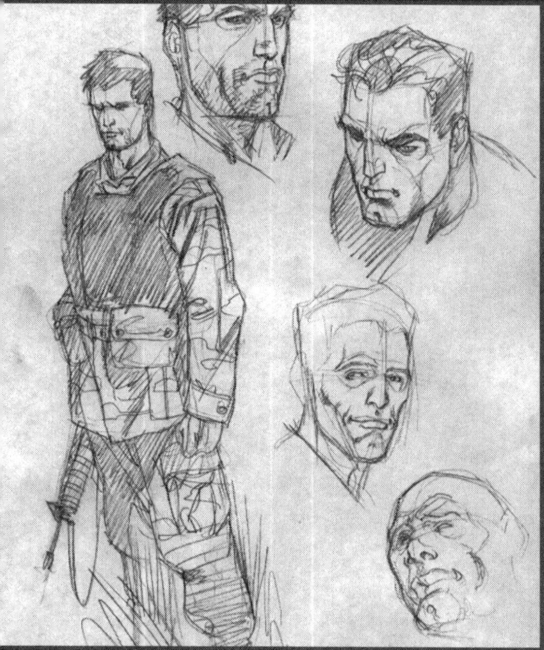

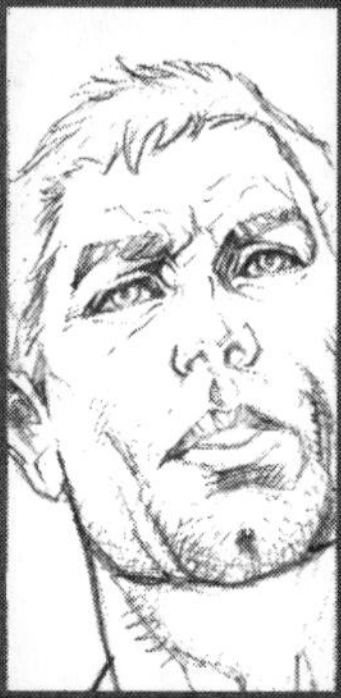

GRIFFIN

He's the tortured soul, so he needed to have a face that could convey emotion better than the others. Bigger eyes tha would show us his inner feelings, but still with the strong jaw that shows his power.

JARVIS

A rugged Texas A&M Aggie Corps grad, his look needed to mirror his strong sense of leadership and dedication to his Team and training.

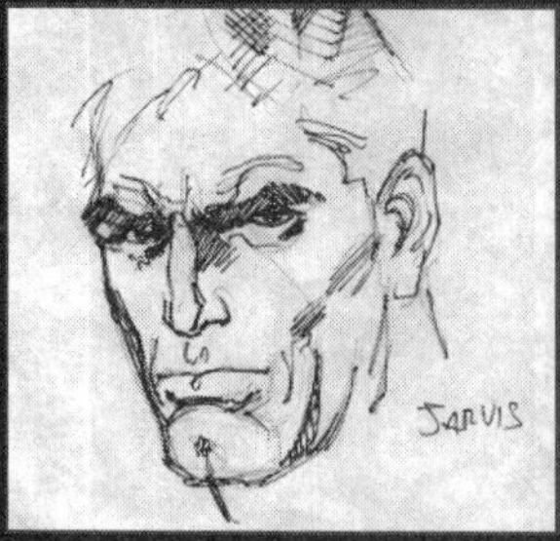
JARVIS

PLATOON FOUR / TEAM SEVEN:

riffin, Jarvis, Taggert, Zeck and Young are the main focus of this book nd it was important to lock down looks that fit their personalities as uickly as possible. Roberto nailed them right out of the gate.

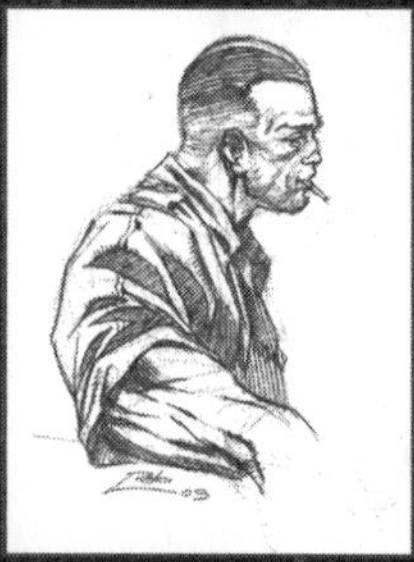

TAGGERT

Older and battle-hardened, Taggert is most experienced member of the Team. He needed to be both wizened-warrior and mentor in his look. A salty sailor, we're were all sorry to see him go.

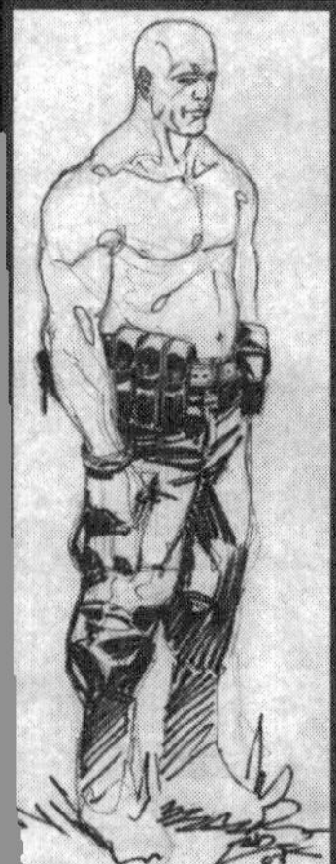

ZECK

Boyish charm but a massive geek, Zeck is both the man you want dating your sister and the one watching your back. He had to have a younger, more boyish look about him than the others, but still be big and tough enough to be a Gunner's Mate.

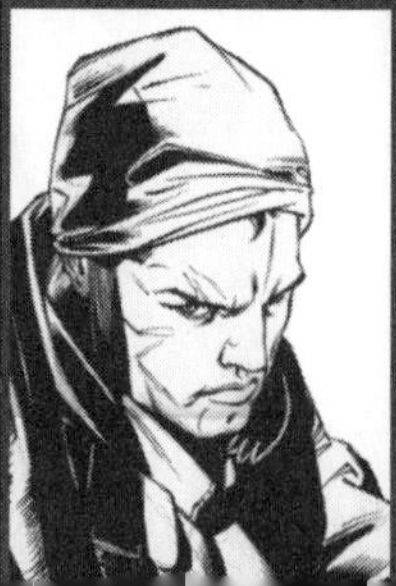

YOUNG

A California-born sci-fi geek, his look needed to be able to change drastically from comic-geek/sci-fi fan to hard-charger in an instant.

ATLANTIANS

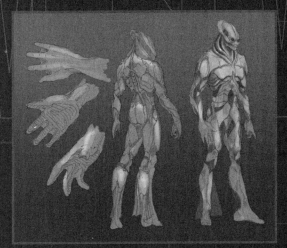

Above: Alex Jaeger's first sketches of the Atlantian. Their faces needed to not only show the emotional sorrow of what they had been through, but also be "alien" enough to not be human. Note the gill slits in the neck.

The Altlantian was to be sleek and powerful, described by Sherman as "a bipedal dolphin able to cut through the water with ease." Alex Jaeger's initial design above captured that concept. Though the ankle fins were later dropped from the design, the over-all shape of the muscular and skeletal systems remained the same from early concept to final art.

Roberto's character studies. Expounding on the initial design, Roberto began trying to capture the feel of the Atlantians. These creatures had endured so much, it was important their emotions came through their harsh exteriors.

The actual city of Atlantis, according to Sherman, was the Capitol City, serving as a hub of government and commerce to the entire kingdom of Atlantis. It was important to Sherman that Atlantis look like no version ever created before. The structures would be built downwards, towards the ocean floor, and be concealed in the out-cropping of reefs and underwater mountains, shielding the Atlantians from the surface world. If looked at from above, humans would see only the rocks and coral of the undersea world. Alex Jager's concept painting for Atlantis captured this, plus more, including complex waterways that act like freeways that connect the outlying cities together.

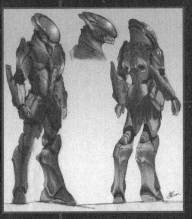

PRESSURE ARMOR

The Atlantian Pressure Armor is designed for several purposes. Foremost, the armor works as a containment suit, able to withstand the reverse pressure a deep-sea creature would have to endure while on the surface. Alex's background is not only in illustration, but mechanical design. It is extremely important to him that everything he designs, if the technology were available, work as envisioned.

THE SYMBOL OF NAMMU

The emblem on the Atlantian army's armor was designed by Sherman as a representation of the goddess Nammu throwing a mighty wave to the heavens that in turn becomes the planet Earth. The wave itself in this final rendering became the inspiration for the Atlantian soldier's k-bar fighting knife.

ATLANTIS

UNDERSEA LIFE

All of the underwater life forms have been impacted by man's neglect. Alex's designs for the massive humpback whale deformed by the remnants of a WWII Japanese battleship that had been fused to it's massive back by toxic waste.

Similarly, a dolphin is mutated by the pollutants in the oceans. Here, Jaeger Has fused a dolphin with the remains of a sunken submarine including its torpedoes.

THE HALL OF RECORDS

The Atlantians keep the entirety of their people's knowledge recorded on stone tablets that individually stand at over 10 feet high and 5 feet wide. They are mounted on massive wooden pikes that allow the reader to rotate them, much like pages in a book. The tablets reside in several different paneled walls, much like the bookshelves in a library, with thousands of tablets making the the majority of this massive room.

ATLANTIS

THE WEAPONS

They Atlantians have weapons that don't fire lasers, they fire explosive rounds tipped with deadly poisons of undersea animals we've yet to discover.

They mostly use a trident-inspired cutting weapon as their main offensive tool that the pistol locks into for increased range and intensified fire power.

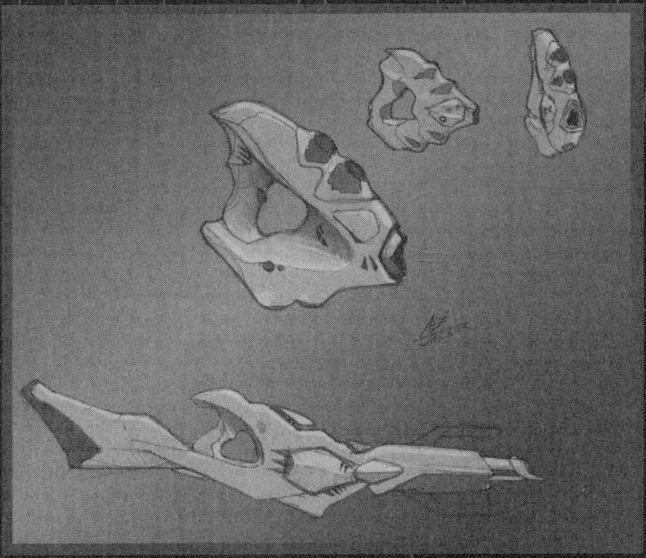

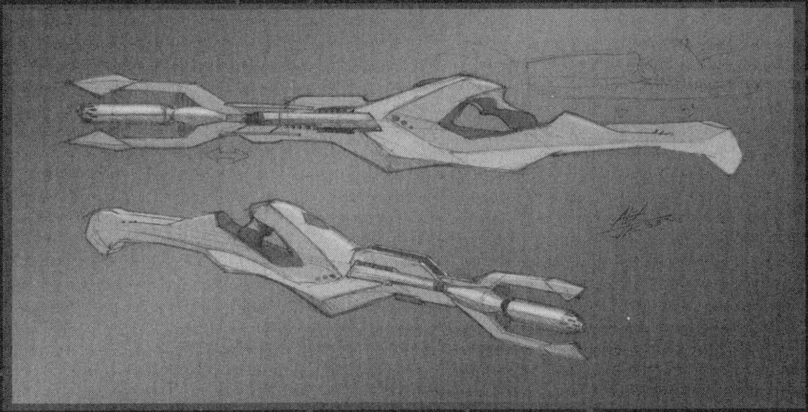

THE TROOP CARRIER

Created to resemble a whale, Jaeger designed the landing craft to be very dynamic in its size and shape. The front doors open like gills, allowin the mass of troops onto the shores very quickly for a massive assault.

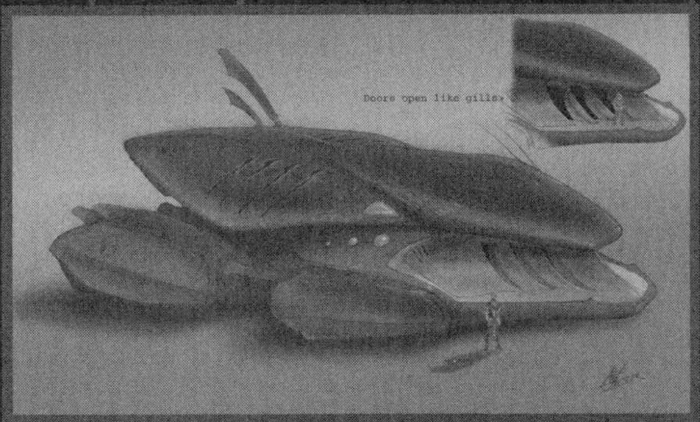
Doors open like gills

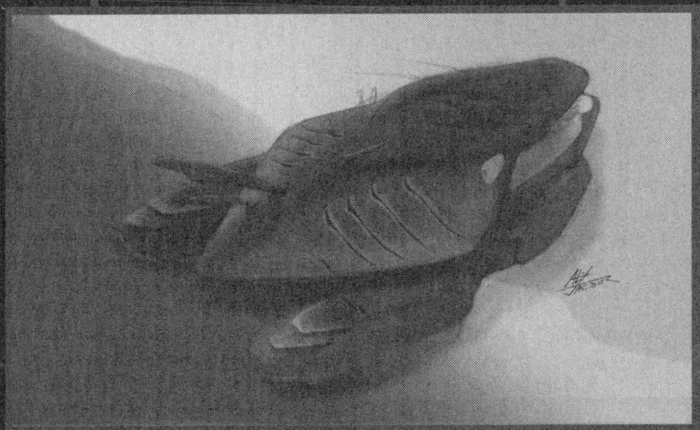

SOCOM: SEAL TEAM SEVEN

FROM TEXT TO PRINT

Here is a quick glimpse into the evolution of Sherman's script to Roberto's final art.

PAGE NINETY-NINE

PANEL ONE

Young and his team of SIX SEALs, and COOPER (who has a BACKPACK on) drop in from a ceiling AIR CONDITIONING VENT into large CUBICAL OFFICE space. The men already on the ground crouch and cover them with their weapons as the others continue to drop. Young and SEAL #1 are crouched.

(1) COOPER: (whisper) What happens if Griffin's wrong?

(2) YOUNG: (whisper) He's never wrong—

(3) YOUNG: (whisper) --he's an officer.

(4) COOPER: (whisper) That's reassuring…

PANEL TWO

Small insert panel. A boot crosses through a LASER BEAM.

(5) SFX: WOOOOP! WOOOOP! WOOOOP!

(6) YOUNG: (off panel, small) …ah crap…

PANEL THREE

Two Air Force Airmen come around the corner, firing! Red ALARM LIGHTS on the wall flash as the SEALs dive for cover behind the cubicals! Young GRABS Cooper by the back of the collar and pulls him behind cover with him.

(7) YOUNG: (yelling) Cover!

PANEL FOUR

Young, back to the cubical wall, reloads his M4 with new magazine. Cooper covers his head with his BACKPACK! Bullets FLY through the wall (they're not very thick). Another Seal (#3) on Young's right peeks around the wall.

PANEL FIVE

The seal team fires from behind cover, hitting the Air Force Guards with the rubber rounds.

PANEL SIX

They run off, down the hallway leaving unconscious soldiers surrounded by small, round black balls.

(8) YOUNG: Sleep well, ladies.

(9) YOUNG: Ya shoulda' joined the Coast Guard…

END PAGE

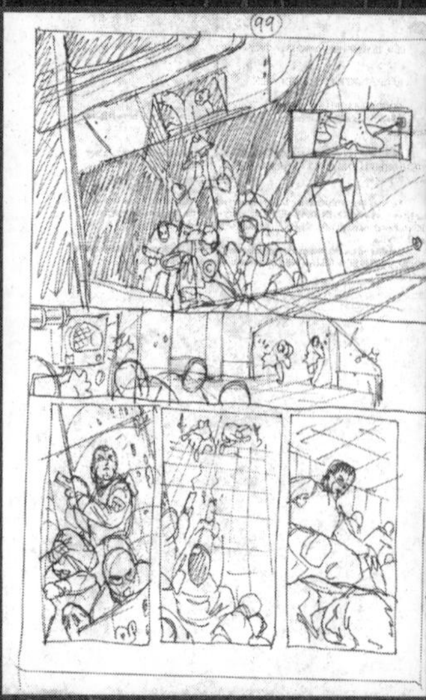

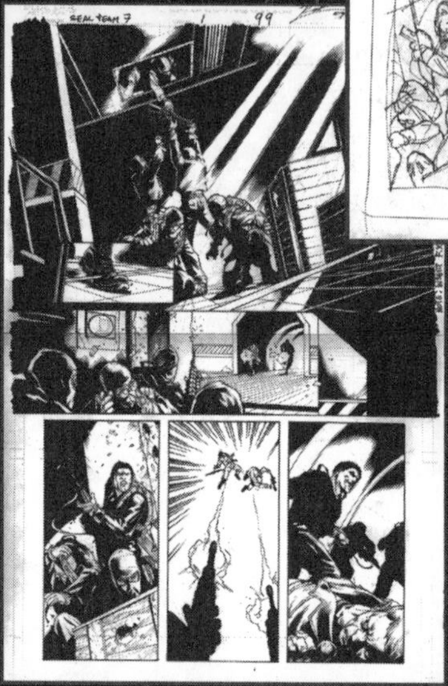

PAGE ONE HUNDERED

HERE'S THE THING. THERE NEEDS TO BE DEATH AND MAYHEM EVERYWHERE ON THIS PAGE BEHIND THE MAIN ACTION! WAR!

PANEL ONE

UNDERWATER – Men fight all around them as JARVIS, TAGGERT, LARCOON and ZECK swim through. Larcoon (still with the FLAG on his CHEST ARMOR) has NO WEAPON, but the others FIRE theirs! A SHOT FLIES BY LARCOON'S HEAD! Jarvis is GRABBING him, pulling Larcoon CLOSER to him!

(1) JARVIS: Stay close to me, damn it!

(2) LARCOON: <I am trying!>

PANEL TWO

An Atlantian comes from nowhere and grabs ZECK around the waist.

(3) ZECK: MASTER CHIEF!!

PANEL THREE

Taggert FIRES!

(4) TAGGERT: Duck kid!

PANEL FOUR

The Atlantian's HELMET BURSTS in a SMALL EXPLOSION! He DROPS ZECK who swims away!

(5) ZECK: Thanks!

PANEL FIVE

The dead carcass sinks to the bottom, BLEEDING, NO HEAD, as the Four swim on towards the Base.

(6) LARCOON: <This shaft leads to an entrance hatch near the bottom!>

(7) JARVIS: Lead the way!

END PAGE

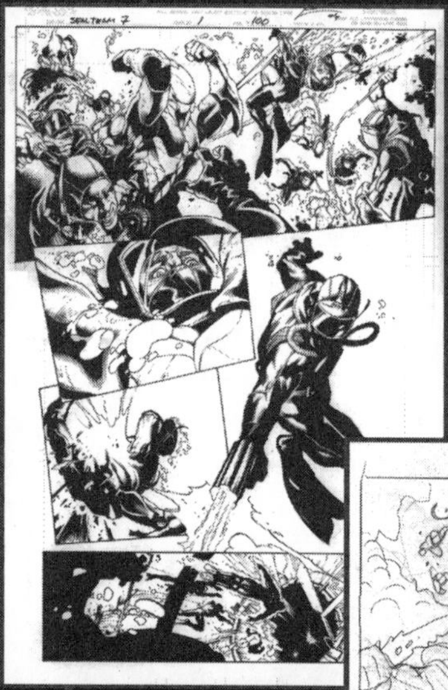

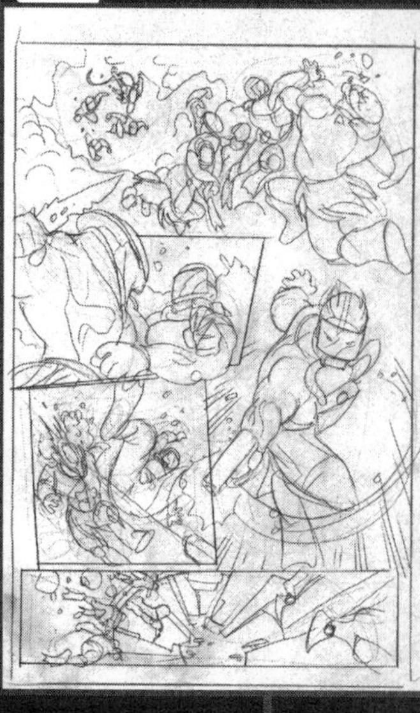

OCOM: SEAL TEAM SEVEN
OVER CONCEPTS

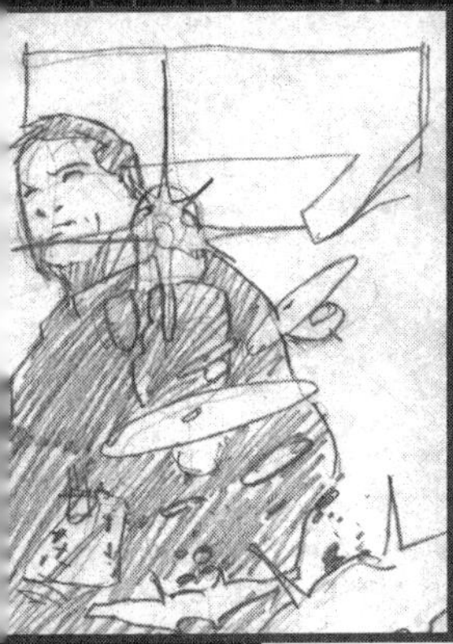

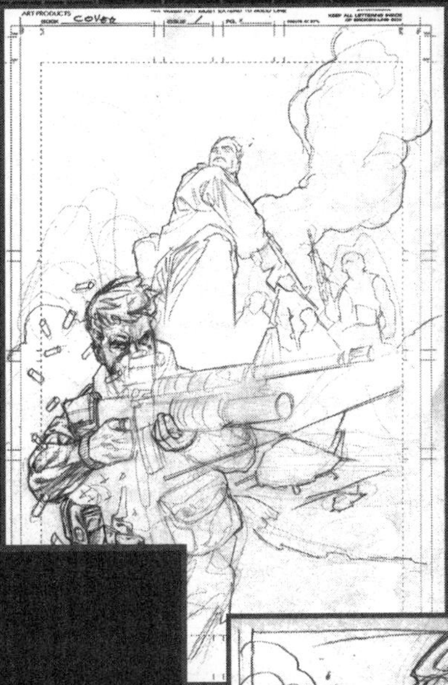

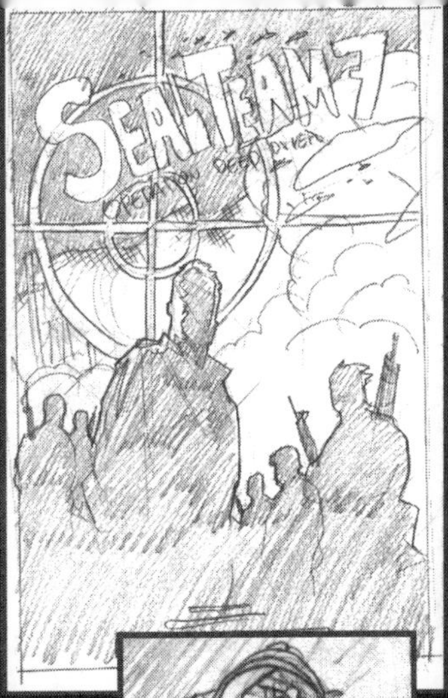
SEALTEAM7

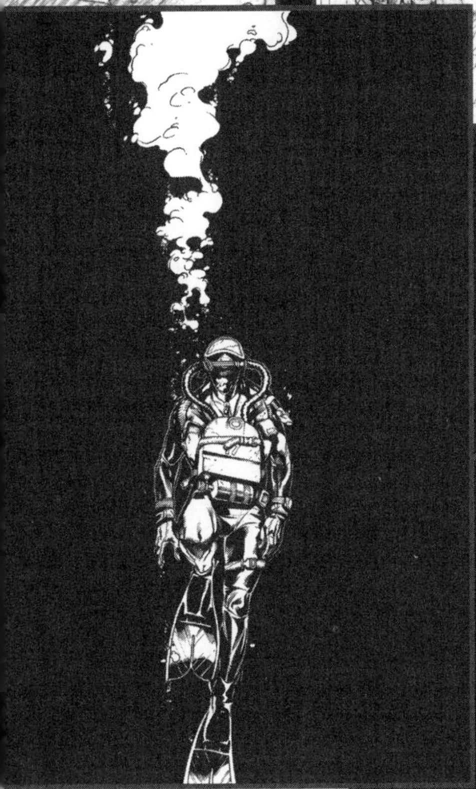

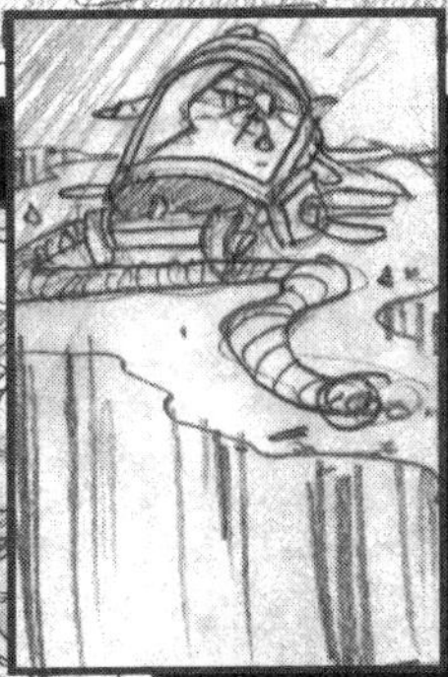

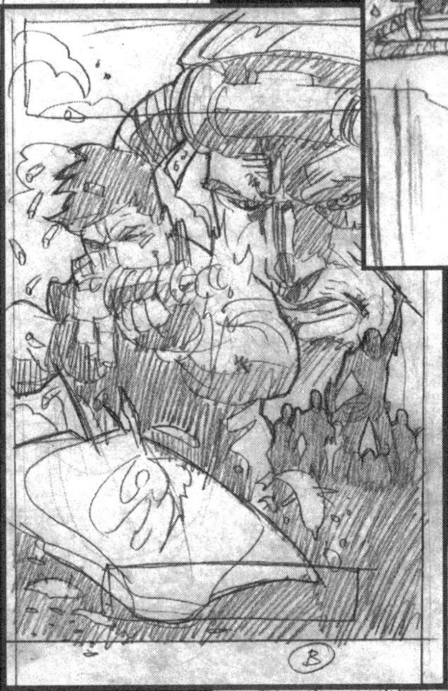

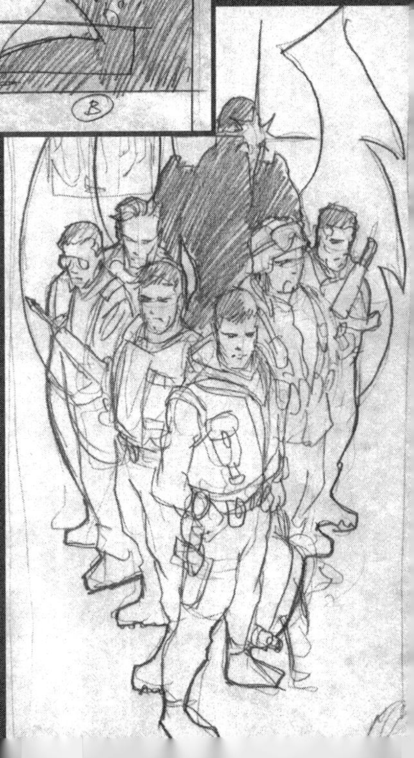

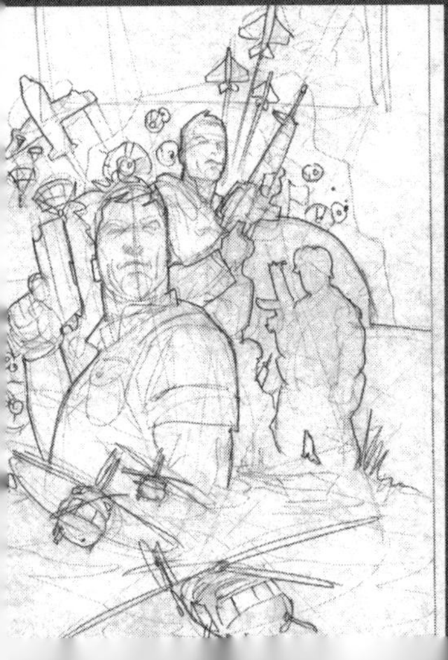

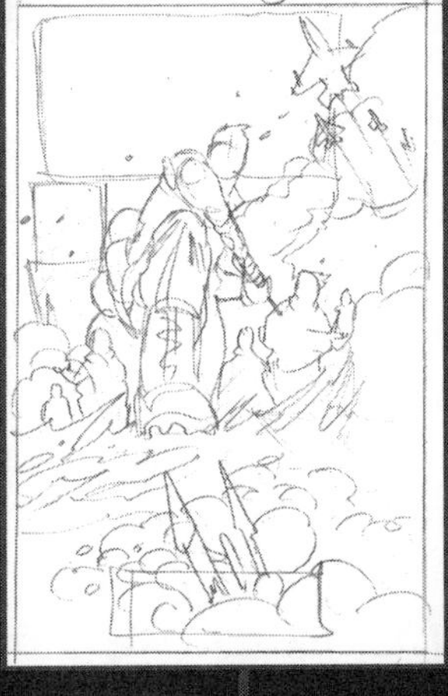

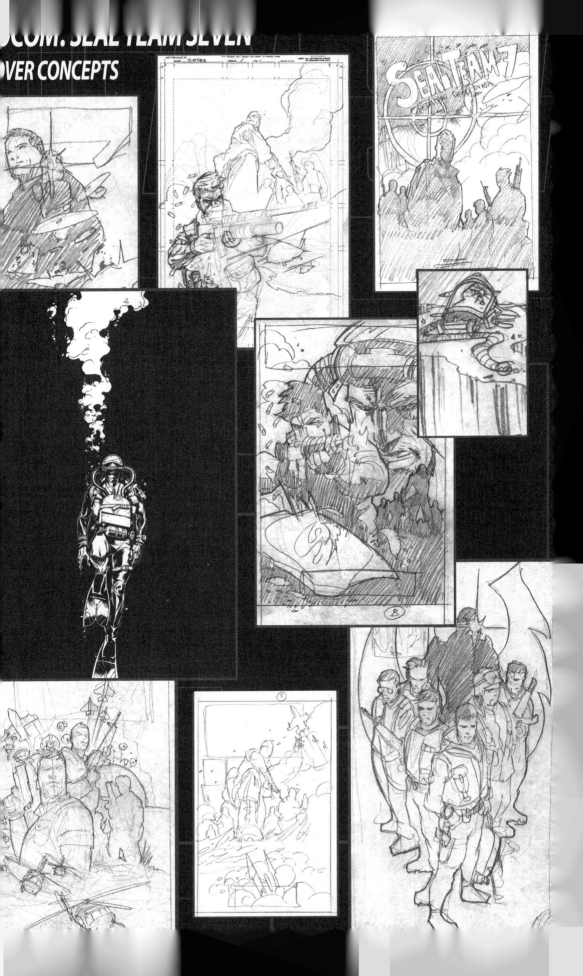

SOCOM: SEAL TEAM SEVEN

SNEAK-PEEK

Here's a quick look into the continuing adventures of SOCOM: SEAL Team Seven in the action-packed second chapter from M. Zachary Sherman and Roberto de la Torre.

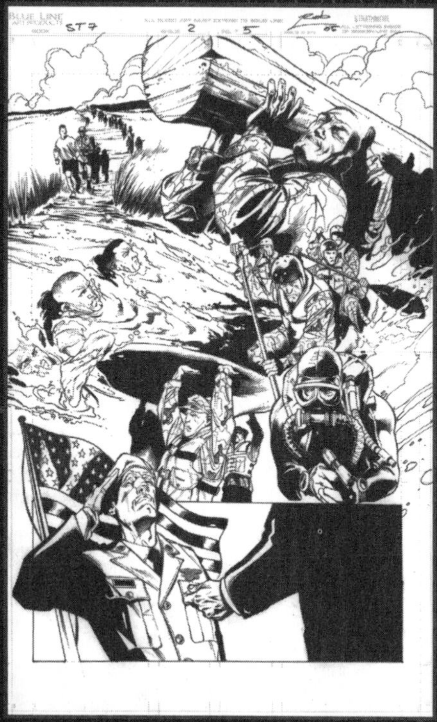

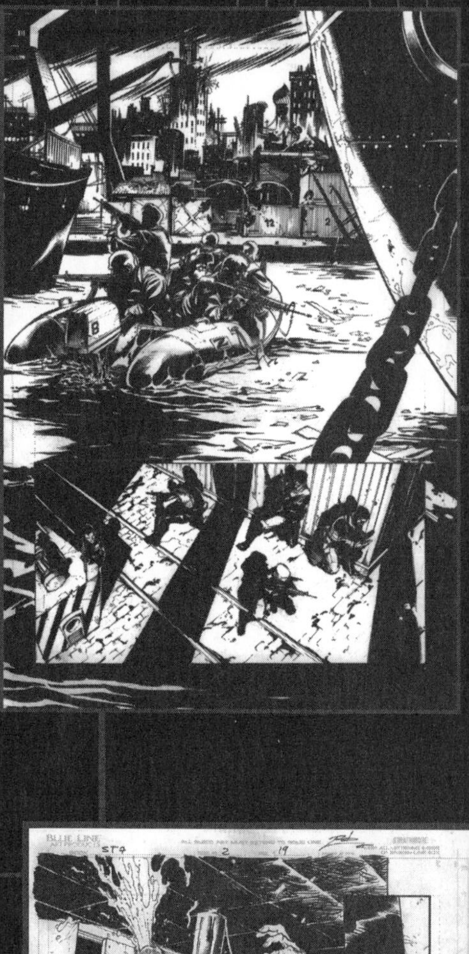

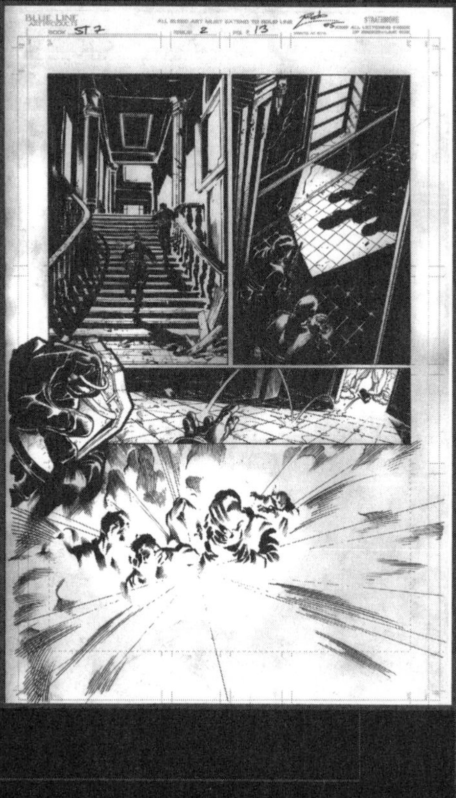

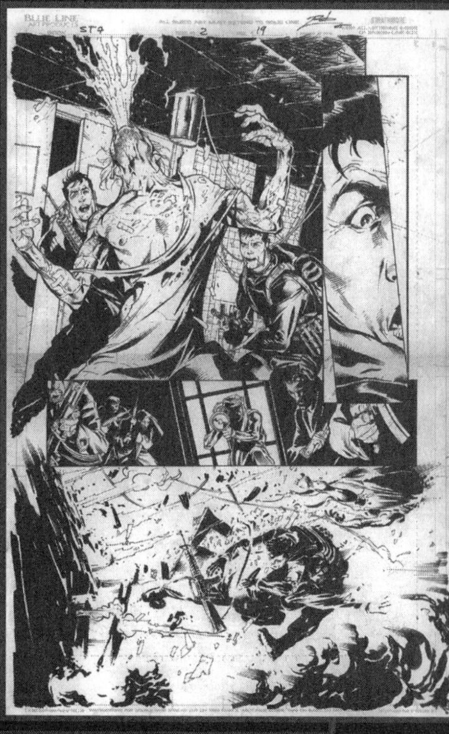

BIOS

M. ZACHARY SHERMAN – Writer

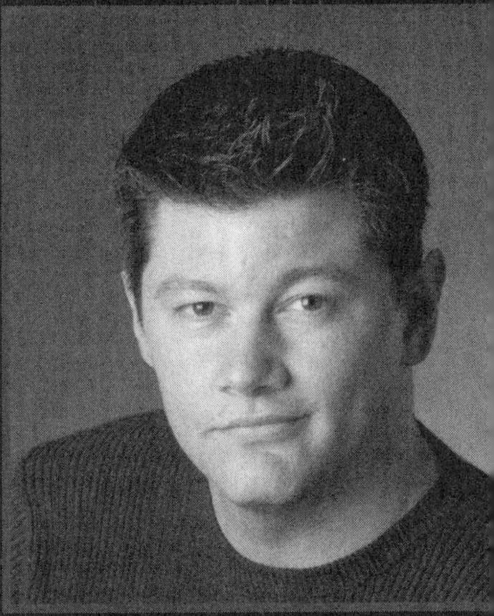

After 16 years of working in the motion picture business, Zachary has had several successes including being a second assistant director, an accomplished screenwriter and a very gratifying career in special effects. In his digital career, he's enjoyed his over nine years at Industrial Light and Magic as a Digital Effects Artist where he is does a plethora of duties, including plate reconstruction using compositing, rotoscoping and digital painting. He has written screenplays for several producers including Ilya Salkind of the *Superman* franchise and penned the screenplay adaptation of Arthur C. Clarke's short story Maelstrom II.

ROBERTO DE LA TORRE - Artist

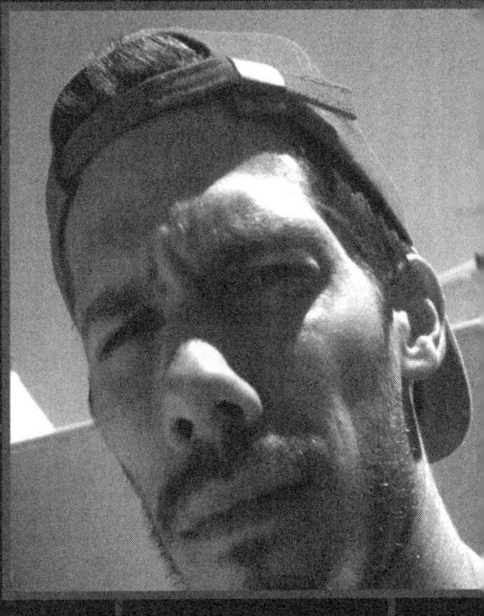

Roberto de la Torre began his amazing ten-year career in comics and animation at the age of nineteen working as a storyboard artist, animator, background painter and character designer for television animation in Madrid, Spain. In 2003, he made his leap into the world of comics, working for European publishers Accion Press, Euro Uniformes, and Altaya on numerous projects. He is currently working on *Ms. Marvel* for Marvel Comics and *SOCOM: SEAL Team Seven Book Two* for *Image*.

MORE GREAT BOOKS FROM IMAGE COMIC

For a comic shop near you carrying graphic novels from Image Comics, please call toll free:
1-888-COMIC-BOOK

AGE OF BRONZE
VOL. 1: A THOUSAND SHIPS TP
ISBN# 1582402000
$19.95
VOL. 2: SACRIFICE HC
ISBN# 1582403600
$29.95

THE AMAZING JOY BUZZARDS, VOL. 1 TP
ISBN# 1582404984
$11.95

THE BLACK FOREST
VOL. 1 GN
ISBN# 1582403503
$9.95
 VOL. 2: CASTLE OF SHADOWS GN
ISBN# 1582405611
$6.99

DAWN
VOL. 1 LUCIFERS HALO NEW ED TP
ISBN# 1582405689
$17.99
VOL. 1 LUCIFERS HALO
SUPPLEMENTAL BOOK TP
ISBN# 1582405697
$12.99

DEATH, JR TP
ISBN# 1582405263
$14.99

EARTHBOY JACOBUS GN
ISBN# 1582404925
$17.95

FLIGHT
VOL. 1 GN
ISBN# 1582403816
$19.95
VOL. 2 GN
ISBN# 1582404771
$24.95

GIRLS, VOL 1: CONCEPTION TP
ISBN# 1582405298
$14.99

GRRL SCOUTS
VOL. 1 TP
ISBN# 1582403163
$12.95
VOL. 2: WORK SUCKS TP
ISBN# 1582403430
$12.95
GUN FU, VOL 1 TP
ISBN# 1582405212
$14.95

HAWAIIAN DICK, VOL. 1: BYRD OF PARADISE TP
ISBN# 1582403171
$14.95

KANE
VOL. 1:
GREETINGS FROM NEW EDEN TP
ISBN# 1582403406
$11.95
VOL. 2: RABBIT HUNT TP
ISBN# 1582403554
$12.95
VOL. 3: HISTORIES TP
ISBN# 1582403821
$12.95
VOL. 4: THIRTY NINTH TP
ISBN# 1582404682
$16.95
VOL. 5: UNTOUCHABLE RICO COSTAS
& OTHER STORIES TP
ISBN# 1582405514
$13.99

LAZARUS CHURCHYARD: THE FINAL CUT GN
ISBN# 1582401802
$14.95

PvP
THE DORK AGES TP
ISBN# 1582403457
$11.95
VOL. 1: PVP AT LARGE TP
ISBN# 1582403740
$11.95
VOL. 2: PVP RELOADED TP
ISBN# 158240433X
$11.95
VOL. 3: PVP RIDES AGAIN TP
ISBN# 1582405530
$11.99

REX MUNDI
VOL. 1: THE GUARDIAN OF THE
TEMPLE TP
ISBN# 158240268X
$14.95
VOL. 2: THE RIVER UNDERGROU
ISBN# 1582404798
$14.95

RIDE, VOL. 1 TP
ISBN# 1582405220
$9.99

RONIN HOOD OF THE 47 SAM
ISBN# 1582405557
$9.99

SEA OF RED, VOL. 1: NO GRAVE BUT THE SEA TP
ISBN# 1582405379
$8.95

SPAWN
SPAWN COLLECTION, VOL. 1 TP
ISBN# 1582405638
$19.95
SPAWN MANGA, VOL. 1 TP
ISBN# 1582405719
$9.99

TOMMYSAURUS REX GN
ISBN# 1582403953
$11.95

ULTRA: SEVEN DAYS TP
ISBN# 1582404836
$17.95

THE WALKING DEA
VOL. 1: DAYS GONE BYE TP
ISBN# 1582403589
$12.95
VOL. 2: MILES BEHIND US TP
ISBN# 1582404135
$12.95
VOL. 3: SAFETY BEHIND BARS T
ISBN# 1582404879
$12.95
VOL. 4: THE HEART'S DESIRE TP
ISBN# 1582405301
$12.99